Protecting Creativity in Fashion Design

Exploring the debate over the benefits of legal protection for fashion design, this book focuses on how a combination of minimal legal protections for design, evolving social norms, digital technology, and market forces can promote innovation and creativity in a business known for its fast-paced remixing and borrowing. Focusing on the advantages and disadvantages of the main US and EU IP laws that protect fashion design in the world's biggest fashion markets, it describes how recent US case law in copyright and trademark cases has led to misaligned incentives for the industry and a lack of clear protection, while, in the EU, the CJEU's interpretation of the pan-European design rights system has created significant overlap with copyright law and risks, leading to the overprotection of design. The book proposes that creativity and innovation in fashion derive some benefit from a limited unregistered design right protection, and that cumulation with copyright protection is unhelpful. It also proposes that there is a larger role for developing social norms relating to sustainability, the ethics of cultural appropriation, and the online shaming of counterfeiters that can also help create a fair equilibrium between protection and borrowing in fashion design.

Susanna Monseau is a Professor at the College of New Jersey. Before becoming an academic, she was as an intellectual property litigator at law firms in London, UK, and Philadelphia and Princeton, US. Her research interests relate to the role of US and European intellectual property laws in technology and fashion. Her scholarship has been published in a range of law journals. She has also written a book, *Law, Technology, and the Future of Business*. Ms. Monseau received a Fulbright award for 2022–23 to conduct research in Finland on how intellectual property laws can help create a more sustainable textiles industry.

Routledge Research in Fashion Law

Protecting Creativity in Fashion Design
US Laws, EU Design Rights, and Other Dimensions of Protection
Susanna Monseau

Artificial Intelligence, Design Law and Fashion
Hasan Kadir Yılmaztekin

For more information about this series, please visit Routledge Research in Fashion Law - Book Series - Routledge & CRC Press

Protecting Creativity in Fashion Design

US Laws, EU Design Rights, and Other Dimensions of Protection

Susanna Monseau

Routledge
Taylor & Francis Group

LONDON AND NEW YORK

First published 2023
by Routledge
4 Park Square, Milton Park, Abingdon, Oxon OX14 4RN

and by Routledge
605 Third Avenue, New York, NY 10158

Routledge is an imprint of the Taylor & Francis Group, an informa business

British Library Cataloguing-in-Publication Data
A catalogue record for this book is available from the British Library

ISBN: 978-0-367-54929-9 (hbk)
ISBN: 978-0-367-54934-3 (pbk)
ISBN: 978-1-003-09140-0 (ebk)

DOI: 10.4324/9781003091400

Typeset in Times New Roman
by Deanta Global Publishing Services, Chennai, India

In memory of my mother, Susan Baker, a real fashion designer

Contents

Figures

Table of Cases

Abbreviations

ACT	– WTO Agreement on Textile and Clothing
AI	– Artificial intelligence
AOIC	– Author's own intellectual creation
Berne Convention	– Berne Convention for the Protection of Literary and Artistic Works, September 9, 1886, *revised* July 24, 1971, *amended* September 29, 1979, 828 U.N.T.S. 221
BGH	– Bundesgerichtshof (the German Supreme Court)
CAD	– Computer-aided design
CBP	– US Customs and Border Protection Agency
CDPA	– The UK Copyright, Designs and Patent Act 1988
CFDA	– Council of Fashion Designers of America
CJEU	– Court of Justice of the European Union
CSR	– Corporate social responsibility
CSR Directive	– European Commission proposal for a directive on corporate sustainability due diligence
CTM	– European Union Community Trademark
DNI	– Declaration of non-infringement
ECHR	– European Court of Human Rights
EPA	– US Environmental Protection Agency
ESG	– Environmental, social, and governance

EUDD	– Directive 98/71/EC of the European Parliament and of the Council of October 13, 1998 on the legal protection of designs, OJ L 289, 28.10.1998
EUDR	– Council Regulation (EC) No 6/2002 of 12 December 2001 on Community designs OJ L 3, 5.1.2002, pp. 1–24
EUIPO	– European Union Intellectual Property Office. Previously known as OHIM – Office for Harmonization in the Internal Market
EUTMD	– Directive (EU) 2015/2436 of the European Parliament and of the Council of December 16, 2015 to approximate the laws of the member states relating to trade marks (Text with EEA relevance) OJ L 336, 23.12.2015, pp. 1–26
EUTMR	– Regulation (EU) 2017/1001 of the European Parliament and of the Council of June 14, 2017 on the European Union trade mark (Text with EEA relevance) OJ L 154, 16.6.2017, pp. 1–99
European Green Deal	– European Commission A European Green Deal Strategy 2019–2024
FHCM	– La Fédération de la Haute Couture et de la Mode
FLSA	– Fair Labor Standards Act 1938 (29 U.S.C. § 203 et seq.)
FOGA	– The Fashion Originators Guild of America
FTC	– Federal Trade Commission
GATT	– General Agreement on Tariffs and Trade, January 1, 1948
GCEU	– General Court of the European Union
Hague Agreement	– Hague Arrangement on the International Deposit of Industrial Designs or Models, November 6, 1925, 74 L.N.T.S. 179
HIPO	– Hungarian Intellectual Property Office
Infosoc Directive	– Directive 2001/29/EC of the European Parliament and of the

	Council of May 22, 2001 on the harmonization of certain aspects of copyright and related rights in the information society, Official Journal L 167 , 22/06/2001, pp. 0010–0019
IPCC	– Intergovernmental Panel on Climate Change
IPEC	– Intellectual Property Enterprise Court
IPR	– Intellectual property rights
Lanham Act	– The Lanham (Trademark) Act of 1946 15 U.S.C. § 1051 et seq.
The Legal Review	– European Commission, Directorate-General for Internal Market, Industry, Entrepreneurship and SMEs, Legal Review on Industrial Design Protection in Europe: final report, Publications Office, 2016, https://data.europa.eu/doi/10.2873/056970
Madrid Agreement	– Madrid Agreement Concerning the International Registration of Marks of April 14, 1891, 828 U.N.T.S. 389 (as amended September 28, 1979)
Member states	– the member states of the European Union (including Austria, Belgium, Bulgaria, Croatia, Republic of Cyprus, Czech Republic, Denmark, Estonia, Finland, France, Germany, Greece, Hungary, Ireland, Italy, Latvia, Lithuania, Luxembourg, Netherlands, Poland, Romania, Slovakia, Slovenia, Spain, and Sweden)
MFA	– Multifibre Arrangement 1974
MSW	– Municipal solid waste
NAFTA	– North American Free Trade Agreement
The New York Fashion Act	– Bill S.7428 (2020). An Act to amend the general business law, in relation to requiring fashion retail sellers to disclose environmental and social due diligence policies; and to amend the state finance law, in relation to establishing a community benefit fund
NGO	– Non-Governmental Organization

NIPO	– Norwegian Industrial Property Office
NFT	– Non-fungible token
OECD	– Organisation for Economic Co-operation and Development
Paris Convention	– Paris Convention for the Protection of Industrial Property of 1883, 21 U.S.T. 1583
PCT	– Patent Cooperation Treaty 19 June, 1970
PEF	– Product Environmental Footprint
PGS work	– Pictorial, graphic, and sculptural works under 17 USC § 101
RCD	– Registered community design right under EUDR
RDR	– National registered design rights in member states
SAC	– Sustainable Apparel Coalition
SDG	– UN Sustainable Development Goals
TFEU	– Treaty on the Functioning of the European Community, December 13, 2007, OJ C 202, 7.6.2016, pp. 1–388
TRIPS Agreement on Trade-Related Aspects of Intellectual Property Rights, April 15, 1994, Annex IC, Legal Instruments	– Results of the Uruguay Round vol. 31 (1994)
UCD	– Unregistered community design right under EUDR
UDR	– Unregistered design rights in member states under other legislation
UKIPO	– United Kingdom Intellectual Property Office
USPTO	– United States Patent and Trademark Office
WIPO	– World Intellectual Property Organization
WTO	– World Trade Organization

Acknowledgments

The author would like to thank her family, friends, and colleagues at the College of New Jersey for all their help and support. In particular, the School of Business Undergraduate Research Assistants' program provided her with four research assistants over the time of writing and researching this book: Elaina Arrechea, Emily Hill, Olivia Schwartz, and Sarah Valdes. Their help was invaluable.

Introduction

Fashion is often treated as something ephemeral and rather silly, all "glamour and frivolity" and not a subject for serious study. Karen Hanson, in her article "Dressing Down, Dressing Up: The Philosophic Fear of Fashion," notes that fashion has systematically been disregarded by philosophers as a subject worthy of research (Hanson 1990). Diane Leenheer Zimmerman says in "Upstairs/Downstairs Fashionwise" that "Women's interest in their appearance is so commonly used to trivialize them that one is apt not to notice when it happens" (Sun et al. 2015, 180).

In spite of this perception that fashion is not deserving of analysis and scholarship, it is our most significant and valuable creative industry, bigger than film, books, or any of the other arts or creative industries. The fashion business is a "relevant and powerful force in our lives. At every level of society people care greatly about how they look" (Agins 2000). Even those who argue they do not follow the whims of fashion are part of the industry. Most, if not all of us, wear clothes.

This book is mainly about the legal protection of fashion design under US and EU intellectual property laws.

Chapter 1 provides an introduction to this major global industry and reviews the main trends and challenges likely to shape the fashion business in the twenty-first century.

Chapter 2 introduces the concepts of creativity and authorship, and fine versus applied art which have played such an important role in the development of laws that protect design. It explains the "piracy paradox" argument that legal protections for fashion design are unnecessary and maps the international harmonization of IP laws over the last 100 years.

Chapter 3 focuses on the legal protection provided to the fashion industry under US intellectual property laws. It reviews the development of US law in the area of copyrights, trademarks, and design patents and explores recent case law on design, including the Supreme Court's *Star Athletica* decision.

Chapter 4 focuses on the development of the EU design rights system. It reviews recent case law on originality and the cumulation of design rights and other intellectual property rights, especially copyright, in relation to fashion design through CJEU cases such as *Cofemel*.

DOI: 10.4324/9781003091400-1

Chapter 5 discusses the few remaining differences between the EU design system and the French, Italian, and UK legal systems (since they are the locations of the European fashion capitals). Most of the chapter is focused on the UK system and the differences between it and the EU system, especially since Brexit.

The last chapter focuses on four dimensions of design protection that go beyond IP laws: Other laws and regulations, social and ethical norms, technology, and the economic dimension. It argues that IP laws are not the main, or even the most important, way of protecting creativity. All these dimensions are important and coexist. The optimal protection for innovation in fashion design would balance encouraging creativity and sustainability without destroying the democratization of fashion that has occurred over the last half-century.

References

Agins, Teri. 2000. *The End of Fashion: How Marketing Changed the Clothing Business Forever*. HarperCollins Publishers.

Hanson, Karen. 1990. "Dressing down Dressing up: The Philosophic Fear of Fashion." *Hypatia* 5 (2): 107–21.

Sun, Haochen, Beebe, Barton and Sunder, Madhavi. eds. 2015. *The Luxury Economy and Intellectual Property: Critical Reflections*. New York: Oxford University Press.

1 Introduction to the Fashion Business
Global Industry, Unclear Rules

Introduction

This introductory chapter describes the history of fashion and the creation of a global fashion industry in the twentieth century to provide a basis for understanding the philosophy and practice behind fashion and design's legal protection in different parts of the world. The chapter also reviews the major trends shaping the twenty-first-century business and some of the current challenges the fashion industry faces. Understanding the trends and challenges facing fashion design in the twenty-first-century is important to the development of protection for creativity and design—both in law and in other dimensions.

The Role of Fashion in Society

Evidence that people created textiles has been found in caves occupied by hunter-gatherers in Europe as far back as 25,000 years ago (Barber 1996, 2). Humans, being mostly hairless, have probably been creating clothing for much longer to protect themselves from the weather in all but the most temperate of climates. For most of human history, people spun and wove fabric from natural fibers (mainly linen, wool, cotton, and silk) to make their own clothes. The function of clothing was mainly practical, although, no doubt, even early man and early woman probably chose to adorn themselves beyond mere practical covering. However, fashions likely changed slowly. Until the last few hundred years, creating fabric was so costly that even the wealthy passed on their clothing to the next generation (Sun et al. 2015, 188).

In many ancient, and not-so-ancient, societies, clothing was used as a means of expression (as it still is today) but also to denote a person's place in the societal hierarchy. Sumptuary codes remained strict in some countries well into the nineteenth century, and clothing was a common method of differentiating social groups. Into the late twentieth century, women, particularly, were restricted in what they could wear: Many UK state schools prohibited female pupils from wearing trousers into the 1980s, and certain New York law firms banned trousers for female attorneys until almost the twenty-first century (Sun et al. 2015, 180). In some Muslim countries, women's choice of clothing continues to be policed

DOI: 10.4324/9781003091400-2

today. They are expected to wear head coverings or even fully veil themselves in public settings or when men outside their families are present.

Clothes have long been important beyond their utility. For many people today, clothing is about personal choice, creativity, aesthetics, and even political symbolism. Fashion has become "one of the most influential phenomena of the modern world, fashion reflects and, at the same time, has a profound role in shaping human culture." (Palandri 2020, 3).

A Brief History of Fashion: The Seventeenth to the Twentieth Century

The Importance of Paris

The first place that comes to mind for most people when they think of the fashion business is Paris. In the seventeenth century, Louis XIV made the French capital the center of luxury, and France the world leader in taste and technology. Louis banned imports of anything that could be made in France and set up highly regulating professional guilds to compete against any foreign products. He required his nobles to buy the new, colorful French fashions to wear at court and made Versailles, previously a dowdy hunting lodge, "into a showplace for the best of French culture and industry" (Chrisman-Campbell 2015, 2). Among other innovations, Louis started the still familiar twice-yearly fashion collections to encourage people to buy more clothing. France stayed more or less at the center of the fashion world for the next 300 years.

In the nineteenth century, Charles Worth, an English dressmaker exiled in Paris, outfitted Napoleon III's wife. He was soon dressing the crowned heads of Europe and fueling the demand for the elegant, elite, luxury world of Paris fashion. Worth developed the system of haute couture (high fashion or dressmaking in French)—the production of individually created clothes for a very small number of rich clients. Although Paris is no longer the only fashion center, this system still operates for couture clothing production: Offering a tiny number of elite customers meticulous fit, opulent fabrics, and garments that are hand sewn by different ateliers (skilled artisans).

During the nineteenth and early twentieth century, new fashion trends would spread from Paris to other parts of Europe and the Americas. Paris was the center for haute couture and attracted designers from all over Europe. Although the Parisian couture houses did not, and still do not, make many garments, their designs had a global impact on fashion trends, from the eighteenth century through to today (Godart 2014, 42). Using Worth's empire as an example, Coco Chanel began her haute couture business, House of Chanel, in Paris, expanding in the 1920s to include perfumes. *Les maisons de la haute couture* exerted a considerable influence over the development of first the Parisian and then the global fashion industry and are still important today.

La Federation de la Haute Couture et de la Mode (FHCM), founded in 1868 as La Chambre Syndicale de la Haute Couture, is the influential governing body of the French fashion industry. It still puts on Paris Fashion Week twice each year and represents *les maisons de la haute couture* at the top of the industry. Its rules determine which design houses fulfill the strict criteria to reach the coveted designation of haute couture. Its control over the Paris industry is still important, as a 2008 case concerning photographing Paris Fashion Week shows.

The FHCM accredits the photographers and other press permitted to attend Paris Fashion Week shows. In 2008, France's highest court ruled that fashion shows were protected by copyright, and FHCM could prevent photographers from publishing photographs and videos of the fashions from the shows before the collections were released to the public. The European Court of Human Rights (ECHR) upheld the decision. It held that the exercise of the freedoms envisaged by Article 10 of the European Convention on Human Rights "is subject to duties and responsibilities and may also be subject to formalities, conditions, restrictions, or penalties only to the extent that they are prescribed by law and are necessary in a democratic society." The ECHR held that, since some of the photographs could be purchased, the photographers' commercial purpose was evident. It denied their application for an exception for freedom of expression and found them liable for copyright infringement of the fashion shows.[1]

The Emergence of Four Fashion Capitals

After the Second World War, the destruction in post-war Europe enabled New York City to become a fashion center for the American market. New York City designers focused on the more casual clothes favored by American women such as sports and athletic wear. However, Europe remained an important center of the luxury and fashion industries. London was important for menswear, and Paris for womenswear. Paris haute couture houses continued to develop subsidiary product lines such as perfumes and beauty products. *Pret-à-porter* (ready-to-wear) clothing became popular owing to the post-war economic depression in Europe.

The preeminence of Paris in the fashion industry started to erode in the 1960s. Labor costs rose, and the French government stopped subsidizing designers; the cheaper ready-to-wear collections were becoming more common; and the mini skirt was born—in London, not Paris. However, Paris remained important. As Godart noted in *The Power Structure of Fashion Industry: Fashion Capitals, Globalization and Creativity*, "[o]ther centers of style were not nearly as influential as Paris and generally followed its dictates" (Godart 2014, 41).

Paris also benefited from the continued importance of France in the luxury industry through the creation, in the late 1980s and early 1990s, of the two major luxury fashion conglomerates, LVMH (Moët Hennessy Louis Vuitton) and PPR (Pinault-Printemps-Redoute). PPR was renamed Kering in 2013, a name meant to reflect its "caring" approach. These luxury business empires allowed Paris to retain its global dominance as a fashion capital despite the emergence of major competing markets and the start of the outsourcing of production to low-cost countries in Asia. Some non-European fashion–luxury conglomerates are now emerging. Recently, the Fosun International Limited-backed Fosun Fashion Group, a Chinese-owned fashion conglomerate, changed its name to the Lavin Group (using the French brand name of one of its well-known subsidiaries). It seeks to become China's largest luxury conglomerate. Despite the increasing size and importance of the Chinese market, Paris remains the most important city for the fashion and luxury industries.

London had become the center for menswear in the nineteenth century, and in the 1960s it became the place for young designers. It was multicultural and filled with young people because of the post-war baby boom, and the city also boasted excellent art and design schools.

By the 1970s, Milan, an industrial city, had beaten Rome, Florence, and other Italian cities with textile industries to become Italy's preeminent city of fashion. Its young population, importance in manufacturing, and fashion pioneers such as Giorgio Armani and Gianni Versace solidified its place as the Italian fashion capital, and it joined the three other fashion capitals of the world.

The tradition of twice-yearly fashion weeks in all four fashion capitals became well established. Godart (2014, 43) noted that "Each of these cities has its own identity and occupies a specific symbolic and economic position in the industry."

The fashion capitals' identities have also shaped how legal concepts have developed to protect fashion design. Fashion has long been treated as art in France and is the focus of strong protection, while in Italy and the UK legal protection focused on industrial design. The EU has now created pan-European design rights which can be used to protect fashion design, and Court of Justice of the European Union (CJEU) decisions have tended to follow French legal tradition as it harmonizes EU law. The US has not considered fashion design to be art, and the law focuses more on branding and trademark protection. Chapter 2 explains how the legal concepts that protect fashion have developed, and the following three chapters focus on the protection of design by US and EU laws.

Today, lots of cities have fashion shows, many are home to fashion designers, and the biggest luxury markets are located in the US and China. However, the shows in Paris, London, New York, and Milan remain the ones covered by major fashion magazines and now also social media influencers. "In the eyes of fashion industry stakeholders, New York, London, Milan and Paris matter much more than Tokyo, Shanghai, Mumbai or São Paulo." Since the fashion shows in Paris, London, New York, and Milan get sustained global attention (Godart 2014), these cities are still where most fashion designers live and work. They are also important centers of law and legal protection for fashion designers.[2]

In the hierarchical fashion world up to the late twentieth century, not only were the fashion capitals important, but the powerful editors of fashion magazines such as *Vogue* and *Harper's Bazaar* held enormous power over the creation of new designs as they covered the big four fashion shows and acted as the "arbiters of taste to the masses" (Agins 2000).

Demographic Changes Bring New Challenges

The late-twentieth-century fashion world continued to change rapidly as women entered the workforce in ever larger numbers. Working women spent less money on high fashion and began dressing less formally. French designers, such as Dior and Pierre Cardin, started to cover their losses on haute couture with licensing deals. They put their trademarks on "handbags, jewelry, shoes and bedsheets," which quickly made them money, but, as licensees cut corners and made substandard products, some names were tarnished. Working women started to turn their backs "on the more foolish and transient aspects of fashion runways and cycles," and casual clothes became popular "and acceptable—even in the office." Women also started to look for cheaper and more utilitarian clothes: "[I]t became a badge of honor to be a bargain hunter." Designer clothes started to look like a "rip-off." Finally, marketability became more important than fanciful haute couture (Agins 2000, 15).

Wall Street Journal reporter Teri Agins argued in her book *The End of Fashion* that these trends have led to the end of fashion, but what they've done is to make designer image, lifestyle branding, and marketing more important to fashion design than creativity and design. All of these trends have been amplified in the twenty-first century by the rise of social media influencers (discussed later in this chapter). The importance of branding can be seen in the focus on trademarks as a means to protect fashion design, particularly in the US market.

The Globalization of Manufacturing

By the late twentieth century, all kinds of companies were finding that shifting their manufacturing to lower labor cost countries in Asia had become very attractive. The cost savings of making clothing, a labor-intensive product, in these countries had been pushed by the US government in the 1970s. Factors such as quality control and time to market meant that, as late as the 1990s, although many manufacturers had shifted production to Asia with lower labor costs, about half of clothes were still manufactured in the US.[3]

The growth of international free trade agreements also made manufacturing in lower labor cost countries more attractive to designers. After World War II, the allies created the General Agreement on Tariffs and Trade (GATT) to bring down tariff barriers. Initially, the Multifibre Arrangement (MFA) established quotas for textiles from countries with cheap labor, such as China, to avoid serious economic damage from rapid increases in imports. In 1995, a new World Trade Organization (WTO) Agreement on Textile and Clothing (ACT) took over from the MFA, and, by 2005, the textiles manufacturing sector stopped getting special treatment and became fully integrated into normal GATT rules, meaning that designers could theoretically shift all clothing manufacturing from high labor cost countries to the lower cost countries, often in Asia.

In 1995, the US also became part of the North American Free Trade Agreement (NAFTA) which enabled manufacturers (including textile and apparel manufacturers) to move production to Mexico. Many companies began producing in Mexico to exploit the cheap labor there. Today, China, Bangladesh, Vietnam, Indonesia, and other poorer, mainly Asian, nations are large contributors of labor in the manufacture of clothing, particularly in fast fashion.

Even though very few apparel manufacturers now make their clothing in the US or Western Europe, most fashion designers have remained based in or around the four fashion capitals. In 2020, three-quarters of fashion designers in the US were based in New York, Los Angeles, and Miami.

In the last decade or so, shifts in global trade have brought back a small number of textile jobs to the US from these countries (a process called "re-shoring"). A small number of foreign textile manufacturers, frustrated by tariffs and rising wages, have moved production to the US South.

So, while fashion design remains focused on the four major fashion capitals in Europe and the US, the manufacture of clothing is now largely divorced from designers and is produced in the Global South, mainly in Asia.

The Twenty-First-Century Fashion Industry

Several of the trends that started in the late twentieth century continue to pull apart the old hierarchy of the industry. Globalization has led to the creation of fast fashion, which has itself led to large increases in piracy and counterfeiting. Digital technology has also wrought major changes to the fashion industry and promises more.

Overproduction in the fashion industry has unleashed concerns about sustainability, and a new focus on circular economy business models for textiles. By the 2000s, many of the economic, technological, and cultural restrictions that once made fashion the province of the elite few had disappeared. According to Italian law professor Barbara Pozzo: "Clothes have been increasingly approached as a means of self-expression, rather than as a signifier of status or profession" (Pozzo 2020).

As the price of clothing manufactured in the Global South has dramatically decreased, the fashion cycle has sped up. Fashion has been democratized. Cheap new clothing reaches the stores not just for the two fashion seasons but almost weekly. The overconsumption of fashion is driven by the creation of meaning in clothes and the transformation of unique to mass-produced clothing which drives new consumption. Capitalism benefits from fashion consumption, and fashion and capitalism are intertwined. Clothing production has doubled over the last 15 years, and we keep it half as long (see Figure 1.1) ("A New Textiles Economy" 2017).

The Birth of Fast Fashion

Mark Brewer of Sheffield Business School explains the fast fashion business model was pioneered by Zara and utilizes "short production times" to churn out "trendy designs." Fast fashion companies don't invest in design but "take inspiration from trends and customer behavior." Brewer states that fast fashion is a drag on innovation that favors established and well-known designers while harming emerging designers (Brewer 2017, 760). Global supply chains enable fast fashion retailers to get more clothing into stores more cheaply and quickly than ever

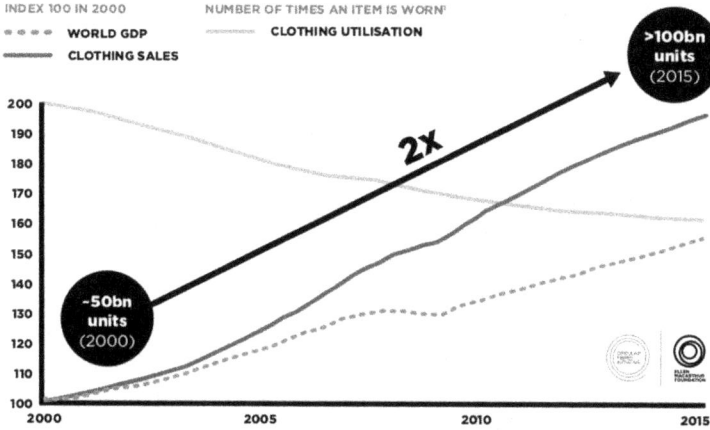

INDEX 100 IN 2000 NUMBER OF TIMES AN ITEM IS WORN[1]

• • • • WORLD GDP ------- CLOTHING UTILISATION
——— CLOTHING SALES

>100bn units (2015)

2X

−50bn units (2000)

1 Average number of times a garment is worn before it ceases to be used
Source: Euromonitor International Apparel & Footwear 2016 Edition (volume sales trends 2005–2015); World Bank, *World development indicators – GD* (2017)

Figure 1.1 Growth of clothing sales and decline in clothing utilization since 2000

before. Fast fashion retailers such as Forever 21, H&M, Topshop, and Primark copied Zara's business model to become household names in a few short years. More recently, they have been joined by online-only offerings such as Shein, Fashion Nova, and Asos.

Fast fashion focuses on the speedy production of already existing styles that have a track record of selling well. It encourages copying and slows innovation and experimentation in design as it speeds up the manufacturing process. Zerbo argued that widespread copying in fast fashion can lead to a "loss of sales and licensing deals" and damage to designers and their brand images (Zerbo 2017, 601).

The Growth of Luxury and Branding

As well as cheap fast fashion, the twenty-first century has seen the bifurcation of the fashion market to include two large segments: fast fashion and luxury. From ancient times, luxury (the income necessary to purchase valuable goods) has been represented as the vice of a tiny group of elites. But luxury has now become democratized. As more and more people can afford to indulge in luxury goods, from fashion to fine wines, social scientists have had to create new categories of luxury from "exceptional or true luxury," through to "accessible or mass-market luxury." Traditional luxury items such as fashion, jewelry, and fragrances are now something that many people can afford. For example, Yves Saint Laurent perfume sales increased 16 times between 1979 and 1989 as it became an accessible luxury. Some argue that this enlargement of the luxury industry means there is no true luxury if many can afford it. However, the market for luxury fashion brands has grown (McNeil and Riello 2016, 252).

In *A Golden Opportunity: Supporting Up-and-Coming U.S. Luxury Designers Through Design Legislation*, Shieva Salehnia said

> The United States and the emerging market of China are currently the biggest players in the personal luxury goods market. The United States is the largest global market for personal luxury goods, accounting for approximately 31 percent of all sales worldwide—greater than the next four markets combined.[4]

Fashion is an important part of the luxury goods market. It "has been an imperative element of the personal (global) luxury goods industry, accounting for 24 percent of all global luxury market sales" (Salehnia 2016, 367).

Although luxury sales dropped during the COVID-19 pandemic, by the end of 2021 many luxury brands were seeing huge increases in their sales. LVMH 2021 sales were up 44% on the year before and 19% on pre-pandemic sales. News reports suggested the luxury conglomerate achieved "record levels of revenue and profitability" (TFL 2022). The luxury market is likely to continue to be important in the fashion industry. More designers in the luxury fashion industry tend to be concerned with counterfeiting and piracy and focus more on the legal protection of their designs.

Counterfeiting and Piracy

With the movement of clothing production to low labor cost countries, one of the most pronounced twenty-first-century trends for designers has been the increase in the number of counterfeit goods in the fashion supply chain. A 2019 OECD–EUIPO study found that counterfeit and pirated products accounted for as much as $509 billion in world trade, which implies that as much as 3.3% of total world trade is in counterfeit and pirated products. A higher percentage of clothing and footwear is fake (see Figure 1.2).

The terms counterfeit and piracy are used to describe a range of illicit activities related to intellectual property rights (IPRs). There are definitions of both these terms in the WTO Agreement on Trade-Related Aspects of Intellectual Property Rights (TRIPS Agreement).

Counterfeiting is the manufacturing and distribution of goods using someone else's name or brand without permission. Under TRIPS,

> Counterfeit trademark goods shall mean any goods, including packaging, bearing without authorization a trademark which is identical to the trademark validly registered in respect of such goods, or which cannot be distinguished in its essential aspects from such a trademark and which thereby infringes the rights of the owner of the trademark in question under the law of the country of importation.

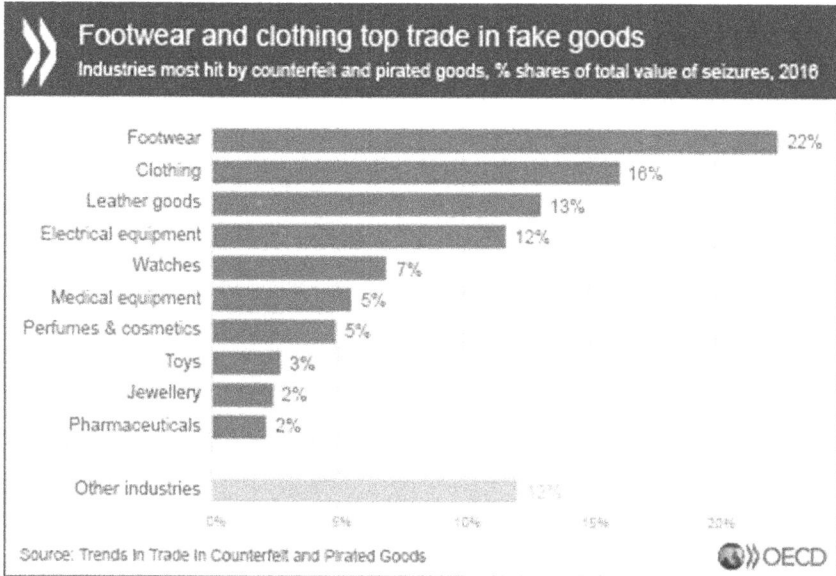

Footwear and clothing top trade in fake goods
Industries most hit by counterfeit and pirated goods, % shares of total value of seizures, 2016

Footwear	22%
Clothing	16%
Leather goods	13%
Electrical equipment	12%
Watches	7%
Medical equipment	5%
Perfumes & cosmetics	5%
Toys	3%
Jewellery	2%
Pharmaceuticals	2%
Other industries	12%

Source: Trends in Trade in Counterfeit and Pirated Goods

OECD

Figure 1.2 OECD top trade in fake footwear and clothing goods

TRIPS defines *piracy* in terms of copyright.

> Pirated copyright goods shall mean any goods which are copies made without the consent of the right holder or person duly authorized by the right holder in the country of production and which are made directly or indirectly from an article where the making of that copy would have constituted an infringement of a copyright or a related right under the law of the country of importation.

Counterfeit goods generally infringe a trademark, design right, or patent, and pirated goods generally infringe a copyright or design right protection.

The growth of e-commerce platforms has also facilitated the rise in sales of fake and counterfeit goods. A bricks and mortar store can vet products and will likely think twice about liability issues before carrying a counterfeit item. However, it's relatively easy for a seller of fakes to set up on Amazon or eBay and sell products directly to consumers. E-commerce essentially allows what were formerly flea market sellers to enter legitimate markets and sell a lot of goods. Third-party sales on Amazon (many of which are legitimate) are now worth $160 billion. The site says that it devotes a substantial amount of time and resources to finding and eliminating fakes and counterfeits with machine learning and data science "to protect our customers from fraud and abuse." However, many investigations have found substantial numbers of fakes for sale on Amazon and other online retailers (Suthivarakom 2020).

Government Policy and Counterfeiting

In both the US and EU, stopping the trade in fake goods has become an important government policy objective. In both regions, the criminal penalties to combat trade in counterfeit goods have been strengthened. For example, in the US, the Stop Counterfeiting in Manufactured Goods Act 2006 (18 U.S.C. §§ 2320) provides for fines of up to $15 million, prison terms of up to 20 years, and mandatory forfeiture, destruction, and restitution provisions for trafficking in counterfeit goods. How fakes are defined is important to creativity and its protection in the fashion industry.

All of the reports produced by governments and international bodies focus on the negative effects of the rise of counterfeiting and piracy. These reports consistently find that around 70% of pirated and counterfeit goods come from China, and the top three categories of fakes are footwear, knit clothing, and leather goods, including handbags (see Figure 1.2). According to the latest OECD–EUIPO report, 16% of counterfeit products are clothing, the second largest category of counterfeit goods behind footwear. The US is the country most affected by counterfeits. Twenty-four percent of fake products seized used US brand names or trademarks, followed by brands from France (17%), Italy (15%), Switzerland (11%), and Germany (9%).

These reports often "translate" lost fashion sales into large job losses in the fashion industry and suggest that the "knock on effects" of counterfeit sales on other sectors are huge. The reports (and also news articles about piracy and counterfeiting) create a sense that counterfeiting and piracy have only negative consequences. The OECD/EUIPO report listed six consequences of IPR infringement, all costly or harmful to the fashion business. They included substantial financial and job losses for the creative industries like fashion, a loss of artistic and technological innovation, damage to competitiveness and the growth of the world economy, health and safety risks, environmental degradation, an undermining of political stability, and even threats to national security from funding terrorism and organized crime (OECD/EUIPO 2019).

The reports also tend to focus almost exclusively on two sets of central bad actors: consumers who knowingly purchase fakes and governments that don't enforce IP laws and allow corruption to flourish. They rarely consider other stakeholders like manufacturers or designers.

However, a close reading of the reports provides some indication that figures on fake goods should be viewed with some caution. For example, the OECD/EUIPO report qualified its high figures for lost sales with a short admission that the hidden and secret nature of counterfeiting make it extremely hard to accurately quantify its costs. It also noted that it cannot always be assumed that "the purchase of a counterfeit good displaces the sale of the corresponding genuine product." The majority (58.5%) "of counterfeit and pirated products traded worldwide in 2016 were sold to consumers who actually knew they were buying fake products" (OECD/EUIPO 2019, 35).

Real or Fake? It's Complicated

The growth in counterfeiting and piracy understandably concerns designers. However, the distinction between real and fake goods is not always simple and clear. They are often hard to tell apart. In most reports on counterfeits, this information is buried.

In reality, there are at least three types of fakes. First, there are counterfeit or knock-off products that are copied by a third party without any input from the original brand owner or designer. These might accurately be termed "real fakes." The second type is produced in the same factories as the "real" products. Often, these products are assembled on the same lines as those created for the legitimate brands on nights and/or weekends. They are sometimes called "third shift" or "ghost shift" products. The factory owner (with or without the brand owners' knowledge) makes the fakes and sells them on the black or grey market on his or her own account. These "over-runs" are particularly hard to spot and to control (Neuwirth 2017, 458). A third type of fake occurs when the original brand owner knowingly strikes a deal which foresees the sale of a considerable number of items on the grey market (of perhaps only slightly inferior quality), with a direct sharing of the profits. These could be called "grey market real products."

Although most of the reports on fakes focus on the damage they do, not all fakes cause lost sales for genuine products and financial losses for designers. As the OECD–EUIPO report noted, many consumers are aware, often owing to the price differential, that they are buying a fake and would not have purchased a genuine product anyway. In fact, fakes can sometimes create positive externalities for producers of real products. They may make some consumers more willing to pay for the better-made real products (a positive effect). Some fashion designers have even faked themselves to get free advertising for their brand. Neuwirth described "One highly 'creative' marketing strategy from a South African fashion designer who deliberately faked their own T-shirt brand called 'Love Jozi' to increase the brand's exclusive appeal. The exercise lasted for two years before being revealed" (Neuwirth 2017, 462). At other times, a consumer may buy a fake and then "gradually gets used to it, feels a connection with it, and later finds him- or herself identifying with the brand name and eventually purchases further items from official flagship stores" (Neuwirth 2017, 455).

Another way that the marketing of fakes may assist designers and brand owners is that it works as "an extension at the lower base of the fashion pyramid which is hierarchically structured from haute couture collections down via designer collections, bridge fashion collections, better fashions, and fashion-basics to basic commodities" (Neuwirth 2017, 452). The lines of differentiation between designers and cheaper fashion have already become blurred as star designers create collections for fast fashion retailers and big box stores. Some commentators argue that the addition of fakes at the bottom simply speeds up the induced obsolescence of old designs which powers innovation in the fashion industry (Raustiala and Sprigman 2006).

Obviously, a fake or counterfeit can create a negative effect. It can diminish the appeal of a real product if the buyer of the fake believes his lower-quality counterfeit to be real and attributes it to the real brand owner. Trade in counterfeits can also be associated with smuggling and criminal activity. How fakes and counterfeits are defined and government policy toward them are important and relevant to the legal protection of design discussed in subsequent chapters.

Digital Technology in the Fashion Business

As in other areas of the economy, the use of digital technology has grown rapidly in the fashion design business, and it is already being used in a variety of ways by fashion designers. Social media platforms and developments in AI are changing how designers create, collaborate, and protect their creations. Some of the effects of these new technologies on design protection are discussed in more detail in Chapter 6.

Social Media

Until the advent of social media, the fashion week shows in Paris, London, New York, and Milan, high-end fashion magazines such as *Vogue* and *Harper's Bazaar*, and perhaps a few fashion icons such as Jackie Kennedy and Princess Diana were the biggest influencers of fashion trends.

Social media platforms, particularly visual platforms such as Instagram, YouTube, and TikTok, have increased the democratization of the once hierarchical fashion industry and moved it further from the system where Paris haute couture houses—and a few elites—dictated style and ushered in the next new thing. Social media sites enable anyone to broadcast their fashion choices instantly around the world. As a result, the social media influencer (including even virtual social media influencers who are avatars, not real people) has become a new force in the world of fashion. Many savvy influencers have amassed huge followings and are able to earn a living by "endorsement deals with major brands, in addition to earning money through advertising and merchandise sales" (Roose 2019).

Several fashion brands and beauty companies have used social media to build their brands almost entirely online. For example, Glossier, the beauty company, "raised $100 million at a valuation of more than $1 billion, and Away, the luggage start-up, has a ubiquitous Instagram ad campaign that helped it reach a valuation of $1.4 billion" (Roose 2019). Fashion Nova, an online-only fast fashion brand, leans on a vast network of celebrities, influencers, and random selfie-takers who post about the brand relentlessly on social media. It is built to satisfy an online clientele with its range of mass-producing cheap clothes that look expensive (Kitroeff 2019).

Young emerging and media-savvy designers have also found other benefits from the rise in the use of social media. For example, it has given them a way to seek relief for the infringement of their designs at less cost than legal proceedings. Social media can spread information about copying and fakes to shame those who do these things. It is faster and cheaper and more accessible than legal proceedings (Palandri 2020, 18). These aspects of social media as a design protection mechanism are discussed in Chapter 6.

Virtual Worlds, AI and 3D Printing

Over the last few years, luxury fashion brands such as Balenciaga and Gucci have teamed up with game designers to offer digital branded clothing for virtual avatars. This area of digital business will likely take off more with the new focus on the metaverse. Many of these luxury conglomerates have set up divisions to focus on this new opportunity.

Luxury brands are also showing great interest in AI and non-fungible tokens (NFTs; unique digital assets whose ownership and authenticity are verified on blockchains and which can be bought and sold in the metaverse, often with cryptocurrency). A major benefit of NFTs is that they can be used to authenticate luxury fashion items, acting as product passports. The possible role of NFTs and AIs in protecting creativity is discussed in Chapter 6.

Fashion's Global Sustainability

The concept of sustainability was first defined in the United Nations 1987 "Report of the World Commission on Environment and Development: Our Common Future":

> Sustainable development is development that meets the needs of the present without compromising the ability of future generations to meet their own needs ... [It] is a process of change in which the exploitation of resources, the direction of investments, the orientation of technological development; and institutional changes are all in harmony and enhance both current and future potential to meet human needs and aspirations.
>
> (Brundtland 1987)

Although this definition is clear and covers both the environment and social aspects of sustainability, there is still a lot of debate in the fashion business over what sustainability means and how it can be measured. Over the last two decades, the overproduction of clothing and the exploitation of fashion industry workers have become well known. Action on these issues is important for the future of the industry, and especially for creativity and design to flourish, but the problems and their solutions are complex and require cooperation between many stakeholders in the fashion industry including designers and government policy makers. Some possible changes are discussed in Chapter 6.

Harmful Effects of Fast Fashion

The biggest difficulty in assessing fashion's environmental, social, and economic (ESG) effects is the accuracy of data on the industry. What quantities of greenhouse gasses (GHGs) are produced in the manufacture of clothing, how much waste the fashion industry produces, how many garments are made per year, and even how many workers make our clothes are all disputed, and accurate statistics are hard to find.[5]

Even if there is dispute about the actual amount of pollution from the fashion industry, "The Environmental Price of Fast Fashion," published in *Nature Reviews* in 2020, states that the fashion industry's high production of GHGs comes from high energy use in manufacture and the fact that clothing is shipped around the world during manufacturing (to take advantage of various free trade agreements) and is then shipped again for global sales (Niinimäki et al. 2020, 190). Fast fashion has accelerated these processes.

Since most clothing, and particularly fast fashion, is produced in countries that lack environmental protection laws, waste and pollution of the earth are also common effects of fashion production. For example, thousands of gallons of toxins are released in the manufacturing processes that make our clothing (Elrod 2017, 593).

Workers who make clothing, particularly fast fashion, are also often exploited. They receive some of the lowest wages in the world. Cheap labor correlates with the lack of safety regulations and harmful working conditions. Many countries chosen by apparel manufacturers do not require workers to receive a living wage or factories to ensure safe working environments. Cheap labor also often means child labor (Elrod 2017, 590).

The huge increase in clothing purchases has sharply exacerbated the harmful effects of the industry. There has been a more than 750% increase in clothing purchases in the US since 1960. For reference, that's nearly ten times more than the increase in the US population over the same time period. Even since 2000, clothing purchases have doubled. This growth in clothing waste coincides with the dominance of fast fashion brands such as H&M and Zara, whose business models are based on selling low-priced items at high volumes.

According to the *Wall Street Journal*, the average person in the US buys 68 pieces of clothing per year, five times more than they did in 1980. By contrast, consumers in India bought five items, and those in Vietnam bought two items each (Thomas 2019). Just ten countries account for three-quarters of all clothes purchased and two-thirds of all footwear. They are the US, China, India, Japan, Germany, the UK, Russia, France, Italy, and Brazil. All four countries representing the fashion capitals are on this list, as is another rich country: Germany. China, India, and Brazil are on the list because of the large size of their populations. Whether or not the figures on the number of outfits purchased are entirely accurate, it is clear that the rich countries buy large amounts of clothing and have increased their purchases significantly over the last two decades as fast fashion has become ubiquitous (see Figure 1.3).

As fast fashion has proliferated, the average number of times a garment is worn before being discarded has shrunk by 36%. The US has a particularly low rate of wear, and garments are often discarded after only seven to ten wears (Thomas 2019). Many discarded garments are not recycled and end their lives in landfills. In 2018, the last year for which the Environmental Protection Agency (EPA) has

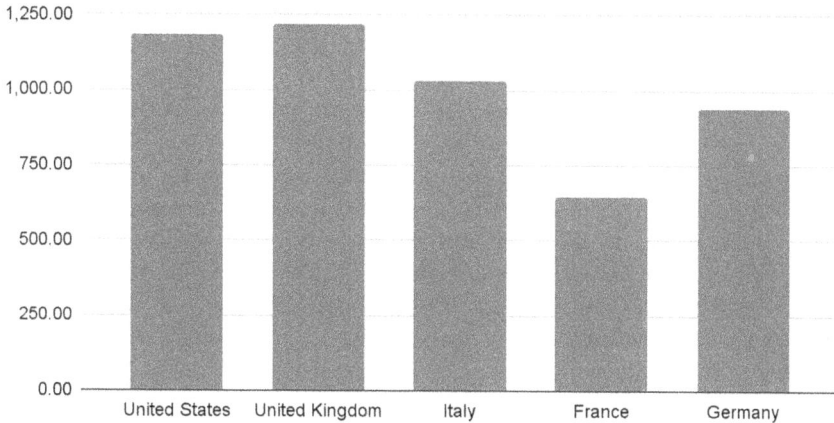

Data from Statistica: Global apparel market - statistics & facts 2020

Figure 1.3 Fashion consumer spending per capita in 2020 (US$)

data, the US generated 11.3 million tons of municipal solid waste (MSW). This equates to around 71 pounds of waste per person per year, and about a third of that waste is textiles, which are mainly old clothing (Pierre-Louis 2019). In the UK, which buys more clothing than any other nation in Europe, consumers discard around 1 million metric tons of clothing per year. Although there is a developed network of charity shops in the UK which recycle some of this, much is discarded, with 80% incinerated and 20% going into landfills ("Fixing Fashion" 2019).

The amount of textile waste created by the fashion industry has led some governments and clothing brands to focus on reducing pollution and dealing with the waste. In 2019, the French government announced a law to ensure that unsold materials—including in the fashion sector—"are not thrown away or destroyed" but are recycled or reused instead. The Anti-Waste Law came into force in 2020. It bans designers and luxury goods companies from destroying any unsold items. In 2020, British luxury brand Burberry announced the ReBurberry Fabric Initiative. It will donate leftover fabrics to fashion students across the UK as part of its ongoing commitment to supporting creative communities (British Fashion Council 2020). Laws and norms that might make fashion more sustainable are discussed in Chapter 6 as, although they focus on reducing waste, they may also protect creativity and design.

The Circular Economy

The circular economy aims to create new models of production and consumption such as renting, recycling, and repair to keep textiles in use for as long as possible. The rising circular economy business models such as reuse and resale are major consumer trends, especially among younger consumers. "Companies that emphasize more sustainable practices make up the slow fashion movement, prizing craftsmanship, good stewardship, and quality products." These companies focus on more ethical sourcing and production techniques, more durable materials, and recycling and reuse (Brewer 2019, 7).

Millennial and Gen Z buying habits are much more focused on sustainability and circular economy models than those of older generations, and so offering these consumers the ability to buy, sell, and switch out second-hand clothing items is becoming a popular business model. Many companies are rushing to fill this space which has led to some concerns as luxury brands particularly attempt to control the second-hand sale of their goods (Kur 2021).

The trends in the fashion industry toward sustainability and the circular economy are changing the industry and likely to have an impact on the way designers create and the protection of design. This is discussed in more detail in Chapter 6.

The Economics and Organization of the Global Fashion Industry

Industry Size

Fashion is now a huge global industry. As with aspects such as the sustainability of the fashion industry, there is a wide variation in measurements of the size and value of the industry ranging from $1.5 to $3 trillion annually. In 2020, Statistica valued the fashion business at over $1.53 trillion, likely rising to $2 trillion by 2026. The UN Alliance for Sustainable Fashion values clothes manufacturing at $2.4 trillion, and Fashion United Business Intelligence (Fashion United) asserts that fashion is a $3-trillion industry. Euromonitor estimates that the global apparel and footwear market will only undergo moderate growth over the next decade and will be worth $3.3 trillion by 2030. The big three retail markets will remain the EU, US, and China, with the main growth occurring in the Chinese and other Asian markets, while the EU and US are steady.

Another area of dispute is the numbers who work in the fashion industry. According to Elisha Teibel in an article entitled "Waste Size: The Skinny on the Environmental Cost of the Fashion Industry," the industry is also one of the most labor-intensive industries on the planet employing over 60 million people (Teibel 2019). The UN Alliance for Sustainable Fashion and Fashion United both put the number employed in the fashion industry substantially higher at over 300 million people worldwide.

The huge variation in measurements for the fashion industry is partly due to what is included in the definition of this industry. Design and designers constitute a small part of the global concern that comprises the fashion industry which, at its broadest, includes design creation, clothes and textile manufacturing, retail, and marketing operations, and even the production of textile raw materials on farms and in factories. Depending on where you draw the line between the business of fashion and other parts of the value chain gets you very different figures on the environmental impact of the industry. Whatever its size, fashion is a major global industry. It dwarfs other creative industries such as film and publishing in size. The film industry as of 2019 was worth a total of $116 billion dollars worldwide, and the publishing industry was smaller at $109 billion.

Unlike most global industries, fashion is not a heavily concentrated industry with a few companies that have huge market shares. The ten leading fashion brands by value are Nike, Inditex (owner of Zara), Adidas, H&M, Cartier, LVMH (Louis Vuitton, Tiffany, etc.), Uniqlo, Hermès, Gucci, and Rolex. These major brands are a mix of fast fashion, sportswear, and luxury brands. Other leading companies include the VF Corporation (owner of 13 brands, as different as Supreme, The North Face, and Timberland), PVH (owners of brands Tommy Hilfiger, Calvin Klein, and Warner's), Hanesbrands (owners of Hanes, Champion, and Playtex), Tapestry Inc (owners of brands Kate Spade, Coach, and other luxury brands), and Ralph Lauren. None control more than a few percent of the market. Many companies compete in this fragmented market, and there are many types of organization. Some companies do not employ designers but commission individual designers. Some companies integrate all operations, from the design of clothing through to the manufacture and retail sales.

The Role of Fashion Designers

Fashion designers make up quite a small part of the global fashion industry. In 2020, there were around 30,000 people working in the fashion design industry in the US (O'Connor 2020). Creative types and designers in fashion often have significantly overlapping roles. A well-known designer may display her designs on a catwalk and in a museum and sell a diffusion line to a mass market store.

The lines between fast and luxury fashion have been blurred, and the industry as a whole is selling more clothes. The twenty-first-century trends related to the globalization and democratization of fashion have led many elite designers and luxury brands to expand their markets by using mass merchants to target a wider audience with limited edition lines. Well-known designers often create special, limited, lower-priced items for sale in big box stores such as Target. Fast fashion brands such as H&M also carry special limited-run lines from well-known designers. These lines capture a demographic that is younger and more price-conscious than the usual luxury purchaser. The result has been a blurring of the line between luxury and mass market and a huge increase in the number of clothes we buy.

Despite its immense size, the fashion industry can still be described as a small club and a "tangled web of conflicts." In 2018, the Fashion Law news site criticized the fashion business as

> a byzantine ecosystem born largely from the industry's failure to look outside of its closest circle of friends (and business collaborators) for talent. The result is a significant overlap of roles—a magazine editor styling a brand's runway show, a critic writing a brand's show notes, an investor acting as a judge in a design competition, or the same handful of casting directors

determining which models walk in shows and appear in ad campaigns during a season.

(TFL 2018)

Only a few major global fashion brands employ large numbers of designers. Gucci and LVMH (owners of 75 luxury brands, including Christian Dior, Louis Vuitton, and Stella McCartney) on the luxury side, H&M and Zara on the fast fashion side, and Nike and Adidas in footwear and sports all employ in-house designers to create their designs. However, most fashion designers work alone or for small companies, and, even though some are famous names, there are few, if any, designers with anything more than a fraction of the global fashion market. Designers often work on commissions, work collaboratively with other designers, and continue to be clustered around the four global fashion capitals.

An understanding of how designers work in practice is relevant to an understanding of the legal concepts which govern the protection of creativity. These concepts are discussed in the next chapter.

Notes

1   The FHCM had created a system to monitor the use of photographs taken during fashion shows. Only photographers who had agreed to specific contract terms were allowed to take photographs at the shows, and the contract prohibited using the photographs for commercial purposes. The three photographers argued that they should be permitted to upload the photographs to the internet for the purposes of reporting current events under the French Intellectual Property Code as well as under Article 10 ("Freedom of Expression") of the European Convention on Human Rights which prevents the author of a copyrighted work from stopping the reproduction of it for news reporting, as long as the author's name is clearly indicated.

2   Shieva Salehnia described how the system of fashion weeks worked in her 2016 article "A Golden Opportunity: Supporting Up-and-Coming US Luxury Designers Through Design Legislation." For about a month every spring and fall, each one of the world's four fashion capitals—New York City, London, Milan, and Paris—host, for one week at a time, the biggest luxury brands' seasonal runway shows. The shows allow designers the opportunity to present their collections as a cohesive experience for the major retailers, the press, and fashion editors traditionally on the guest list. After seeing a collection, retailers place orders for the clothes, which are then manufactured and shipped to retail locations within four to six months of the presentation time. Fashion magazines then run spreads with the new collections three to four months before the clothes arrive in stores.

3   The American Apparel and Footwear Association reported that, in 1991, American-made apparel accounted for 56.2% of all clothing purchased in the US. In 2020, it was estimated at less than 3%.

4   Statistica data from 2021 shows that the US remains the top-ranked personal luxury goods market with an estimated market value of about €55 billion ($63 billion). China has grown to be the second biggest luxury market with an estimated €44 billion ($50 billion) in market value.

5   McKinsey, the United Nations, the Ellen MacArthur Foundation, and the World Bank all give figures for GHGs which vary widely. They attribute 2–10% of GHG emissions to the fashion industry. The highest figure of 10% is more than the emissions of Germany, France, and the UK combined. However, it is hard to find any scien-

tific evidence or accepted measurements on which these figures are based, and more recently they have been challenged by a large number of people, including Wicker (2020).

References

"A New Textiles Economy: Redesigning Fashion's Future." 2017. Ellen MacArthur Foundation. https://archive.ellenmacarthurfoundation.org/assets/downloads/A-New -Textiles-Economy.pdf.

Agins, Teri. 2000. *The End of Fashion: How Marketing Changed the Clothing Business Forever*. HarperCollins Publishers.

Barber, Elizabeth Wayland. 1996. *Women's Work: The First 20,000 Years Women, Cloth, and Society in Early Times*. WW Norton.

Brewer, Mark K. 2017. "Fashion Law: More than Wigs, Gowns, and Intellectual Property." *San Diego Law Review*, 54 (4): 739–84.

———. 2019. "Slow Fashion in a Fast Fashion World: Promoting Sustainability and Responsibility." *Laws* 8 (4): 24. https://doi.org/10.3390/laws8040024.

British Fashion Council. 2020. "Burberry Announces the Launch of Reburberry Fabric in Partnership with the British Fashion Council." December 8, 2020. https://www.bri tishfashioncouncil.co.uk/bfcnews/4350/burberry-announces-the-launch-of-reburberry -fabric-in-partnership-with-the-british-fashion-council.

Brundtland, Gro Harlem. 1987. "Report of the World Commission on Environment and Development: Our Common Future." United Nations General Assembly document A/42/427.

Chrisman-Campbell, Kimberley. 2015. "The King of Couture: How Louis XIV Invented Fashion as We Know It." *The Atlantic*. September 1, 2015. https://www.theatlantic.com /entertainment/archive/2015/09/the-king-of-couture/402952/.

Elrod, Cassandra. 2017. "The Domino Effect: How Inadequate Intellectual Property Rights in the Fashion Industry Affect Global Sustainability." *Indiana Journal of Global Legal Issues* 24 (2): 575–96.

"Fixing Fashion: Clothing Consumption and Sustainability." 2019. HC 1952. House of Commons Environmental Audit Committee. https://publications.parliament.uk/pa/ cm201719/cmselect/cmenvaud/1952/1952.pdf.

Godart, Frederick. 2014. "The Power Structure of Fashion Industry: Fashion Capitals, Globalization and Creativity." *International Journal of Fashion Studies* 1 (1): 39–55.

Kitroeff, Natalie. 2019. "Fashion Nova's Secret: Underpaid Workers in Los Angeles Factories." The New York Times, December 16, 2019, sec. Business. https://www .nytimes.com/2019/12/16/business/fashion-nova-underpaid-workers.html.

Kur. 2021. "'As Good as New': Sale of Repaired or Refurbished Goods: Commendable Practice or Trade Mark Infringement?" *GRUR International*, 70 (3): 228–236.

McNeil, Peter, and Giorgio Riello. 2016. *Luxury A Rich History*. Oxford University Press.

Neuwirth, Rostam. 2017. "Counterfeiting and Piracy in International Trade: The Good, the Bad and the … Oxymoron of 'Real Fakes.'" *Queen Mary Journal of Intellectual Property* 7 (4): 444–67.

Niinimäki, Krisi, Greg Peters, Helena Dahlbo, Patsy Perry, Timo Rissanen, and Alison Gwilt. 2020. "The Environmental Price of Fast Fashion." *Nature Reviews. Earth & Environment* 1 (April): 189–200.

O'Connor, Claire. 2020. "Fashion Designers in the US." 54149. IBIS World.

OECD/EUIPO. 2019. "Trends in Trade in Counterfeit and Pirated Goods, Illicit Trade." OECD Publishing, Paris/European Union Intellectual Property Office. https://doi.org /10.1787/g2g9f533-en.

Palandri, Lucrezia. 2020. "Fashion as Art: Rights and Remedies in the Age of Social Media." *Laws* 9 (1): 1–9. https://doi.org/10.3390/laws9010009.

Pierre-Louis, Kendra. 2019. "How to Buy Clothes That Are Built to Last." The New York Times, September 25, 2019, sec. Climate. https://www.nytimes.com/interactive/2019/ climate/sustainable-clothing.html.

Pozzo, Barbara. 2020. "Fashion between Inspiration and Appropriation." *MDPI Laws*, February. https://www.mdpi.com/2075-471X/9/1/5.

Raustiala, Kal, and Christopher Sprigman. 2006. "The Piracy Paradox: Innovation and Intellectual Property in Fashion Design." *Virginia Law Review* 92: 1687–1775.

Roose, Kevin. 2019. "Don't Scoff at Influencers. They're Taking Over the World." The New York Times, July 16, 2019, sec. Technology. https://www.nytimes.com/2019/07 /16/technology/vidcon-social-media-influencers.html.

Salehnia, Shieva. 2016. "A Golden Opportunity: Supporting Up-and-Coming US Luxury Designers Through Design Legislation." *Brooklyn Journal of International Law* 42, no.1: 367–424.

Sun, Haochen, Barton Beebe, and Sunder Madhavi. 2015. *The Luxury Economy and Intellectual Property*. Oxford University Press.

Suthivarakom, Ganda. 2020. "Welcome to the Era of Fake Products." Wirecutter: Reviews for the Real World (blog). February 11, 2020. https://www.nytimes.com/wirecutter/ blog/amazon-counterfeit-fake-products.

Teibel, Elisha. 2019. "Waste Size: The Skinny On The Environmental Costs Of The Fashion Industry,." *William & Mary Environmental Law and Policy Review* 43: 595–638.

TFL. 2018. "The Fashion Industry: A Small Club, A Tangled Web of Conflicts." The Fashion Law. January 3, 2018. https://www.thefashionlaw.com/fashion-industry-a -small-club-a-tangled-web/.

———. 2022. "LVMH Sales Top $71 Billion in 2021, Helped by Fashion and Leather Goods." The Fashion Law, January 27, 2022. https://www.thefashionlaw.com/lvmh -sales-top-71-billion-in-2021-helped-by-fashion-leather-goods.

Thomas, Dana. 2019. "The High Price of Fast Fashion." *Wall Street Journal*, August 29, 2019, sec. Life. https://www.wsj.com/articles/the-high-price-of-fast-fashion -11567096637.

Wicker, Alden. 2020. "Fashion Has a Misinformation Problem. That's Bad for the Environment." Vox. January 27, 2020. https://www.vox.com/the-goods/2020/1/27 /21080107/fashion-environment-facts-statistics-impact.

Zerbo, Julie. 2017. "Protecting Fashion Designs: Not Only 'What?' But 'Who?'" *American University Business Law Review* 6 (3): 595–626.

2 Creativity, Authorship, Design, and IP Law

Introduction

This chapter discusses the concepts of creativity, authorship, and copying, and the division between fine arts and design. These concepts play important roles in the development of laws to protect design. It also explains the development of different legal traditions to protect design in the major fashion markets of France and the US. Lastly, it briefly describes the international harmonization of IP law over the last 100 years.

Creativity

The Concept of Authorship

Our conceptions about how fashion (and other) designers create are undoubtedly extremely inadequate. There has been very little research into how designers work, and what role legal protections play in creative endeavors. Systems of intellectual property law envisage creativity as involving a single individual. This creator's job is to come up with new and original designs. But the reality of creativity, in any sphere, whether fashion design or a work of fiction, is much more complex. No designer or author starts from scratch to create a new and unique work. Creating almost always involves the borrowing and mixing of previous work and may involve more than one author. This is even more true of fashion design than other creative endeavors.

Jessica Litman, in "The Public Domain," pointed out that:

> To say that every new work is in some sense based on the works that preceded it, is such a truism that it has long been a cliche, invoked but not examined. Cinematographers, actors, choreographers, architects, and sculptors all engage in the process of adapting, transforming, and recombining what is already "out there" in some other form.
>
> (Litman 1990, 696–7)

DOI: 10.4324/9781003091400-3

Fashion designers could very easily be added to this list as they engage in adapting and transforming existing styles to create something new.

The concepts of authorship and how creativity operates are in fact quite recent. In her 1984 article "The Genius and the Copyright," Martha Woodmansee explained that although we think of an author as "an individual who is solely responsible—and therefore exclusively deserving of credit—for the production of a unique work," this is an eighteenth-century invention. Prior to this time, two concepts existed for creativity. The creative person either was a craftsman or had received inspiration from a divine source. Both concepts could co-exist in the same person, and both concepts viewed creativity as a process for which the creative person was a vessel rather than an initiator. The modern writer and artist who earn a living from their creative works only began to emerge when the centuries-old systems of aristocratic and ecclesiastical patronage disappeared (Woodmansee 1984, 426).

In the world of fashion design, creativity is rarely the work of one person—the solitary genius working alone. Julie Zerbo, among others, has argued that copyright laws that focus on authorship and exclude useful articles miss these realities and are not helpful in protecting design. According to Zerbo, fashion designers really need legal protection for the "value-added" part that they contribute to a useful item (clothing) (Zerbo 2017, 620). Zerbo does not challenge authorship and creativity as concepts, but her argument is clearly based on the view that they are inadequate to describe what fashion designers actually do.

In reality, the most important requirement for creativity to occur is that the creator has access to the work of others. Original works are based on access to prior works, says Wendy Gordon in "On Owning Information: Intellectual Property and the Restitutionary Impulse," particularly in something like fashion, which is part of culture, art, and commerce. She explains: "A culture could not exist if all free riding were prohibited" (Gordon 1992, 167).

What Is Design: Art or Craft?

Like creativity and authorship, the division between what is art and what is craft is fraught with assumptions and complexity. This debate over whether the fine arts (literature, painting, music, and sculpture) are inherently different from applied or industrial arts, including crafts and fashion design, has consumed lawyers, academics, and others since the first industrial revolution mechanized the production of objects.

The start of the first industrial revolution in much of the Western world created "a sharp distinction between the world of the arts and that of technology. As a result, culture has been split into two, mutually exclusive branches: one scientific, quantifiable and 'hard,' the other aesthetic, evaluative, and 'soft'" (Coles 2005, 18). The difficulty is that design is a practical art, and the activity where creativity and industry come together. A design can be creative and artistic like fine art even while it is also created for the purpose of being one of many as an industrial product.

By the end of the nineteenth century, the difficulties with the concept of "design" became more and more obvious. Design often "came to form a bridge between the two" worlds of art and industry (Coles 2005, 18). People such as William Morris, and others in the Arts and Crafts movement in the UK, argued that art was about creating beautiful objects, whether designs for useful articles (such as a dress or a lamp) or fine art, such as sculpture. William Morris felt that "the divisions made between the arts of the 'intellect'—architecture, sculpture, and painting—and those of the 'decorative'—interior architecture and the crafts—were based on a false presupposition." In his essay "The Lesser Arts," Morris asserted that his agenda was to study the subject that is the "great body of art, by means of which men have at all times more or less striven to beautify the familiar matters of everyday life" (Morris and Morris 2012, 2). The debate about the division between applied and fine art continues to this day.

Modern design complicates the debate further by focusing on the unity of form and function. Designers today do not see design as a secondary decorative feature added to a product to make it more pleasing to the eye but as an integral part of an object. French-born Raymond Loewy, a fashion illustrator by training, was one of the first people to convince American manufacturers in the early twentieth century that the appearance of their products mattered, and that focusing on design resulted in products that were easier and cheaper to manufacture and more pleasurable to use (Monseau 2012, 499).

Today, we recognize that good design reaps economic benefits. Many governments promote it through industrial policies. There are awards for it, and much research tells us that companies that are effective users of design outperform the stock market (Monseau 2012, 502). Many consumers have sufficient disposable income that they don't buy products solely based on necessity; rather, they consider design in their decisions which results in competitiveness and innovation based on design.

The Role of Copying in Fashion Design

Creativity does not happen in a vacuum, and few, if any, authors create new and unique work. This is particularly true of fashion designers who are known for copying (in both good and bad ways). Appropriation, referencing, derivation, imitation, and recontextualization are terms commonly used to describe the creative methods of fashion designers. All of these words are essentially synonyms for using prior work in some way in the design process. For most designers, these words denote activities that are common and permissible. Some level of copying is understood as an integral part of the design process. It is both necessary and beneficial to the cyclical trends that distinguish the creation of fashion. In the past, fashion designers have been content to tolerate even some level of close copying as normal, or perhaps treat it as an ethical violation rather than a legal one, because the process of design relies on borrowing from previous works.

If explanations of creativity are accurate, then overbroad intellectual property rights, instead of encouraging creativity, will do the opposite. Strong rights will distort markets away from competition by interfering with the ability of secondary creators to use the work of those who went before them.

However, most designers are able to see a distinction between the normal design processes of deriving inspiration from earlier designs and the unethical process of making a close or exact copy of an earlier design. Close copying is about free riding on the work of others simply to make money. Recontextualizing or remixing earlier work is one of the ways designers work and create fashions.

There is a widespread (although legally inaccurate) belief in the fashion industry that, if you change at least a percentage of a design (between 3 and 20% are the usual amounts given) or make a certain number of changes (often five is the suggested number), you can claim to have created something new and you have a legal defense to a copyright lawsuit. Well-known designers such as the late Virgil Abloh of Off-White have alluded to this "rule": Abloh called it "the three percent approach" and said that changing a design by that percentage was enough to qualify it as new (TFL 2020).

Even though the rule has no basis in law, it illustrates the way in which many designers think about copying; Some copying is reasonable as long as something new is added or some changes are made to the original. This kind of copying should be tolerated and should not count as an infringement of an earlier design.

As the industry has globalized, there has been a significant increase in the speed at which the industry operates, and as the fashion cycle has sped up so has the amount of close copying, often by purveyors of fast fashion. Many designers, particularly in the midrange, are hurt by copying and want the law to draw a bright line between the creative remixing and copying that they consider permissible and the close copying, which they don't (Hemphill and Suk 2009, 1176).

These debates about authorship and copying, and whether design differs from fine art, create arguments about how and where to protect design under intellectual property laws that have been going on for more than 200 years. The main difficulty in the legal protection of design is that it lies at the intersection of art and commerce and so it does not fit neatly into any of the intellectual property law categories.

Does Creativity Benefit from Copying?

The fact that the fashion industry appears to thrive in spite of the difficulties of protecting it is also the subject of much academic debate. In 2006, Kal Raustiala and Christopher Sprigman reignited a debate in the US about the legal protection of fashion design. They argued that fashion design in the US benefits from a lack of legal protection in their influential article, "The Piracy Paradox: Innovation and Intellectual Property in Fashion Design." They believe that the lack of intellectual property protection for the fashion industry in the US is not detrimental to the industry; on the contrary, it is what drives creativity in fashion design (Raustiala and Sprigman 2006, 1718).

In "The Piracy Paradox," Raustiala and Sprigman argue that two interrelated concepts, which they call "anchoring" and "induced obsolescence," drive innovation and creativity in the fashion industry. The concept of "anchoring" means that a set of definable styles or trends emerge to define a season which drives consumer buying. The free appropriation or copying of these styles then results in the "induced obsolescence" of earlier designs. The fashion industry thus creates styles that fall out of fashion and are replaced, often seasonally, by new styles. Raustiala and Sprigman use these concepts to explain why copying is actually beneficial to the fashion industry. In their view, induced obsolescence and anchoring help explain the otherwise puzzling persistence of continuous fashion creativity in the face of extensive copying. Some designers will suffer from the pirating of their designs, but, overall, copying is helpful, not harmful, to the industry (Raustiala and Sprigman 2006, 1733).

The purpose of Raustiala and Sprigman's inquiry is to understand how innovation persists without legal protection. This is an extremely important task given the costs of IP protection. In an update to their article in 2009, they stated: "Copying and derivative reworking produce a faster creative cycle and more consumption of fashion due to the quicker deterioration of apparel's status-conferring value." According to Raustiala and Sprigman "both line-by-line copying and the more limited appropriation involved in derivative reworking feed this process" (Raustiala and Sprigman 2009, 1207).

Flaws in the "Piracy Paradox"

Many scholars have pointed to flaws in the arguments in "The Piracy Paradox." The most common criticisms are that Raustiala and Sprigman underestimate the new technologies of copying, and they misunderstand the effect of various other changes in the fashion business, especially the motivations and buying habits of consumers. Changes in the industry discussed in Chapter 1, such as the speed of communication with factories in the Global South, which are ready and able to execute commissions from fashion design pirates instantly, have significantly affected the dynamics of the business. In some cases, knockoffs and counterfeits can reach the stores before the originals. When this happens, the original designers are being denied the economic fruits of their creative labors, which could in turn provide a disincentive to innovate.

C. Scott Hemphill and Jeannie Suk point out in "The Law, Culture, and Economics of Fashion" that Raustiala and Sprigman "treat close copying and shared trends as indistinguishable for their purposes, referring to both phenomena as 'copies'" (Hemphill and Suk 2009, 1181). Hemphill and Suk contend that piracy and counterfeiting in the globalized fashion industry now take place on a vastly different scale than they did at the beginning of the twentieth century when designers were perhaps content to have little legal protection for fashion design.

Piracy and counterfeits have increased greatly with the globalization of the industry. Copying has been going on for the whole of fashion's history, but, today, the industry is less club-like. The globalization of the industry and advent of "fast fashion"—clothing brands such as Zara, H&M, and Forever 21 that reproduce the latest trends quickly and cheaply—have made global piracy a major concern for many designers.

At the turn of the twentieth century, the big American department stores—Saks Fifth Avenue, Bergdorf-Goodman, Neiman Marcus, etc.—were already sending scouts to the Paris fashion shows to sketch the latest styles. These designs would then be copied and produced as part of the store's next seasonal collection. As fashion became more accessible, it also became easier to copy from sketches. In the mid twentieth century, the American industry created its own watchdog, the Fashion Originators Guild of America (FOGA), to police copying within the industry. It checked labels of designs to ensure authenticity. In Paris, a similar organization undertook the same role (Pouillard 2011, 337 and 332). These organizations no longer exist; the industry is global and hard to police, and the number of fake goods has multiplied.

The "Piracy Paradox" argument fails to account for the havoc the accelerated fashion cycle of a globalized industry brings to designers. In the post-war twentieth century, American designers generally produced and presented collections twice a year. In the twenty-first century, fashion houses have had to increase the pace of their design and production schedules to meet growing customer demands. Large luxury conglomerates such as LVMH and the Gucci Group have also contributed to the fast pace by consolidating much of the luxury goods market and building portfolios across industries.

Raustiala and Sprigman may be correct that

> extending copyright is likely to harm, not help, new or small designers. Relatively unknown and poorly funded entrants are at a disadvantage, relative to a rich and well-known incumbent, in most any market ... [The] fashion's low-IP equilibrium does at least deprive large fashion firms of one anticompetitive tool that big firms operating in high-IP markets often use to grind down upstarts: lawyers.
>
> (Raustiala and Sprigman 2009, 1221)

Is Fashion Design (Law) Frivolous?

As fashion design exists at the difficult intersection between art, commerce, utility, and adornment, it has not until very recently been taken seriously as a force for creativity and artistic work. Discussing the recent elevation of fashion to a creative and artistic endeavor, Melissa Taylor, in "Culture Transition: Fashion's Cultural Dialogue between Commerce and Art," states: "It is in its newly found presence in both high and popular culture that fashion finds itself located across both commerce and art, and now seems to be entering into a new cultural dialogue of previously opposing cultural contexts" (Taylor 2005, 446). In Taylor's view: "Divisions between artist and fashion designer could be deemed as unnecessary in this climate of creativity, in which boundaries are crossed into other production areas" (Taylor 2005, 448).

Fashion has long suffered from a perception that it is insignificant, unimportant, and unworthy of study. Fashion plays a large role in economic competitiveness and is one of the most recognizable and pivotal art–design industries in the world. It dwarfs other creative industries such as film and music. However, it continues to be viewed as unimportant and insubstantial.

Thus, fashion suffers, not only from the conceptual difficulties that derive from the long-running distinction between applied and fine art, but also from a lack of study. Until recently, academics focused on the frivolous nature of fashion to exclude it from academic study. Discussing why studying the history of art is seen as more legitimate than studying the history of fashion, Sandra Miller, in "Fashion as Art; Is Fashion Art?" stated, "[t]he study of clothes from a historical perspective … has not yet acquired a status equal to that of the fine arts; this may well have something to do with the perceived lower status of craft" (Miller 2007, 30).

Karen Hansen explained, in "Dressing Up, Dressing Down," that many scholars have concurred with the view that fashion is a superficial, and worse, mostly female pastime, and so not a serious subject of study. "Philosophy does indeed manifest sustained scorn for attention to personal appearance and fashionable dress" (Hanson 1990, 107). Perhaps this is why the legal protections provided by intellectual property laws for fashion and clothing remain significantly below those provided for the more "serious" creative endeavors such as sculpture and painting.

The lowly status of fashion design in the artistic sphere is clearly changing. Increasingly, art museums display work by well-known fashion designers in their collections. In October 2020, the Metropolitan Museum of Art in New York opened an exhibition, *About Time: Fashion and Duration*, which surveyed 150 years of fashion and was sponsored by Louis Vuitton. The exhibition clearly treated the fashions displayed as art forms. Melissa Taylor noted that "Many designers working at the innovative end of the haute couture market are accepted as artists, yet some refuse to qualify their work as belonging to either art or fashion" (Taylor 2005, 448). The Met followed its 2020 exhibition with another the next year: *In America: A Lexicon of Fashion*. The description stated that it "establishes a modern vocabulary of American fashion based on its expressive qualities." Again, in this exhibition, works of fashion were displayed as art forms.

Fashion design is becoming a two-tier endeavor. Some high-end designers have found their place as artists and even display their work in museum exhibitions. Taylor notes that: "Few can afford a Versace dress or an Armani suit, but that shouldn't blind us to the artistry of the design, just as the price tag on a Picasso shouldn't hinder our enjoyment of the painting" (Taylor 2005, 454). Other designs have become commodified for the mass market. They are not placed in museums and have a much more utilitarian status as disposable clothing for the masses.

High-end fashion designers who view themselves as artists of a sort argue that fashion design deserves copyright-like protection. As Pouillard stated: "[W]hen the high-end fashion industry lobbies for increased protection of design, it typically argues that it is different from industrial design, thus claiming to be something else, most often art or applied art" (Pouillard and Kuldova 2017, 344).

The recency of fashion design as a subject worthy of study has meant that the discipline of fashion law is also a new one. Susan Scafidi, now academic director of the Fashion Law Institute at Fordham University and author of "Who Owns Culture? Appropriation and Authenticity in American Law," as well as many articles on intellectual property and fashion law, is a pioneer of fashion law as a legal discipline. When Scafidi first taught fashion law in the early years of the twenty-first century, she faced the same difficulties as those who have argued that fashion is an art and a subject worthy of study. She had to fight for the inclusion of fashion law in the law school curriculum as a serious field of study. However, there are now courses in fashion law, law for designers, and others that acknowledge the importance of the industry and the necessity of focusing on how it is affected by law and policy.

A Lack of Evidence-Based Research on Creativity and Law

The question of whether fashion design would benefit from stronger IP protection, or at least more harmonization of the French and US legal traditions, is one of the many areas where there are many theories, but little in the way of empirical evidence. We really don't know that much about whether intellectual property rights incentivize creativity, although that is generally considered to be their purpose.

In a 2017 article, "Copyright and Creative Incentives: What We Know (and Don't)," Christopher Sprigman reviewed various studies and natural experiments that examine the links between copyright and incentives to create new works. He found a lack of empirical research on whether copyright protection increases creativity, which he noted is mainly because we've only been asking the question at all in the last 25 years. In reviewing various natural experiments and studies, he found that, while some support the theory that copyright incentivizes creativity, others do not. He noted that high fixed-cost endeavors (his example was the creation of Italian operas and Bollywood movies) appear to benefit from copyright protection. Lower-cost endeavors do not show the same need for copyright protection. Studies show little to no evidence that copyright or its lack affected the quantity of new pop music created during the time period when Napster enabled many to avoid paying for music (Sprigman 2017, 464).

Sprigman also discussed his "Piracy Paradox" research with Raustiala on the "negative spaces" occupied by fashion and other creative industries. He argued that the vibrant state of these industries is a testament to the fact that innovation often occurs without intellectual property protection. In fact, innovation is often generated through factors unrelated to laws, such as social norms that promote sharing, first mover advantages, and user involvement in the creative process. In fashion, copying is an important part of the trend cycle that drives innovation according to Sprigman. He said, "[c]opyright is a tax on learning. It is a tax on culture. It is a tax on speech. And this tax is more than an inconvenience. It is a barrier to those who cannot, or will not, pay it." Since copyright makes creative work more expensive, "the necessity of the tax cannot simply be assumed. It must be evidenced" (Sprigman 2017, 455–6).

Intellectual Property Protection and Fashion Design

The Public Benefit of IP

The types of property that fall under the umbrella term intellectual property[1] are generally non-rivalrous and non-excludable. Non-rivalrous property means property that cannot be exhausted or consumed by use. A book is not used up because one person reads it; it can be consumed many times, whereas an apple can only be consumed once. A book is thus non-rivalrous. An apple is not.

Not all, but some intellectual property is also non-excludable. This means that there isn't a good mechanism for excluding those who don't or can't pay for the property. Air and public defense fall into this category, but it is also often true of some types of property that can be protected by intellectual property laws such as art, music, design, and other types of content and information. This has become especially true in an internet age where the costs of duplication and dissemination of this type of property have dropped significantly.

Inventions, new designs, and other creative works which are generally non-rivalrous, and are often non-excludable, are public as well as private goods. They benefit others in addition to their owners. This is one of the biggest differences between intellectual property and other types of property, and why IP is subject to legal protection for only a limited time period.

Balance between Public and Private Benefits

Property is a somewhat misleading term for the rights provided by intellectual property. Copyrights and patents are essentially an attempt to achieve a balance between the private rights of creators and the public benefit of encouraging new ideas, creativity, and inventions. This is the reason the law provides the rights holder with only a limited term of protection before her property enters the public domain. The creator can limit access to her work for a period of time to recoup the economic costs of creation. Then, the work should become available for all to use. Since most types of intellectual property are non-rivalrous and non-excludable, the main concern for the creators of new works of authorship, such as fashion design, or new scientific discoveries or inventions is that, "once copies are available to others, it is often inexpensive for these users to make additional copies" (Landes and Posner 2003, 49).

Thus, copyright and patent protection involve a trade-off. Providing rights to intellectual property owners makes creative works more expensive for the public, but the prohibition on use or costs of access provide the "incentives to create the work in the first place." According to Landes and Posner in "The Economic Structure of Intellectual Property Law," "striking the correct balance between access and incentives is the central problem in copyright law" (Landes and Posner 2003, 11).

The result of this trade-off (at least for patents and copyrights) has historically been intellectual property rights that are limited in time, limited in scope, and granted only to authors and inventors who meet certain minimum requirements.

On this view, the proper goal of intellectual property law is to give as little protection as possible consistent with encouraging innovation. For fashion design, as well as many other creative endeavors, the concept of the sole author is not necessarily an accurate way of conceiving of how creativity works.

Trademarks, as informational signs, are even less like property than other intellectual property rights. They are signs used in commerce in connection with a product or service. They should not be considered as property rights on their own because their role is linked to the business or products that they identify. In the US, particularly, the focus on branding has made trademark law very important to fashion designers.

The Evolution of Legal Protection of Design

The three areas of intellectual property law that protect creativity and innovation are copyrights, patents, and trademarks. Each grants a type of monopoly right to the creator or innovator of some type of "work of the mind" or industrial or artistic property for a period of time. Copyrights protect art, patents protect industrial inventions, and trademarks protect reputation and act as a carrier of information. Design can fit into all of these categories (see Figure 2.1).

Design and law have had an unstable relationship since the beginnings of intellectual property law because design can be part of the artistic and industrial spheres or fall somewhere between the two. Consequently, the three main

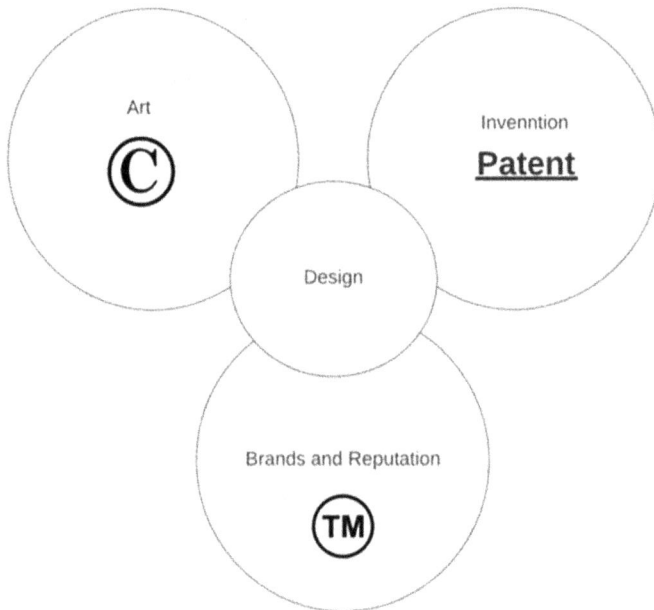

Figure 2.1 Where to protect design in IP law

branches of IP law have not developed a clear and harmonized theory of design protection. Pouillard and Kuldova describe the "interconnected fields of fashion and design" as being

> at the meeting point between art and industry, design and utility, economic interest and creativity, where, in practice, they become increasingly difficult to tell apart as each feeds on the other in order to increase its imaginary value—both attempting to capitalize on the imaginary association with fine arts and its residual aura of quality, importance and value.
>
> (Pouillard and Kuldova 2017, 344)

How different legal systems protect design, especially fashion design, is often primarily based on the importance of the applied arts or design to a particular economy. In the US, fashion design tends not to be considered as fine art but, rather, as an applied art or craft that involves the creation of useful objects. Consequently, US law does not, in general, deem fashion and other design industries worthy of the same legal protection as fine arts. It separates creativity and design from the function of an object. Under US law, embellishments to a useful article can be protected but not the useful article itself. The facts of *Brandir International, INC., v. Cascade Pacific Lumber Co.* provides an illustration of the division of creativity and function. The plaintiff turned his sinuous metal sculpture into a bike rack with a few modifications. The court held that the bike rack was not protectable by copyright as there was no separation between the design (the sculpture) and the useful object (the bike rack).

French law treats design in the same way as fine art and provides much stronger legal protection for many types of commercial creations, such as fashion. It developed in a country with strong and important fashion and luxury design-intensive industries. To complicate matters, in many legal regimes, design has vacillated between copyright protection and patent protection. French legal tradition has influenced the development of EU law, discussed in Chapter 4.

Although it is a global industry, fashion design is protected by different and partly overlapping legal regimes in different parts of the world. The different laws and their development do not seem to have had a major effect on how the global industry operates today, which perhaps gives weight to the argument in Chapter 6 that law is not the major regulator of design.

US Legal Tradition and Design

In the Anglo-American legal tradition going back to the English Statute of Anne of 1709, copyright is primarily viewed as an economic right that protects artistic expression for a limited period to enable authors/creators to benefit economically from their creativity. Patents protect new inventions for a limited period to enable inventors to exploit their economic benefits. Trademarks have a slightly different purpose. They protect consumers from confusion about the origin of goods. Despite some recent copyright cases which open the possibility of more protection for applied art and design, trademarks tend to be the focus of those seeking to protect fashion design in the United States.

US lawmakers have considered the question of whether to extend some type of copyright-like legal protection to fashion and design on many occasions over the last 100 years but have yet to do so. Discussions about protecting design by a copyright-like law continued most recently in 2012 with a bill promoted by the Council of Fashion Designers of America (CFDA) called the Innovative Design Protection and Piracy Prevention Act. To date, Congress has failed to pass this bill or any version of fashion design protection.

Copyright is not ideal for design protection mainly because of the length of the term of protection. Currently, most members of the Berne Convention protect copyrights for the life of the creator plus 70 years. This term is long even for the protection of fine art, and it is doubtful whether that length is needed to encourage creativity. When applied to design, copyright law could protect the most mundane, everyday objects for an inordinate length of time.

As the author argued in a 2012 article, "Congress should not focus on protecting a single industry—such as fashion—from design copying: rather, it should create a coherent, unified approach to the protection of all industrial design" (Monseau 2012, 543).

The subject matter and terms of all intellectual property rights in the US have expanded considerably in the last three centuries, but protection is still focused on the protection of the economic value of these rights.

French (and European) Legal Tradition and Design

In much of Europe, IP law has traditionally offered "far greater protection to fashion design in comparison to the United States." As Pouillard and Kuldova explained in "Interrogating Intellectual Property Rights in Post-war Fashion and Design," "France has the strongest fashion design protection available. The historical importance of fashion as a national industry supported by the government has played a fundamental role in the building of strong protection for fashion design in France" (Pouillard and Kuldova 2017, 349). In the French design protection system, even when "litigation is low, this does not signify that an intellectual property rights system does not exist" (Pouillard and Kuldova 2017, 348). Strong norms protected those creating fashion design in France, at least in the twentieth century.

From the nineteenth century, creative practices and norms surrounding design showed an understanding of the conceptual separation between close copying, and remixing and other forms of creativity such as homage and borrowing that fuel the fashion and design industries. Close copying was prohibited by both law and practice, where interpretations were given much more leeway. Although it is not always apparent from legal cases, if you look at the norms, customs, and practices that govern groups and clusters of designers, it is possible to see that these concepts form part of practice. For example, the FHCM allowed "a zone of flexible practices" around design. This included an understanding that designers would not prevent home sewists who found inspiration in haute couture from copying their garments (Pouillard and Kuldova 2017, 349–50).

In contrast to US law, French copyright law provides both economic and moral rights to the author of a copyright work. Moral rights require creators to be recognized as the creators of their work even after sale. While economic rights generally end after the first sale, moral rights allow an author to prevent changes to his or her work even after sale.

The Growing Strength of Intellectual Property Rights

As well as the lack of clarity in the legal protection of design in different jurisdictions, intellectual property rights owners of all types have worked to strengthen their rights. Mark Lemley says in his 2004 article, "Property, Intellectual Property and Free Riding," that American intellectual property owners are constantly "petition[ing] Congress to give them still more rights." Lemley points out that

> This sort of legislative rent seeking has proven to be a real problem in intellectual property, particularly in the copyright field, where Congress of late seems willing to give copyright owners whatever they ask for, at least as long as there is no large vested interest making demands on the other side.
>
> (Lemley 2005, 1063)

The strengthening of IPRs is not simply an American phenomenon.

The terms of rights for both copyright and patents have increased internationally owing to the harmonization of laws by international treaties. It is easier for work to qualify for copyright protection, and there is no registration requirement for copyright protection. There have also been increases in the harshness of penalties.

Trademarks have always received protection that is potentially unlimited in time, but the right to protect against consumer confusion

> has increasingly taken on the character of a property right, with the result that trademark "owners" now have the power to prevent various kinds of uses of their marks, regardless of whether consumers will be confused, or search costs increased.
>
> (Lemley 2005, 1042)

Many of the exclusions or limitations on IP rights which developed to prevent the overprotection of copyrights, trademarks, and patents have also been worn away recently by court decisions.

Lemley argues that treating intellectual property like real property with strong exclusive rights is a mistake that is counterproductive to the goal of producing more creative work.

> Economic theory offers no justification for awarding creators anything beyond what is necessary to recover their average total costs. Unlike real

property, intellectual property is a conscious decision to create scarcity in a type of good in which it is ordinarily absent in order to artificially boost the economic returns to innovation.

However, as Lemley notes, there are others who have suggested that copyrights should last forever, relying on the economic theory that property ownership promotes the most efficient use of resources: These commentators believe that "[a]ll valuable resources, including copyrightable works, should be owned, in order to create incentives for their efficient exploitation and to avoid overuse" (Lemley 2005, 1042).

Many academics and legal commentators now question whether strong intellectual property protections really incentivize creativity. Raustiala and Sprigman argue that the fashion industry particularly benefits from the "piracy paradox" and that it is better to leave some intellectual property unprotected.

(Many) Attempts at Harmonizing IP Laws Internationally

Over 100 years of international harmonization treaties mean that IP rights are similar in terms of the duration and the type of protection provided in most countries in the world, certainly in the EU and US, which are members of all the major harmonization efforts. However, despite harmonization, differences in the philosophy behind rights and the subject matter of protection remain.

IP laws still, for the most part, create national rights for specific territories. Useful design which exists at the intersection between art and industry provides difficult subject matter for protection. As discussed below, French and US laws take different approaches; US tends to view design as part of an industrial process and requires a high level of innovation and protection via patent law, and French jurisprudence views design as a creative, artistic process and provides a copyright-type system of legal protection for design.

The global harmonization of IP laws started over 100 years ago with the Paris and Berne Conventions in 1883 and 1886, respectively. The Paris Convention attempted to define and harmonize the protection accorded to useful inventions (through patent law), and the Berne Convention did the same for creative works (through copyright law). The Madrid Agreement of 1891 added trademark rights to a more global system. It created a centrally administered system for obtaining registration in 134 countries in 1989. The newer field of industrial design first figured in a legal treaty in the 1920s.

Today, four main international agreements and two international organizations uphold the internationally agreed principles of the protection of industrial design. None of them provide a clear international standard for the protection of design, and their history illustrates the ongoing conflict between the creativity and innovation approaches to the protection of design.

The Hague Agreement

In 1925, the Hague Agreement Concerning the International Registrations of Industrial Designs became the first treaty to specifically focus on the international protection of industrial design rights. The Hague Agreement does not attempt to harmonize design laws or set any standards for the legal protection of industrial design. Its aim is simply to streamline the legal procedure for obtaining protection for industrial designs by creating a centralized international deposit of industrial designs. This change makes it easier to register designs for designers who are nationals of, or domiciled in, the approximately 75 countries and supranational groups that are part of the Hague Agreement. Under the Hague Agreement, renewable protection of a design for a period of up to 25 years is possible, depending on the law of the nation-state member.

There have been three revisions to the Hague Agreement, and the treaty is now administered by the World Intellectual Property Organization (WIPO; discussed later in this section). Even after three revisions, the Hague Agreement has not added any clear theory of protection to the law of industrial design. The revisions have simplified procedures, but membership of the Hague Agreement remains low partially because the Hague mechanism does not provide a single harmonized system of protection. It gives countries a maximum of six months to refuse protection to a deposited design, but they do so under their own existing laws. This short time limit does not leave much time for a substantive examination of a design (like design patent law in the US). The agreement also provides no harmonized standards for protection, so that a designer could be unable to protect their design in one country because a standard of the law in that country is not met. The system is also limited to registered design rights. It does not protect any unregistered design rights.

Not all EU member states are members of the Hague Agreement. The 2016 EU Commission Legal Review on the Protection of Industrial Design recommends that all member states should be encouraged to join (Dumortier et al. 2016). When those outside the EU apply for international design protection under the Hague Agreement, the most common country or region designated for protection is the EU.

The Berne Convention

The Berne Convention for the Protection of Literary and Artistic Works was signed in 1886 by a group of countries wishing to enshrine certain basic principles of copyright protection. It did not originally protect applied art or industrial design. In fact, from the 1900s, there was a forceful debate between the members about whether to include applied art as copyrightable subject matter. Initially, the convention specifically left out design from the types of property protectable by copyright because disagreements over whether to protect it in the same way as fine art were so common.

There are three basic principles in the Berne Convention. The first is the principle of national treatment, meaning that "works originating in one of the Contracting States must be given the same protection in each of the other Contracting States." The second principle is the principle of "automatic" protection, meaning that "protection must not be conditional upon compliance with any formality." The final principle is the one of "'independence" of protection. This means that "protection is independent of the existence of protection in the country of origin of the work." The convention also mandates a list of minimum standards of protection for the works that are protected. These include that the length of the copyright term must be at least the life of the author plus 50 years.

At the 1948 meeting, the French delegates succeeded in securing a compromise on the protection of design. They managed to obtain the agreement of the other delegates to the concept that designers of all ornaments, whatever their merit or purpose, should be entitled to legal protection. Protection for "applied art" was added to Article 2 of the convention. However, protection of design is not mandatory. Although, to be a contracting state of the Berne Convention, a country must satisfy certain minimum standards for the protection of literary and artistic works, sub-section 2(7) states "it shall be a matter for legislation in the countries of the Union to determine the extent of the application of their laws to works of applied art and industrial designs and models, as well as the conditions under which such works, designs and models shall be protected."

Many delegates were concerned that it would be anticompetitive to provide industrial designers with the long period of copyright protection afforded to creative works. Ultimately, since agreement could not be reached, this awkward compromise added works of applied art to the protectable subject matter of the convention, but allowed each country to retain the right to define applied art, to limit the duration of copyright in applied art, and also to distinguish between protectable applied art and a category called "designs and models"—which could be subject to a more restrictive industrial property regime. Signatories could choose to write *sui generis* design laws to protect industrial design and, even if they used the copyright scheme as a basis for design protection, they could still choose to limit the duration of protection of applied art as opposed to fine art.

The US did not join the Berne Convention until 1988 and, even then, it did not change its law to include design among the types of property protected by copyright law. Globally, the Berne Convention provides a reasonable degree of agreement and harmonized laws for the protection of literary or artistic works by copyright law, but there remains no such global consensus about design.

The Paris Convention

The Paris Convention was the beginning of ensuring the protection of inventions internationally. It required contracting states to "grant the same protection to nationals of other Contracting States that it grants to its own nationals." It gave a right of priority in the case of patents, marks, and industrial designs so that, as long as a first application is filed in one of the contracting states, the applicant may apply for protection in any of the other contracting states within a year, and those applications are treated as having the same date as the first application. The additional applications are then treated as if they had been filed on the same date as the original application. The Paris Convention also harmonizes some parts of patent law with a set of common rules.

In 1958, the Paris Convention on Industrial Property also extended its provisions to cover industrial design. It adopted a new article at its Lisbon Conference that provided that all member states should protect "industrial designs," but, as at the 1948 Brussels Conference of the Berne Convention, it was agreed that each state could determine the nature, subject matter, and conditions of such protection. Thus, the standard for the protection of industrial design, and the tension between design as an innovative industrial or artistic creative process remain unclear under these two international conventions which are intended to harmonize IP laws.

The World Intellectual Property Organization

In the 1960s, the WIPO was created. At the same time, there was an international effort to develop a model design law or agreed set of principles for the protection of industrial design. Growing post-war globalization meant that many countries became interested in creating specific design protection laws. However, the reform movement was short-lived and ended without any clear international standard. The WIPO itself remained in existence and now oversees the Hague Agreement for registering industrial designs internationally, the only global agreement on design protection. The Hague Agreement does not harmonize design law. It simply provides inventors and creators with a single international application to protect design rights in all its signature members. The US and most European countries are members. WIPO also oversees the Berne and Paris Conventions, the Madrid international trademark registration system, and the Patent Cooperation Treaty (PCT).

The additions to the Paris and Berne Conventions mostly serve to illustrate the continuing debate about where to place design in IP law, rather than helping in terms of the actual international protection of design.

The WTO and TRIPS

The Trade-Related Aspects of Intellectual Property Agreement (TRIPS) is the first international agreement to lay out a somewhat more focused set of principles for the protection of design. The TRIPS provisions envisage that design protection should be short (like patents and other industrial property rights) but focused mainly on protection against copying (like copyright law). Thus, the TRIPS provisions are perhaps evidence that a modified copyright approach to the protection of design is becoming the international standard.

In 1994, the Uruguay Round of trade talks created the World Trade Organization (WTO) and adopted the Trade-Related Aspects of Intellectual Property Agreement. After nearly seven years of talks, this was the biggest reform of the world trading system set up by the General Agreement on Tariffs and Trades (GATT) after World War II. The newly created WTO was a permanent organization with the power to settle disputes between member nations, and TRIPS added intellectual property to world trade rules as part of the GATT agreements. All members of the WTO were required to harmonize their IP rights to encourage and assist globalization by ensuring the effective and appropriate enforcement of IP rights.

The TRIPS Agreement covers a comprehensive list of IPRs: copyright and related rights, trademarks including service marks, geographical indications, industrial designs, patents, the layout-design of integrated circuits, and undisclosed information including trade secrets and test data. The three main areas that TRIPS harmonizes are standards, enforcement, and dispute settlement. The most important area for understanding the protection of design is standards since this refers to how "the Agreement sets out the minimum standards of protection to be provided by each Member." For industrial designs, TRIPS requires that member countries provide protection for at least ten years for any industrial design which is new or original. "New" is a patent standard while "original" is a copyright standard. Thus, TRIPS sidesteps the question of whether design is an industrial or creative process and so whether it should be protected under patent or copyright laws.

TRIPS is an important addition to the international agreements that contain provisions for intellectual property, not least because it covers the vast majority of world trade (there are now 164 country signatories). It is also the first agreement to provide some direction on the type of protection that should be provided to design—whether a copyright-like right or a patent-like right. TRIPS requires member countries to protect these "new or original" designs through either industrial design law or copyright law. Although the agreement appears not to clearly mandate a particular standard for protectable subject matter by using both the words "new" and "original," it contains hints that it is focused on the protection of creativity under a copyright-like standard because it requires designs to be protected from copying for a minimum of ten years. The requirement for protection against copying appears to recognize that a copyright-type approach, focusing on protecting originality rather than the more innovative novelty standard, is the most relevant for industrial design. The minimum term requirement is much less than the full copyright term, suggesting a recognition of the commercial application of design and a rejection of the full copyright approach.

Under TRIPS, as long as members provide ten years' protection from copying, they remain free to determine the subject matter and type of design protection they will provide, and the method of implementation. When President Clinton signed legislation implementing TRIPS into US law in 1995, he determined that existing US design patent law already protected industrial design sufficiently to comply with TRIPS—although it only protects the most novel designs at the more innovative end of the design spectrum. The US did modify its copyright law to protect architecture to comply with the treaty, but, for design, it held that design patents were sufficient to fulfill its obligations to protect industrial design.

After over 100 years of harmonization, differences in design laws remain. The concepts of authorship and the understanding of how creativity occurs don't fit the reality of creative activity, particularly for design. Thus, it remains difficult to fit it neatly into the IP framework. US laws protecting designers and the EU design rights system are discussed in more detail in Chapters 3–5. A variety of other methods for protecting creativity in fashion design are discussed more fully in Chapter 6.

Note

1   Intellectual property is a quite recent name for copyrights, patents, and trademarks.

References

Coles, Alex. 2005. "On Art's Romance with Design." *Design Issues* 21 (3): 17–25.

Dumortier, Jos, Davide Parilli, Uma Suthersanen, David Musker, and et al. 2016. "Legal Review on Industrial Design Protection in Europe." MARKT2014/083/D. European Commission.

Gordon, Wendy J. 1992. "On Owning Information: Intellectual Property and the Restitutionary Impulse." *Virginia Law Review* 78 (1): 149–281.

Hanson, Karen. 1990. "Dressing Down Dressing Up—The Philosophic Fear of Fashion." *Hypatia* 5 (2): 107–21.

Hemphill, C. Scott, and Jeannie Suk. 2009. "Law, Culture, & Economics of Fashion." *Stanford Law Review* 61: 1147–99.

Landes, M. William, and Richard A. Posner. 2003. *The Economic Structure of Intellectual Property Law*. The Belknap Press of Harvard University Press.

Lemley, Mark A. 2005. "Property, Intellectual Property, and Free Riding." *Texas Law Review* 83 (4): 1031–76.

Litman, Jessica. 1990. "The Public Domain." *Emory Law Journal* 39: 965–1024.

Miller, Sandra. 2007. "Fashion as Art; Is Fashion Art?" *Fashion Theory* 11 (1): 25–40.

Monseau, Susanna. 2012. "The Challenge of Protecting Industrial Design in a Global Economy." *Texas Intellectual Property Law Journal* 20 (3): 495–544.

Morris, William, and May Morris. 2012. *The Collected Works of William Morris: With Introductions by His Daughter May Morris: Volume 22: Hopes and Fears for Art; Lectures on Art and Industry. Vol. 22. Cambridge Library Collection—Literary Studies*. Cambridge University Press. https://doi.org/10.1017/CBO9781139343145.

Pouillard, Véronique. 2011. "Design Piracy in the Fashion Industries of Paris and New York in the Interwar Years." *Business History Review* 85 (2): 319–44. https://doi.org /10.1017/S0007680511000407.

Pouillard, Véronique, and Tereza Kuldova. 2017. "Interrogating Intellectual Property Rights in Post-War Fashion and Design." *Journal of Design History* 30 (4): 343–55.

Raustiala, Kal, and Christopher Sprigman. 2006. "The Piracy Paradox: Innovation and Intellectual Property in Fashion Design." *Virginia Law Review* 92: 1687–1775.

———. 2009. "Piracy Paradox Revisited." *Stanford Law Review* 61 (5): 1200–1226.

Sprigman, Christopher. 2017. "Copyright and Creative Incentives: What We Know (And Don't)." *Houston Law Review* 55 (2): 451–78.

Taylor, Melissa. 2005. "Culture Transition: Fashion's Cultural Dialogue between Commerce and Art." *Fashion Theory* 9 (4): 445–59.

TFL. 2020. "The 3% Rule: The Reality Behind One of Fashion's Favorite Rules-of-Thumb." The Fashion Law. March 24, 2020. https://www.thefashionlaw.com/the-rule -one-of-fashions-favorite-rules-of-thumb-is-little-more-than-a-bit-of-fake-news/.

Woodmansee, Martha. 1984. "The Genius and the Copyright: Economic and Legal Conditions of the Emergence of the 'Author.'" *Eighteenth Century Studies* 14 (4): 425–48.

Zerbo, Julie. 2017. "Protecting Fashion Designs: Not Only 'What?' But 'Who?'" *American University Business Law Review* 6 (3): 595–626.

3 US IP Law

Vibrant Industry with Little Legal Protection?

Introduction

The US fashion market is one of the two largest in the world. The domestic market value is $406 billion according to Fashion United's 2016 figures (Fashion United 2021). The US is also the largest luxury market in the world. US consumers consistently buy the most items of clothing in the world per capita, although, as noted in Chapter 1, like most fashion figures the numbers are disputed.

Until World War II, US designers had a reputation for copying the trends coming out of Paris, but, for at least the last 50 years, New York City has been a major fashion capital in its own right. The US and Europe now compete to be the center of the global fashion industry.

This chapter focuses on how US intellectual property laws currently protect fashion design. It describes the development and purposes of the major intellectual property rights of copyright, patent, and trademark law, and how these legal concepts have evolved to protect aspects of fashion design. Although the "piracy paradox," discussed in Chapter 2, suggests that US law barely protects the fashion industry, this is not entirely true. This chapter reviews developments in US intellectual property law and cases as they apply to fashion design, to show how it is currently protected by US law. It also discusses proposals for a *sui generis* protection for fashion design in US law[1] which, if passed, would take IP protection of design in the US in the direction of the EU laws discussed in Chapter 4.

The Purpose of Intellectual Property Protection under US Law

The standard justification for the protection of copyrights and patents is set out in the Patents Clause—Article 1, Section 8, Clause 8—of the US Constitution. It states that Congress shall have power "To promote the progress of science and useful arts, by securing for limited times to authors and inventors the exclusive right to their respective writings and discoveries."

This legal protection enables "authors and inventors" to monetize their "writings and discoveries." The assumption is that the ability to make money from their creations will encourage further creativity and thus lead to the production of more new works. In US law, both copyright and patent laws provide limited

DOI: 10.4324/9781003091400-4

monopolies to individual creators based on a utilitarian or economic rationale that these monopolies will encourage creativity.

Trademarks, a much older form of intellectual property, tracing their history back to the marks of medieval guilds, have a slightly different legal justification. There is no obvious public benefit in encouraging the creation of more trademarks. The legal purpose of a trademark is to provide information to consumers. Traditionally, the law protects trademarks because they are signs and symbols that inform consumers about the source of goods or services. Trademarks are a shorthand way to indicate the source of origin to potential consumers. Of course, prohibiting the use of the marks of another in commerce also provides benefits for trademark owners. It protects their reputation and deters free riding on their economic efforts. Federal trademark law is derived not from the Patents Clause but from the Commerce Clause of the US Constitution.

Although US law does not provide any IPR focused specifically on fashion design, it is not accurate to say that design is entirely unprotected by the US legal system. The problem is more that the IPRs used to protect design in the US are often intended to protect something else, and they can be misaligned with the goals and creativity incentives in the fashion industry.

Copyright

The obvious place for fashion designers, especially those who consider themselves as kinds of artists, to seek protection for their designs is copyright law since copyright protects original artistic work. The range of subject matter and duration of copyright protection have expanded enormously since the first US Copyright Act in 1790.

Modern copyright law covers many types of creators and types of work. It now provides very strong rights and a long term of protection with no requirements for registration. Creators, from artists and choreographers to software programmers and YouTubers, are able to invoke copyright protection for their works. Under US law, the subject matter protectable by copyright has expanded from books and maps to almost any creative endeavor expressed in a tangible form and includes subject matter as diverse as buildings and software programs.

Copyright used to be viewed mainly as a negative right to prevent copying, but it has morphed into an exclusive right to control all types of exploitation of a creative work. The copyright term today can also barely be called "limited." Most work is now protected for approximately a century (the term in both the US and Europe for an individual owner of copyright is the life of the author plus 70 years. If the copyright is owned by a corporate entity, the term is 95 years). The length of protection is a far cry from the original 14 years in the 1790 Copyright Act. Since the US joined the Berne Convention, there is no longer a requirement for registration to obtain protection.

History and Purpose of Copyright Law's Protection of Design

Congress framed the first Copyright Act as being "for the encouragement of learning, by securing the copies of maps, charts, and books, to the authors and proprietors of such copies." This first act contained no distinction between useful and artistic items. Maps and charts certainly have both functional and artistic qualities.

There have since been many revisions to the law. During the nineteenth century, the main changes were the gradual additions of various new types of creative works, for example, dramatic work and photographs, to the list of protectable subject matter. Through case law, some limitations on copyright protection developed. In 1880, in *Selden and Baker*, the Supreme Court held that ideas were not copyrightable. Cases also added new categories of copyrightable work. In 1903, in *Bleistein v. Donaldson Lithographing Company*, in a case about circus posters, the Supreme Court first held that commercial art could be subject to copyright.

The Copyright Act of 1909 provided a major overhaul to copyright law. It added the explicit requirement that a protected work should be original, added a new category of "pictorial, graphic, and sculptural work" that could potentially add design to the categories of protectable subject matter, and extended the maximum term of copyright to 56 years.

Originality in copyright law is not the high standard of novelty or nonobviousness required in patent law. In *Feist v. Rural Tel. Serv. Co.*, the Supreme Court defined originality in copyright to mean that the work is "independently created by the author" and "possesses at least some minimal degree of creativity." The standard of originality under US law is more generous than the standard under EU law (which is discussed in the next chapter). A work that is not a copy generally rises to the minimal degree of creativity required.[2] The requirement of originality means that independent creation operates as a defense.

In 1954, the Supreme Court decided an important case for copyright in design, *Mazer v. Stein* (discussed in more detail later in the chapter). The justices held that a work of art embodied in a useful article could be protected by copyright.

In 1976, after the US joined the Universal Copyright Convention, the third major revision of copyright law, the Copyright Act 1976, extended copyright protection to all works, both published and unpublished once fixed in tangible form. This removed the requirement for registration, although registration of a copyright work still provides the owner with important advantages such as the right to enforce his or her rights through litigation. The 1976 act also changed the term of copyright protection to the life of the author plus 50 years. In 1988, the US became one of the last major industrial countries to join the Berne Convention. In 1998, it increased the copyright term again to the current term of the life of the author plus 70 years.

The 1976 bill also contained a second part which did not become law. Part II would have extended a *sui generis* type of legal protection to designs. The bill was later used as the basis for the legal protection of specific types of design: Architectural works and boat hulls. Some have argued that copyright law should also be extended to cover fashion designs, but this has yet to happen.

Doctrines in Copyright Law Limiting Protection for Design

Several doctrines have developed in copyright law that limit the broad protection of its exclusive rights. By far the most important and developed limitation for fashion design is that of separability, which prohibits the protection of "useful articles" or functional items by copyright. Two other doctrines, the ideas/expression dichotomy and the defense of fair use, have also been used to limit the application of copyright law to design.

Separability

Copyright legislation and judicial decisions have developed the concept that the functional and non-functional aspects of a useful article must be capable of physical or conceptual separation. Only the non-functional aspects of the article are eligible for copyright protection. The doctrine of separability is very much focused on limiting copyright protection for industrial design and applied art, and so it is particularly relevant to any discussion of fashion design and copyright law.

The doctrine got its start in the *Bleistein v. Donaldson* case in 1903. In his opinion, Justice Wendell Holmes made an oft requoted statement about how courts should determine what constituted an original work for the purposes of copyright protection: "It would be a dangerous undertaking for persons trained only to the law to constitute themselves final judges of the worth of pictorial illustrations, outside of the narrowest and most obvious limits." In the case, the Supreme Court majority held that the circus posters, even though commercial rather than fine art, "promoted the useful arts" and thus could be the subject of copyright protection.

After Justice Holmes construed the term "work of fine art" to protect a work used in a commercial setting, the term "fine art" disappeared from the 1909 Copyright Act. This next act created a category of "[w]orks of art, models, or designs for works of art." The Copyright Office initially kept the distinction between fine and industrial arts in its rules and continued to exclude works of industrial art. In 1917, the Copyright Office finally modified its rule to allow the registration of drawings even if later used for industrial application (Donahue 1990, 330).

In the 1940s, the Copyright Office started to register copyrights in "works of artistic craftsmanship in so far as their form but not their mechanical or utilitarian aspects are concerned."

Finally, in 1954, in *Mazer v. Stein*, the Supreme Court got a chance to consider whether copyright should protect only fine art or should also protect the aesthetic elements of useful objects. Succinctly phrasing the issue in the case as whether a lamp base manufacturer could copyright his lamp bases, the Court reasoned that simply because a work of art is incorporated into the design of a useful article does not remove it from copyright protection. Justice Reed said, "We find nothing in the copyright statute to support the argument that the intended use in industry of an article eligible for copyright bars or invalidates its registration." The *Mazer* ruling potentially put the US on the path of creating a general design protection. After this case it was clear that, if art was *later* incorporated in a useful article, the artistic design did not lose copyright protection. The Court did not answer the more difficult question of whether the design of a simultaneously artistic but also useful article was entitled to protection.

The Supreme Court's holding in *Mazer* removed the idea that copyright protection could be applied only to a "narrow or rigid concept of art." It also made clear that aesthetic elements of useful articles "were eligible for copyright protection."(See Figure 3.1)

After *Mazer*, the Copyright Office apparently favored protecting designs through new legislation rather than as part of the existing copyright law. It felt that a broad judicial approach to protecting industrial designs under copyright law would have anticompetitive effects given the long duration of copyright protection. It was also concerned that judicial activism in this area would likely reduce the chance of Congress passing a specific design statute (Denicola 1983, 718).

In 1960, the Copyright Office introduced a regulation to clarify when copyright could be registered in respect of a work of art used in commerce:

> If the sole intrinsic function of an article is its utility, the fact that it is unique and attractively shaped will not qualify it as a work of art. However, if the shape of a utilitarian article incorporates features, such as artistic sculpture, carving, or pictorial representation, which can be identified separately and are capable of existing independently as a work of art, such features will be eligible for registration.
>
> (Ginsburg 2018, 304–350).

This rule formed the basis of the separability requirement which has become the principal method for ascertaining the legal protection of aesthetically pleasing functional objects under copyright law.

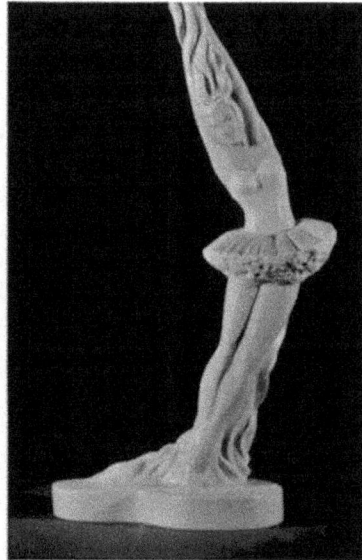

Figure 3.1 The lamp base statue from *Mazer v. Stein* case

The separability rule was codified in Section 101 of the Copyright Act of 1976:

> [T]he design of a useful article, as defined in this section, shall be considered a pictorial, graphic or sculptural work only if, and to the extent that, such design incorporates pictorial, graphic, or sculptural [PGS] features that can be identified separately from, and are capable of existing independently of, the utilitarian aspects of the article.
>
> (Ginsburg 2018, 304–350).

The Copyright Office proposed Title II of the Copyright Act 1976 to provide limited protection for original, commercial designs[3] but it failed to pass in the House on the basis that it created an unnecessary monopoly and would likely raise prices for consumers.

Courts have created and applied such a variety of separability tests that the 1976 Act's codification of the copyright protection of useful articles cannot be said to have resulted in clarity for the protection of industrial design under copyright law. And, although numerous attempts have been made over the years, Congress has failed to pass a law specifically protecting design.

(Too) Many Tests for Separability

In the petition for a writ of certiorari in the most recent Supreme Court case to consider the separability doctrine and the limits of copyright protection for design, *Star Athletica* (see Figure 3.2, a case about cheerleading uniforms), the petitioners described the interpretation of the statutory language regarding separability as "the most vexing, unresolved question in copyright law."

In its decision in *Star Athletica*, the Sixth Circuit reviewed the nine different tests created since *Mazer* by the Copyright Office, appellate courts, and various legal scholars. The Sixth Circuit went on to create and apply a new tenth test that simply recombined various of the conceptual separability tests utilized by other circuits and scholars.

Using the many different separability tests below, various US appellate courts have held that belt buckles and mannequin heads could be copyrighted based on the separability of their artistic elements from the useful article, but that mannequins, bike racks, and casino uniforms were inseparable and could not be copyrighted.[4] Obviously, these determinations are somewhat fact-specific, but the cases illustrate how the tests are often confusing and fail to offer much assistance to designers.

The main separability tests that have developed since *Mazer v. Stein* are briefly described below (using the names given to them by the Sixth Circuit in *Star Athletica*):

1. **The Copyright Office approach** is that "[a PGS] feature satisfies the [conceptual-separability] requirement only if the artistic feature and the useful article could both exist side by side and be perceived as fully realized,

Design 299B
Registration No. VA 1-319-226

Figure 3.2 One of Varsity's designs from *Star Athletica* case

separate works—one an artistic work and the other a useful article." In 1991, to try and clarify the principle of conceptual separability as it related to clothing, the Copyright Office issued a policy decision explaining that the office generally refused to register copyright in "three-dimensional aspects of clothing or costume design," as clothes were useful and ordinarily contained "no artistic authorship separable from their overall utilitarian shape." But the office stated that it would register fanciful costumes "if they contain separable pictorial, graphic, or sculptural elements."

2. **The primary-subsidiary approach**: In 1980, the Second Circuit held in *Kieselstein-Cord v. Accessories by Pearl, Inc.* that a sculpted metal belt buckle was copyrightable because the "artistic features of the [belt] design [were] 'primary' to [its] 'subsidiary utilitarian function.'"

3. **The objectively necessary approach**: In 1985, the Second Circuit created a new, more stringent standard for conceptual separability in *Carol Barnhart Inc., v. Economy Cover Corp.*, a case about mannequins. The majority held that a design is conceptually separable "if the artistic features of the design are not necessary to the performance of the utilitarian function of the article." The majority held that the artistic features of the mannequins were necessary for the performance of their utilitarian function, and so the design was not copyrightable.

4. **The ordinary-observer approach**: Judge Newman's dissent in *Carol Barnhart* gave rise to another test. After surveying the earlier tests, Judge Newman used the perspective of the "ordinary, reasonable observer" to ask whether the article "stimulate[s] in the mind of the beholder a concept that is separate from the concept evoked by its utilitarian function." He determined that an ordinary observer would conceive of the nude mannequins as sculptural art. In this test, the factfinder must consider the aesthetic concept without "simultaneously contemplating the utilitarian function" of the article.

5. **The design approach**: In *Brandir v. Cascade Pacific Lumber* in 1987, the Second Circuit used an article by Robert Denicola to reconcile earlier conceptual separability tests. Denicola had suggested that there was no bright line between works of industrial design and artistic works made into useful articles. The court adopted his test that considered "the extent to which the work reflects artistic expression uninhibited by functional considerations." In the case, a sculptor had modified a wire sculpture to optimize its use as a bike rack. The court held the bike rack was not copyrightable. "[I]f design elements reflect a merger of aesthetic and functional considerations, the artistic aspects of a work cannot be said to be conceptually separable from the utilitarian elements. Conversely, where design elements can be identified as reflecting the designer's artistic judgment exercised independently of functional influences, conceptual separability exists." This is a test which requires judges to engage in subjective artistic judgments in a way which would have concerned Justice Holmes.

6. **The stand-alone approach**: In 2004, in another case concerning mannequins, *Pivot Point International v. Charlene Products*, the Seventh Circuit addressed the issues of conceptual separability and held that "the features of Pivot Point's mannequin could be conceptualized as existing independently from the mannequin's use in hair and makeup training because they were the result of the designer's artistic judgment." This test is process-oriented in that it considers how the useful article was created. It is similar to the design approach in *Brandir* in requiring the factfinder to consider how the article was made. Since the design process for most industrially designed useful articles such as clothing requires functional considerations to be taken into account, the *Pivot Point* test would likely prevent clothing from being granted copyright protection.

7. **The likelihood of marketability approach**: In 2005, the Fifth Circuit adopted Professor Nimmer's marketability test in the context of clothing design. In *Galiano v. Harrah's Operating Company*, a case about casino uniforms, the Fifth Circuit said "[t]here is little doubt that clothing possesses utilitarian and aesthetic value" but a "clothing design that is intended to be used on clothing is copyrightable only to the extent that its artistic qualities can be separated from the utilitarian nature of the garment." The Nimmer test considers whether "there is substantial likelihood that even if the article had no utilitarian use it would still be marketable to some significant segment of the community simply because of its aesthetic qualities." Adopting this test,

the Court held that there was no evidence that the uniforms were "marketable independently of their utilitarian function as casino uniforms." Nimmer has criticized his own test on the grounds that a "likelihood of marketability standard is foreign to copyright, could disproportionately favor more conventional or popular forms of art, and is very difficult to prove" (Chatterjee 2018, 564).

8. **Patry approach**: *Patry on Copyright* states that, "[w]hen determining whether [PGS] features are protectable under the Copyright Act, the focus should be on whether those … aspects are separable from the 'utilitarian *aspects*' of the article, not the [entire] 'article' because the protected features need not be capable of existing apart from the article, only from its functional aspects." This test has two additional steps, first a determination of the PGS features and second a determination that they can exist independent of the utilitarian aspects of the useful article or are dictated by the form or function of the useful article.

9. **The subjective–objective approach**: This approach to conceptual separability is determined by balancing (a) "the degree to which the designer's subjective process is motivated by aesthetic concerns" with (b) "the degree to which the design of a useful article is objectively dictated by its utilitarian function." This test requires judges to weigh how much the design is dictated by function and how much by aesthetic concerns.

Several of these tests are problematic because they require judges to undertake subjective and/or complicated and unrealistic evaluations of art and creativity of the kind that Justice Holmes felt were outside the capabilities of the judiciary more than 100 years ago. Even if they have the skill, in many cases judges will not have the evidence needed to apply many of these tests. How is a judge to determine the extent to which the work reflects artistic expression, whether the artistic features of the design are "primary" or "secondary" to its "subsidiary" utilitarian function, or whether there is a likelihood that it is marketable? A judge would also be hard pressed to determine who is an "ordinary observer" and how this observer could have two *separate* concepts in his mind about the useful article at one time.

In its opinion in *Star Athletica*, the Sixth Circuit did not criticize the many tests; it simply noted that other circuits had used multiple different approaches in analyzing conceptual separability which meant that it was difficult to select one approach to answer the question of whether an artistic design is conceptually separable from the utilitarian aspects of the article. It then went on to lay out yet another test for determining the conceptual separability of clothing design consisting of five questions. The test first asks whether the design is a PGS work. If it is, it inquires whether it is the design of a useful article, and what the utilitarian aspects of this article are. The fourth and most important question is whether the viewer can identify those features separately from the utilitarian aspects of the article. And, if this is possible, the fifth question is whether these features can exist independently of the useful article. The Court suggested that courts should use the "objectively necessary" and "design process" approaches to determine the answers to these questions.

Using its new test, the Sixth Circuit held that Varsity's cheerleading uniforms were protectable by copyright since its designs "of stripes, chevrons, color blocks, and zigzags [can] exist[ ] independently of the utilitarian aspects of a cheerleading uniform" and the arrangement of the designs are "wholly unnecessary to the performance of the garment's ability to cover the body, permit free movement, and wick moisture." The Sixth Circuit noted that "it is impossible either physically or conceptually to separate a 'dress design,' which 'graphically sets forth the shape, style, cut, and dimensions for converting fabric into a finished dress or other clothing garment,' from the utilitarian aspects of clothing, i.e., to cover, protect, and warm the body." But it stated that Varsity's "designs are more like fabric design than dress design."

Star Athletica: The Supreme Court Addresses Separability

Star Athletica appealed the Sixth Circuit decision upholding Varsity's copyright in its chevron designs, and the Supreme Court finally got its first chance since *Mazer* to address this "most vexing, unresolved question in copyright law," one that one appeals court had described as a "metaphysical quandary."

Unfortunately, the long-awaited Supreme Court opinion did not resolve the vexing question, nor bring much clarity to the copyright standards for the designs of useful articles such as clothing.

During legal argument, Justice Sotomayor, clearly cognizant of the stakes for established fashion designers and the fast fashion industry, stated:

> You're killing knock-offs with copyright. You haven't been able to do it with trademark law. You haven't been able to do it with patent designs. We are now going to use copyright law to kill the knockoff industry. I don't know that that's bad. I'm just saying.
>
> (Mann 2016)

Justice Thomas, writing for the majority, did not revisit the lower courts' recitation of the nine tests for separability. He started by stating the general view of almost every court that has considered the question—"[t]he line between art and industrial design, however, is often difficult to draw." Then, he attempted to simplify the test to determine the copyrightability of a PGS feature of a useful article by basing it only on the Copyright Act's language. Thomas dismissed the distinction between physical and conceptual separability, stating,

> we reject the view that a useful article must remain after the artistic feature has been imaginatively separated from the article, we necessarily abandon the distinction between "physical" and "conceptual" separability, which some courts and commentators have adopted based on the Copyright Act's legislative history.

Thomas's test is essentially a rewording of the statute. He articulated his new test in the simplest terms:

> a feature of the design of a useful article is eligible for copyright if, when identified and imagined apart from the useful article, it would qualify as a pictorial, graphic, or sculptural work either on its own or when fixed in some other tangible medium.

Applying this test to the cheerleading uniforms in the case, Thomas held that "imaginatively removing the surface decorations from the uniforms and applying them in another medium *would not replicate the uniform itself*" (italics added). Thomas noted that the cheerleading designs had, in fact, been applied to different types of clothing, so clearly the decorations were separable from the uniforms and could be protected by copyright. Only the two-dimensional surface decorations of chevrons on the uniforms were copyrightable. Thomas held that copyright owners did not have the right to stop others from manufacturing "a cheerleading uniform of identical shape, cut, and dimensions to the ones on which the decorations in this case appear."

Ginsburg concurred with the majority, but because the designs at issue were not, in her view, the designs of useful articles. She held that the chevron designs in question were themselves "copyrightable pictorial or graphic works reproduced on useful articles." Essentially, Ginsburg viewed the designs on the cheerleading uniforms as fabric designs.

Justice Breyer dissented, joined by Justice Kennedy. Using the same test articulated by Thomas for the majority, Breyer held that Varsity's cheerleading uniforms were not copyrightable. A separable design feature must be "capable of existing independently" of the useful article as a separate artistic work that is not itself the useful article. Breyer demonstrated the flaw in the test, asking: "What design features *could not be* imaginatively reproduced on a painter's canvas?" He stated that, if the chevrons and stripes (of the cheerleading uniforms) were applied to a "painter's canvas that painting would be of a cheerleader's dress." In Breyer's words: "Congress did not intend a century or more of copyright protection" imposing costs on others for useful articles such as these. Quoting Lord Macaulay's famous statement on the importance of limiting legal protection because of its costs for the public, that copyright in books is a "tax on readers for the purpose of giving a bounty to writers," Breyer explained that "it is clear that Congress has not extended broad copyright protection to the fashion design industry." He believed that, if the court did so, it would be providing "the designer protection that Congress refused to provide. It would risk increased prices and unforeseeable disruption in the clothing industry."

Breyer's use of the same test for conceptual separability as Thomas to come to the opposite conclusion suggests that the test is no more helpful than the various earlier tests it is supposed to replace. As Justice Breyer pointed out: "virtually any industrial design can be thought of separately as a work of art: Just imagine a frame surrounding the design, or its being placed in a gallery."

If Thomas's intent was to create a simple test for separability that all lower courts could uniformly follow and eliminate the confusion of the nine to ten previous separability tests, he failed. The lower courts will continue to have difficulty applying this new test as they did previous ones. As Samantha Burdick says in "Star Athletica Tells the Fashion Industry to Knock-it-Off with the Knockoffs," "in its attempt to settle the separability paradox, [it] opens the door to copyrightability of design features that are intertwined with the useful articles they are depicted on" (Burdick 2019, 403). It does appear that after *Star Athletica*, notwithstanding the added confusion, it will become easier to obtain copyright protection for clothing designs.

Separability post Star Athletica

In April 2017, athletic shoemaker Puma sued fast fashion retailer Forever 21 for producing "lookalike versions of footwear from Rhianna's Fenty line for Puma." The lawsuit was based on the fact that Forever 21 had mimicked three of Rhianna's bestselling designs for Puma, the Creeper, Fur Slide, and Bow Slide styles, that were in Rhianna's collection for Puma. Forever 21 argued that the three-dimensional contours of the shoe were not copyrightable because they could not be separated from the shoes without destroying the "basic shape of the useful article." Unfortunately, the case was settled in 2018, and the terms of the settlement were confidential, and so we do not know if a court would have decided that separability requires that the decoration be entirely detachable in some way from the totality of the design, like the fabric patterns in *Star Athletica*, or whether it can be part of the cut or style of the design.

In 2019, the Third Circuit held that the district court in New Jersey had been correct to grant an injunction to prevent the sale of a copyrighted banana costume. Rasta Imposta sued Kangaroo for copying its design of a banana costume. In fact, Kangaroo had bought some overruns of the Rasta Imports design to resell. Rasta Imposta held a copyright for the costume. Its complaint contained claims of copyright infringement, trade dress infringement, and unfair competition. The Third Circuit, applying *Star Athletica*, held that the banana costume's combination of colors, lines, shape, and length (i.e., its artistic features) were both separable and capable of independent existence, and thus were copyrightable. The court held that the shape of Rasta's costume did not "effectively monopolize the underlying idea" of a banana and contained a separable design that was original.

In 2019, perhaps emboldened by the *Star Athletica* decision, luxury fashion house Versace sued online fast fashion purveyor Fashion Nova in a much-publicized lawsuit in a California federal court over several closely copied outfits including Versace's "jungle print" dress made famous by Jennifer Lopez in 2000.

Versace claimed that the dress was protected by copyright for its fabric patterns and design. It described the copyrightable subject matter as a "green tropical leaf and bamboo pattern, plunging neckline extending to the navel, high-cut leg slit, circular brooch where the plunging neckline meets the high-cut leg slit, and long, flowing sleeves." Versace argued that "Fashion Nova's ability to churn out new clothing so quickly"—and so cheaply—"is due in large part to its willingness to copy the copyrighted designs, trademarks and trade dress elements of well-known designers, and trade on their creative efforts in order to bolster [its own] bottom line." Fashion Nova fought back, claiming that Versace's design lacked originality and was widely used in the industry. Fashion Nova wanted to depose Donatella Versace, the brand's creative director and sister of its late founder Gianni Versace. The judge sided with Versace in disallowing the deposition of creators or designers for purposes of supporting an invalidity defense.

The parties settled the case in late 2021 just days before the trial. Unfortunately, it is not clear if the *Star Athletica* decision played a part in the parties' decision to settle, and especially whether Fashion Nova was concerned about the dress design and pattern combinations being protectable by copyright. The patterns on the two dresses were very similar, supporting the view that Versace had a relatively strong case of infringement if elements of the design were protectable as separate from the functional aspects of the dress.

The Complexity of Separability and Function in Clothing

Several commentators have attempted to define separability in clothing by considering what the function of clothing is or whether an outfit can be conceived without a particular feature. The doctrine of separability depends on a definition of functional. If it is part of fashion's function to be beautiful, or at least to accentuate the body of the wearer, as Christopher Buccafusco and Jeanne Fromer argue in their article "Fashion's Function in Intellectual Property Law," then aesthetic aspects of the design would not be separable from its utility. Many, if not most, elements of aesthetic clothing design would be excluded from copyrightability.

Clothing design can be both expressive and functional. Most clothing, even when it is expressive, is designed in service of a particular function, whether that function is to look good for a special occasion (such as an evening dress) or to be protective against inclement weather (such as a rain coat). Sometimes, whether clothing is expressive or functional depends on the context and the audience. For example, camouflage serves a utilitarian purpose on an army uniform (Buccafusco and Fromer 2017, 74), but the same camouflage may be expressive on a purse. If an element of design is expressive in a way that is separable from the clothing's function, then it should be protectable by copyright. The camouflage design of the army uniform should not be copyrightable because that would remove a utilitarian or functional feature from the designers' toolkit. However, on the purse, there is no similar reason to prevent the designer from obtaining a copyright on the design.

Buccafusco and Fromer argue that, since the chevrons, patterns, and stripes (such as those at issue in *Star Athletica*) are added to a cheerleading uniform to emphasize the fitness and athleticism of the wearer, they should not be copyrightable. This is the function of cheerleading uniforms. Granting copyright for these designs would enable the designer to "monopolize functional aspects of garments without satisfying the exacting demands of patent law" (Buccafusco and Fromer 2017, 89).

Mala Chattergee, in her article "Conceptual Separability as Conceivability," suggests using a conceivability framework for assessing separability in fashion design. Conceivability means asking whether, when you conceive of the design without the particular design feature, it still functions in the same way. If so, the feature is expressive and can be copyrighted. It is not necessary to the article's function and so it is conceptually separable from the article's utilitarian aspects and should be entitled to copyright protection. If the answer is no, then the design element has failed the test. It is at least partly functional and should not be protected by copyright law (Chatterjee 2018, 560).

Burdick noted that the test of separability in *Star Athletica* is not a strong test or one supported by a large majority of judges: "Star Athletica purports to offer the first uniform test to assist clothing manufacturers in determining the copyrightability of their clothing features. Yet, the Court's decision came from only a five-Justice majority, with one Justice concurring." Perhaps more importantly, Justices Breyer and Kennedy used the same separability test as the majority to find that the chevrons and stripes were not separable and, thus, not eligible for copyright protection (Burdick 2019, 393–4).

The doctrine of separability still fails to provide a clear or workable guide for courts or designers as it doesn't answer the important question of how to protect design where form and function are intertwined, as in much of fashion design. Certainly, *Star Athletica* has failed to clarify the doctrine of separability, but it may have added a higher level of copyright protection to fabric patterns and designs applied to clothing that could be used to protect fashion design against knock-offs, as suggested by Justice Sotomayor in her questioning.

The Ideas/Expression Dichotomy

Copyright cannot protect an idea, but it can protect the expression of that idea. A historical date, a cake recipe, or other fact or basic idea is not copyrightable because no one should be able to monopolize the building blocks of creativity. However, the way in which the idea is expressed may be protectable. Put another way, no one owns the facts, but they can make the packaging their own. In a post *Star Athletica* law journal article, "Give Me a ©: Refashioning the Supreme Court's Decision in *Star Athletica v. Varsity* into an Art-First Approach to Copyright Protection for Fashion Designers," Jared Schroeder and Camille Kraeplin suggest the use of the ideas/expression dichotomy as a way to resolve the confusion created by the separability test: Fashion designs can be conceptualized as art applied to useful objects, facts, or ideas, rather than as useful articles. They explain that news articles, although not the facts on which they are based, are eligible for copyright protection because they are the result of the author's work. They suggest that a shirt or a dress should not be copyrighted since it is "essentially a *fact* with insufficient originality," while a fashion design should be copyrightable because "[t]he choices and arrangement of different elements, or facts, elevate it to an original work, despite its composition being substantially of utility items such as cloth, thread, or plastic" (Schroeder and Kraeplin 2019, 38).

The use of the ideas/expression dichotomy in a design context is on display in a 1992 case about photography, *Rogers v. Koons*. The plaintiff photographer, Rogers, had taken a picture "of a typical American scene—a smiling husband and wife holding a litter of charming puppies." Rogers licensed this print to a company selling postcards. Jeff Koons, the famous, and sometimes controversial artist, copied the postcard, which he viewed as a typical, commonplace "mass culture" scene, as a sculpture. The Second Circuit Court of Appeal held that Roger's photo was original as it was "the product of plaintiff's artistic creation," and that Koons copied it without authorization. The court held:

> We recognize that ideas, concepts, and the like found in the common domain are the inheritance of everyone. What is protected is the original or unique way that an author expresses those ideas, concepts, principles or processes. Hence, in looking at these two works of art to determine whether they are substantially similar, focus must be on the similarity of the *expression* of an idea or fact, not on the similarity of the facts, ideas or concepts themselves.

Applying the *Rogers* decision to fashion design would require consideration of how a particular design worked in an original or unique way to express the generally utilitarian concept of clothing. This demonstrates another legal concept that could be used to protect the execution of an idea by a designer without "extending a monopoly regarding that concept or idea to the copyright holder."

Some fashion cases have, in fact, used the ideas/expression dichotomy as a method of determining the dividing line between protectable art and unprotectable functional design. In 1990, Knitwaves, a manufacturer of knitwear, launched a collection of sweaters including two with copyright protection, the "Leaf Sweater" with puffy leaf appliqués and the "Squirrel Cardigan" with a squirrel and leaf appliqués. In 1992, a competitor, Lollytogs, released a competing line of sweaters with similar leaf and squirrel designs. Evidence showed that a Lollytogs design executive had provided the Knitwaves sweaters to the design department with a request for them to create sweaters with the "same feel" as the Knitwaves sweaters. The Lollytogs's designer testified that she had made changes to the original Knitwaves sweater, including rearranging the placement of the leaf appliqués and adding acorns to the design. It is not clear, but she may have been working under the assumption that this made her designs new under the oft touted "three percent rule" (described in Chapter 2) that many designers believe protects them from copyright infringement claims if they make a small number of changes to a garment.

The district court concluded that Lollytogs set out to knock off the Knitwaves sweater design and, without referring to the separability test, *Mazer*, or any other PGS cases, found in favor of Knitwaves, stating: "[T]he plaintiff must show that the defendant appropriated the plaintiff's particular means of expressing an idea, not merely that he expressed the same idea." The court used the substantial similarity test, concluding that, despite the limited differences between the two sweaters, Lollytogs's arrangement was "substantially similar" to that of Knitwaves. It decided that, while clothes are "useful articles" and not copyrightable, "fabric designs, such as the artwork on Knitwaves' sweaters, are like 'writings' for the purpose of copyright law."

By avoiding the conception of the sweater as a PGS work, the court created a far less complex way of looking at fashion design under the "literary works" part of Section 102 of the Copyright Act. This required the court to consider first whether the designs were creative and original, and then to consider whether the Lollytogs design was substantially similar to the Knitwaves design. It did not have to perform the mental gymnastics of considering whether the design was separable from the useful article of the sweater.

Fair Use

The doctrine of fair use, now codified as Section 107 of the Copyright Act 1976, allows some unlicensed uses of copyright-protected works. The statute sets out four factors:

- The purpose and character of the use.
- The nature of the copyrighted work.
- The amount of the work used.
- And the effect of the use on the potential market for the copyrighted work.

Fair use could protect designers using earlier garment designs in later work. However, fair use does not provide much certainty. The Supreme Court has described it as "a holistic, context-sensitive inquiry ... not to be simplified with bright-line rules." Courts often give the different fair use factors different weights, sometimes even deciding that these factors are merely illustrative and other factors may be pertinent in determining whether a use is fair. This gives rise to the criticism that fair use is not a helpful test and operates as the "right to hire a lawyer," rather than a sure way of knowing whether the use of a copyrighted work will be permitted.

Fair use has only rarely been used in fashion-related cases. It has been successful where the secondary use was a commentary on the first use, and it could potentially be successful if the secondary use of the design was transformative of the first.

The defendants in several lawsuits brought by Louis Vuitton to prevent the use of its luxury brand on dog toys and other similar products used fair use as a defense. Haute Diggity Dog created and sold parody products "Chewnel," "Sniffany & Co," and "Chewy Vuiton." Louis Vuitton sued alleging trademark infringement, trademark dilution, and copyright infringement. The Fourth Circuit spent little time on the copyright claim, simply holding that, applying the fair use factors, Haute Diggity Dog's parody of certain altered elements of Louis Vuitton's multicolor design was fair use.

In 2017, Louis Vuitton lost a similar lawsuit against a company called My Other Bag which used the illustration of a Louis Vuitton purse design on its canvas tote. The court agreed that the use of the Louis Vuitton design was a clear parody of the expensive luggage company. My Other Bag's design was essentially a commentary on Louis Vuitton's expensive purse.

Where the secondary use is not a commentary on the first use, courts have focused on the first fair use factor—the purpose and character of the use. The main question is whether the secondary use is transformative of the first.

In 2021, in *The Andy Warhol Foundation for the Visual Arts, Inc., v. Goldsmith*, the Second Circuit decided that Warhol's use of Goldsmith's photographs of Prince was not fair use (see Figure 3.3). The Court explained that, in determining whether a new use was transformative, it was not enough that the artist had put his or her own stamp or style on the work. It held that a court must consider all four fair use factors in determining if a new use of the original work was fair. Warhol was not commenting on the original photographs or using them for an entirely different purpose, and the Court decided that "the secondary work itself must reasonably be perceived as embodying a distinct artistic purpose, one that conveys a new meaning or message separate from its source material." It is not enough that the new work has a different style or aesthetic if it uses the same source material. Fair use requires something more transformative of the original work.

It is not clear how courts are to determine whether a secondary user transforms an original work without making artistic judgments about the secondary user's work. The Supreme Court heard argument on this case in October 2022. Its decision is not yet published, but during oral argument several of the justices asked questions that made clear that they felt that even transformative uses like creating a film from a book (Justice Kagan's example) require permission. Thus, suggesting that where the purpose of the use is essentially the same as the original work (a picture of Prince) then the new work is unlikely to be transformative. Many groups filed amicus briefs (mostly in support of the photographer Goldsmith arguing that Warhol's use was not transformative. The government's brief in support of Goldsmith argued that for a use to be fair all of the fair use factors should be considered, not just the purpose and character of the use. It seems likely that the Supreme Court will uphold the Second Circuit decision that Warhol's painting was not sufficiently transformative to be a fair use of Goldsmith's photograph.

Proving transformative use of an earlier design is far easier if a second commercial use has a different purpose or character (i.e. it either comments on the first use) or uses it in an entirely different market (for example, the parody bags in the Louis Vuitton cases). Otherwise, a secondary user must fundamentally transform the design, rather than recreate it in a different style or aesthetic.

Given the difficulties of assessing transformative use, particularly of a design used in a similar way to an earlier design, without a court case, designers will likely avoid using earlier works rather than hope that they can argue that they fit within the vague parameters of the increasingly important first fair use factor.

Figure 3.3 Andy Warhol's Prince work and the Goldsmith Prince photographs

Sui Generis Protection for Fashion Design

Since 1914, numerous bills have been proposed, but Congress has never passed a comprehensive design protection law. Even when the US joined the Berne Convention (which required the protection of applied art), Congress did not act.

Probably the closest US law came to adding protection for industrial design, including fashion, was in 1976. The Copyright Office favored adding a short-term protection for artistic design of a useful article with some formalities. The Senate agreed and proposed Title II of the 1976 Copyright Act: A five-year protection for "ornamental designs of useful articles." It defined a useful article as "an article which in normal use has an intrinsic utilitarian function that is not merely to portray the appearance of the article or to convey information." A design consisted of "those aspects or elements of the article, including its two-dimensional or three-dimensional features of shape and surface, which make up the appearance of the article." Designs would be deemed ornamental if they were "intended to make the article attractive or distinct in appearance." Protection would attach to original designs, not commonplace or minor variations of existing designs, and would apply as long as the design was not dictated solely by a utilitarian function. It was possible to apply for an additional five years of protection at the end of the original term.

The House of Representatives Judiciary Committee deleted Section II in its entirety on the basis that this design bill could not be considered to be copyright protection and thus had no place in a copyright revision bill. The Judiciary Committee was also concerned about the patent-like monopoly that would be created by the new protection without showing that its benefits outweighed the disadvantage of removing designs from free public use. In the final copyright bill, the House Judiciary Committee went on to revise Section 101 to include the definition of a PGS work (from the Supreme Court decision in *Mazer*) and the definition of a "useful article" (from the Copyright Office 1960 regulation). It narrowed the Copyright Office definition from an article having "a *sole* intrinsic utilitarian function" to an article with "an intrinsic utilitarian function." Even a highly decorative article could not be protected by copyright if it also had a useful function. This set a higher bar for the protection of PGS works than the simpler test for the protection of literary works—originality.

Since 1976, two specific design industries have been successful in obtaining *sui generis* design protection. Lobbyists for architects and boat builders have obtained protection for their industries using the framework set out by the deleted Title II of the Copyright Act 1976. Architectural works were added to the list of categories of work protected by copyright law in the Architectural Works Copyright Protection Act, enacted in 1990, and boat hulls were added in the Vessel Hull Protection Act of 1998.

Fashion designers have lobbied for similar protection on multiple occasions but, so far, to no avail. The difficulty of protecting fashion designs under US law with copyright has led designers to turn to another intellectual property right—trademarks.

Copyrights Disadvantages for Fashion Design

Using copyright protection for fashion design in the US is difficult mainly because the doctrines that are supposed to ensure that copyright only protects the creative parts of a design remain unclear and hard for courts to apply with any consistency. Traditionally, copyright protects original and purely artistic works from copying to ensure that their economic value can be exploited by their creators. Separability is an attempt to avoid the creator gaining a long period of legal protection for purely functional aspects of their design so that these remain available to all. The law has developed the already existing distinction between the purely decorative fine arts and the more useful crafts and applied arts to create this concept. It has proved to be almost unworkable in practice, particularly in an area such as fashion design where a garment seamlessly merges artistic and functional elements.

Two other copyright concepts—the ideas/expression dichotomy and the doctrine of fair use—may provide more workable methods of protecting artistic design without providing unnecessary legal protection to functional clothing. However, these concepts have not been well developed by court decisions to create a clear and workable division between protectable art and unprotectable functional design.

The length and increasing strength of copyright protection offer further reasons why copyright does not provide a legal mechanism well suited to protecting creativity in design. When a design gains copyright protection, it is removed from the artistic and cultural references available to other designers for the life of the originator plus 70 years. One of the most important requirements for creativity in design is that designers have access to the work of others.

Trademarks

Trademarks are probably the most important US intellectual property right for fashion designers. Margaret Chon states in "Slow Logo: Brand Citizenship in

Global Value Networks": "trademark and trade dress laws are the principal regulatory mechanism in the area of design (including fashion) in jurisdictions such as the United States" (Chon 2014, 954). As explained in Chapter 1, the US fashion industry has developed with a focus on branding and marketing more than design, and the use of trademark law for design protection reflects that focus.

History and Purpose of Trademark Law's Protection of Design

Although trademark law is the oldest branch of intellectual property law, going back to the medieval craft guilds, the philosophy behind, and purpose of, trademark protection have not been the subject of as much scholarly discussion as other intellectual property rights. In fact, there is almost no discussion of the purpose of trademarks, particularly compared with the extensive academic literature on the philosophies, history, and purpose of both patent and copyright protection.

The incentive rationale of intellectual property works for copyrights and patents but not for trademarks: "We don't protect trademarks to encourage the creation of more trademarks" (Lemley 1999, 1694). As far back as 1879, the Supreme Court noted another major distinction between trademarks and other forms of intellectual property in that a trademark does not itself "depend upon novelty, invention, discovery, or any work of the brain. It requires no fancy or imagination, no genius, no laborious thought." In other words, a trademark is not protected because it is creative.

The law conceives a trademark's function as simple. It is informational. Trademark law is intended primarily to protect the consumer from being misled as to the source of origin of the goods or services with which it is associated. Secondarily, a trademark protects the goodwill of the trademark owner from those who seek to free ride on his reputation. The legal understanding of trademarks tends to focus on the economic function that a trademark has to convey information to consumers about brands. The law protects trademarks so that the public can use them to identify the source of origin of particular goods or services. Producers can thus use trademarks to create a reputation and thus "compete on the basis of experience characteristics of goods, and so on" (Lemley 1999, 1695). Trademark law focuses on false designations of origin, and the standard in litigation is not whether the customer is actually confused or mistaken as to the origin of particular goods, but whether such confusion is likely given the relevant circumstance. Design's purpose is not to indicate where particular designs come from.

In his seminal book on trademarks, *The Historical Foundations of the Law Relating to Trademarks* written in 1925, Frank Schechter described a somewhat broader purpose for trademarks. He said the real value of a trademark lay in its selling power, which depends on the psychological hold the mark has on the consumer. Professor Schechter argued that the more well known and unique a mark is, the more powerful it is.

Trademarks in the modern world certainly function as Schechter noted in many more ways than simply providing information to the consumer. Among other things, we use trademarks or brands to express who we are, that we belong to a particular group, or that we hold certain ideals or support particular causes (Schechter 1925). It is easy to see this if we consider any number of modern brands. Chon argues that the role of brands goes far beyond the legal boundaries of trademarks and has cultural, social, and political impacts and functions (Chon 2014, 938). Trademarks provide information not just about the brand to the consumer but also about the consumer to others. For this reason, brands are pervasive in the modern world. It sometimes seems that everyone seeks to brand themselves; even countries have marketing and branding campaigns.

Lemley described how trademarks enable companies to build community, identity, and culture around organizations. They provide "a very efficient way of communicating information to customers" and play a key role "in allowing the growth of complex, long-term organizations spread over a wide geographic area" (Lemley 1999, 1690).

Branding and the protection of its trademarks have become increasingly essential to the modern consumer company. Fashion brands expend much time and money on promoting and protecting their brands through trademark law. This is demonstrated most clearly in the luxury sector. Luxury brand owners focus on maintaining strong trademarks and are likely to turn to trademark litigation to protect their brand names. Using trademarks to protect brand names and product designs is a strategy used by many well-known designers. Trademark law makes it much easier to demonstrate the required customer confusion if a mark is famous.

Kuldova and Pouillard confirm the importance of trademarks and branding in the fashion industry in the US in their article, "Interrogating Intellectual Property Rights in Post-War Fashion and Design," "[I]nvesting in the creation of powerful brands with easily recognizable logos associated with seductive brand mythologies has become one of the most effective intellectual property rights strategies in the fashion industry." As they also explain, there is another benefit of using trademarks in the fashion business: "[T]rademarks also remain the most popular way of protecting fashion, because they can be used as an inherent design element in a final product" (Pouillard and Kuldova 2017, 348).

Trademark law's strong protections encourage luxury brand owners, particularly, to display visible trademarks prominently on their merchandise. This would not be necessary if the design, rather than the brand, was the subject of legal protection. Trademark law changes creative choices.

The focus on trademarks is particularly important for fashion designers since clothing is so often intended by its creators and those who wear it to communicate identity. Clothing may signal political identity, class, culture, and other expressions of who we are. Trademarks provide a shorthand for communicating messages both about us and about the causes we believe in. A BLM t-shirt and Trump red hat provide a lot of information about the wearer, as does an expensive power suit or a flowing kaftan. How we dress is important to how we experience aspects of our identity, values, and culture and is a vital part of our experience as human beings. Brands, and their legal protection via trademarks, are used by consumers as much as by the corporations who own them.

The Lanham Act and the Non-Traditional Trademark

In the US, the principal federal statute protecting trademarks is the Lanham Act, passed in 1947. The act was intended to protect traditional trademarks (words) and, to a lesser extent, to protect trade dress (designs). In the 70 years since the passage of the Lanham Act, the economic rationale for trademarks has not changed significantly, but the law and how it is applied by courts have changed.

Before the Lanham Act, trademark law protected so-called traditional or technical trademarks: Words, emblems, or symbols, affixed to, or emblazoned on, products. A separate branch of the common law, the law of unfair competition, could be used to protect against the imitation of packaging designs and other product attributes. However, to succeed in an unfair competition case, the plaintiff had to show deception or fraud, i.e., that customers actually believed that the copied product designs came from another source.

The legislative history of the Lanham Act shows that Congress intended to keep this traditional approach. It expanded the definition of a technical trademark to encompass descriptive word marks, but it also expressly barred the registration of trade dress (the shape or configuration of products or their packaging) on the Principal Register or its protection. Congress clearly did not intend for the Lanham Act to protect trade dress any further than it was already protected by the common law doctrine of unfair competition. The act permitted the registration of trade dress on the Supplemental Register simply to help companies trying to register trade dress in those foreign jurisdictions that chose to recognize it.

The Development of Trade Dress Protection

Section 43(a) of the Lanham Act expanded the statutory protection to trade dress by providing relief against "false designation of origin, false or misleading description of fact, or false or misleading representation of fact, which are likely to cause confusion." This section created a federal statutory tort of unfair competition that did not require a showing of fraud, but simply that a false designation of origin or misleading statement was likely to cause confusion. Crucially, Section 43(a) removed the requirement for the plaintiff to own a federal trademark registration to invoke trademark law protection, and so Section 43(a) has developed to protect non-traditional trademarks such as design.

The federal courts' expansive interpretations of Section 43(a) over the last 50 years have significantly expanded trademark law beyond the traditional protection of the informational value of specific marks to avoid consumer confusion. The law now protects an array of non-traditional trademark subject matter against many uses that are not likely to cause consumer confusion. The law has protected product configurations, designs, packaging, and design choices such as colors, among other non-traditional trademark subject matter. Courts also no longer require the plaintiff to be able to show that the defendant's conduct is causing harm to the plaintiff's business. This has caused some commentators to argue that the Lanham Act risks becoming a "general anti-copying statute" (Lemley 1999, 1714).

The term "trade dress" is used, but not specifically defined, in the Lanham Act. It is generally taken to refer to the visual appearance of a product or its packaging. In the 1995 Supreme Court case *Two Pesos Inc. v. Taco Cabana, Inc.*, trade dress was defined broadly as including the total image of a product including features such as size, shape, color or color combinations, texture, graphics, and other aspects of a product's design. These have all been protected as trade dress on the basis that these visual signs can work as an indicator of the source of a product, just like a traditional word mark. There are some instantly recognizable fashion designs that indicate the source of origin of the design. The shape of the Hermès Birkin bag is registered as a trademark in a number of jurisdictions because its shape conveys a message about its origins. However, there is a danger that broad protection of the visual appearance of a design can be used to limit legitimate competition and should be the exception rather than the rule.

Trade dress owners were not happy with the Lanham Act's initial exclusion of trade dress from the Principal Register and pushed for the courts or the US Patent and Trademark Office (USPTO) to recognize trade dress as worthy of registration on the Principal Register just like traditional or technical trademarks. In 1958, the new commissioner of trademarks, Daphne Robert Leeds, overturned the distinction so important for fashion designers and allowed trade dress to be registered on the Principal Register (Lunney 2000, 1133). Many businesses have since successfully claimed trademark protection for product configurations and designs. These include the décor in restaurants and stores, the shape of lollipops, knitwear patterns, and even the color of the soles of shoes.

For the next 40 years, although the USPTO made efforts to restrain the registration of trade dress, the Court of Customs and Patent Appeals ignored them, and, in 1976, the Eighth Circuit joined in, followed by other circuits. In all of these decisions, the fact that Congress specifically amended the language of Section 43(a) during the legislative process to preclude trade dress protection was not even raised (Lunney 2018, 225). This history of Section 43(a) explains how trademarks have become so important to fashion designers.

Doctrines in Trademark Law Limiting Protection for Design

Like copyright law, trademark law provides a variety of exceptions that are designed to avoid the detrimental effects on competition of overly strong trademark protection. These limits on trademark protection include the doctrines of functionality, descriptiveness, secondary meaning, and inherent distinctiveness. They are discussed here in relation to fashion design.

Functionality

Functional subject matter cannot be protected as a trademark. This is the main bar that prevents fashion designers (and others) from protecting the configuration or design of their goods using trademark law. Unfortunately, as in copyright law, courts have struggled to create a clear and workable definition of what functional means.

Courts used to be extremely wary of granting trademark protection to any functional objects. In the nineteenth century, a New York court refused to grant a trademark for an ornamental tin pail used to sell merchandise. The judge claimed that the danger of granting trademarks to packaging meant that "someone, bolder than the others, might go to the very root of things, and claim for his goods the primitive brown paper and tow string, as a peculiar property." The view was that protecting packaging or design too broadly would enable one designer or producer to monopolize a commonplace design.

In 1982, this sentiment was revisited in *In re Morton Norwich Products inc.* The US Court of Customs and Patent Appeals recognized that, if all packaging was registrable as a trademark, "the effect would be to gradually throttle trade." In *In re Morton*, the Court held that there needed to be "a fundamental right to compete through imitation of a competitor's product, which right can only be temporarily denied by the patent or copyright laws."

Functionality is meant to prevent the registration of aspects of a product design or packaging which should remain open to all designers. In this case, the Court determined that the shape of a container for a spray cleaner was registrable because, although it had some functionality, it was not the only way to make this spray bottle, and it also served to indicate the origin of the product. The court created two different types of functionality—*de facto* functionality and *de jure* functionality—and held that only one of them barred the registration of a trademark. It defined *de facto* functionality as where "although the design of a product ... is directed to performance of a function, it may be legally recognized as an indication of source." Essentially, the idea of *de facto* functionality is that such items are functional, but there are many other designs that could also be used to bring about the same function. However, an item that is *de jure* functional cannot be protected as a trademark. *De jure* functionality means that the item works specifically because of its functional shape.

Although the distinction between *de facto* and *de jure* functionality seems to have fallen out of favor, it could be applied in the fashion context. Basic clothing designs would be considered *de jure* functional because they are designed to fit the human form (and thus should not be registrable as trademarks). Couture clothing, or more innovative and creative designer wear, would be *de facto* functional (and thus potentially registrable). Such clothing has to fit the human body, but it is intended to go beyond simply providing functional attributes such as warmth and covering. Innovative designs come in many different varieties. However, trademarks should not protect these designs simply for being creative but only if these designs were also being used to indicate the origin of the goods.

In 1995, the Supreme Court considered functionality in terms of the use of a color in a design in *Qualitex Co. v. Jacobson Products Co.* Qualitex used a green-gold color on its dry-cleaning pads and sued to enjoin a competitor from using a similar color. The question before the court was whether color alone is capable of acting as a trademark. The Court held that if the color chosen "is not essential to a product's use or purpose and does not affect cost or quality" of the product, then the color is not functional and can, where secondary meaning is demonstrated, be registered as a trademark.

However, an aesthetic aspect of the product such as its color can clearly have an effect on a product's utility or cost. Where a color serves more than an aesthetic function, its registration as a trademark should be restricted. If one producer is able to monopolize a color, this risks hindering competition, even if the color also has a source-identifying role. The Supreme Court in *Qualitex* believed it had dealt with the problem of aesthetic functionality by requiring that any color used as a trademark must be non-functional and have acquired secondary meaning. However, in clothing, particularly, color is clearly one of the designer's most important design choices.

In *In re Becton* in 2012, the Federal Circuit Court of Appeal once again revived the *de facto/de jure* distinction. Applying *In re Morton*, it determined that the design of a medical collection tube was not protectable as a trademark. The Court said that "Whenever a proposed mark includes both functional and non-functional features, as in this case, the critical question is the degree of utility present in the overall design of the mark." The court used the example of the Coca-Cola bottle to illustrate this point, "noting that the bottle's significant overall non-functional shape would not lose trademark protection simply because 'the shape of an insignificant element of the design, such as the lip of the bottle, is arguably functional.'" In dissent, Judge Linn argued that, although "certain individual features of [Becton's] closure cap design are functional," the design as a whole was not simply functional and should be registrable. This dissent demonstrates that it is somewhat difficult to apply a test which essentially asks how important a feature is to the function of the product.

Perhaps as a result of problems with the concept of *de jure* and *de facto* functionality, the Supreme Court did not use this test in its 2001 decision in *TrafFix Devices, Inc. v. Marketing Displays, Inc.* This case concerned the design of a traffic sign on which the patent had expired but which the company wanted to continue to protect as a trademark. The court held that the *de facto* and *de jure* distinction "was incorrect as a comprehensive definition" of functionality. It stated that functionality means that a feature "is essential to the use or purpose of the product or affects its cost or quality." Those features are functional, regardless of the availability to competitors of other alternatives.

The Supreme Court adopted this narrower definition of functionality in the *TrafFix* case to avoid extending the term of a utility patent indefinitely via trademark law. This would undermine the legislature's intent in patent law to limit the protection of functional features to a fixed term. However, the Supreme Court held that, if

> a manufacturer seeks to protect arbitrary, incidental, or ornamental aspects of features of a product found in the patent claims, such as arbitrary curves in the legs or an ornamental pattern painted on the springs, a different result might obtain.

This decision has limited the ability of designers to register as trade dress a design that contains functional features. Under *TrafFix*, if there is any functional component to the design, it cannot be registered.

However, the test for functionality in a product still assumes a strict division between the functional and aesthetic parts of a design, which modern design generally seeks to avoid. In modern design, aesthetics often can and do serve a purpose. As Orit Afori explained in "Reconceptualizing Property in Designs,"

> [M]any contemporary designs combine functional and aesthetical elements, and it is impossible to separate the two. These designs follow the "Form-Follows-Function" artistic school and the philosophy of functionalism which originated in the 1920s ... According to functionalism, the best designs are those in which the appearance springs truly from the structure and is a logical expression of it.
>
> (Afori 2008, 1121–1122)

Arguably, aesthetics has, in fact, always played a functional role in product design. All the choices made by a designer tend to contribute something real to the product and justify the consumers' choices to buy it. If the term "function" is defined as "a way for achieving an aim," we must go beyond the narrow definition of "function" as something only technical or physical and include aesthetic choices such as color as contributing to the function of a product. The functional components of a design should not be able to obtain protection as trademarks because that would limit the universe of features from which designers can choose their next design. Buccafusco and Fromer argued for a similar broad conception of functionality to include beauty and aesthetic choices. They quote fashion designers, explaining that

> [b]y using art components in [their design] [designers] can alter the frame of reference in which we see the human form, and in so doing, [they] can create illusions or effects that would not be possible in any other way.
>
> (Buccafusco and Fromer 2017, 60)

They argue that these comments show that beauty and art serve a functional role in fashion design.

Secondary Meaning (and Color)

Although a functional mark can never be protected as a trademark, a descriptive or generic mark can be protected if it is shown to have acquired sufficient secondary meaning. Distinctiveness, or secondary meaning, is not defined in the Lanham Act, but lack of it can act as an additional bar to the registration of an aspect of design such as color or shape. Courts can infer secondary meaning from types of information such as sales and advertising budgets, the popularity of the product, its uniqueness, or simply because the design has been imitated.

In *Qualitex*, the Supreme Court determined that color was not functional and could be registered as a trademark. However, Qualitex had to show that its green-gold dry cleaning pads had achieved a secondary meaning, which it defined as the process through which customers, over time, "come to treat a particular color on a product or its packaging ... as signifying a brand."

In long-running litigation about French designer Christian Louboutin's red-soled shoes, the Second Circuit determined in 2012 that the color red used by Louboutin had acquired secondary meaning through its distinctiveness and customer recognition of it as a signifier that shoes with this color soles came from Louboutin.

The Second Circuit decision in this case answered the "difficult and novel" question of whether a single color can serve as a trademark in the fashion industry. Color is such an important creative design choice in fashion that the law should make it difficult to remove a particular color from the design lexicon by giving it trademark protection.

YSL had created and marketed a completely red shoe and challenged Louboutin's trademark registration for red soles. It argued that Louboutin's red sole was not distinctive but ornamental, or alternatively, color should be viewed as functional in fashion. Thus, red-soled shoes were a functional aesthetic choice to which all designers should have access. The district court agreed, stating: "whatever commercial purposes may support extending trademark protection to a single color for industrial goods do not easily fit the unique characteristics and needs—the creativity, aesthetics, taste, and seasonal change—that define production of articles of fashion." In applying a different test to the fashion industry as far as color marks were concerned, Judge Marrero said that allowing a fashion designer to protect a specific color was like allowing Picasso to bring suit against Monet for using a shade that Picasso was known for. Creative fashion designers needed access to all colors, and thus color is functional in fashion. Fashion is defined mainly by cut, color, and fabric choices. Limiting color would be anticompetitive.

Louboutin appealed, and the Second Circuit Court addressed whether a single color was protectable as a trademark, the doctrine of aesthetic functionality, and whether a single color is necessarily functional.

The Second Circuit described Louboutin's striking bright lacquered red soles as a signature item regularly adorning celebrities and fashion icons. It noted that Louboutin had invested substantial amounts of capital in building a reputation and goodwill, holding that this had created a shoe sole that was instantly recognizable to "those in the know." The court reversed the lower court decision and held that the lipstick red color of Louboutin's shoe soles could function as a trademark.

While the Second Circuit agreed that trademark law should not be used to inhibit legitimate competition by giving monopoly control to a producer over a useful product design, it said that, in *Qualitex*, the Supreme Court had determined that there was no bar to single colors functioning as trademarks and it admonished the district court for creating an industry-specific test for fashion.

The Second Circuit applied *Qualitex* and determined that the color of the shoe soles was not functional and had acquired secondary meaning. It crafted a threefold test including aesthetic functionality: Was the color "essential to the use or purpose" of the goods? Second, did the color "affect the cost or quality" of the product at issue? Third, if the design feature is not "functional" from a traditional perspective, it must be shown not to have a significant effect on competition. A "mark is aesthetically functional, and therefore ineligible for protection under the Lanham Act, where protection of the mark *significantly* undermines competitors' ability to compete in the relevant market." The court decided that this functionality defense did not guarantee a competitor "the greatest range for [his] creative outlet, but only the ability to fairly compete within a given market."

The Court went on to limit the breadth of Louboutin's mark. It concluded that the red sole had acquired the necessary secondary meaning—and thus the requisite "distinctness" to merit protection—but only when used as a red outsole *contrasting* with the remainder of the shoe, not when both sole and upper shoe were red. After it modified Louboutin's trademark registration, the Court decided that YSL's use of a red outsole on monochromatic red shoes did not infringe Louboutin's trademark. This suggests that the Second Circuit might have been uncomfortable about allowing a single-color trademark in fashion. It also gave both parties the ability to declare victory. The decision certainly extends the protection of trademark law for what are design choices. Fashion design is driven by aesthetic appeal, an area in which color plays a large part.

The decision also encouraged something already prevalent in the world of fashion design: The classification of design choices as branding exercises. Before the case was decided, Jeannie Suk wrote an op-ed in the *New York Times* arguing that "Louboutin's claim spotlights the pressure on fashion designers to frame their aesthetic choices as brand identifiers, and the legal contortions that result" (Suk 2012).

There has been significant criticism of this decision in terms of its potential for anticompetitive effects. The main concern is that specific designers could monopolize particular colors with effective marketing, essentially removing them from use in certain segments of the market. Savvy designers could convert public recognition and strong market shares into secondary meaning for the color palettes they use. The unlimited duration of trademark rights would narrow the spectrum of usable colors, which would hinder competition and limit innovation and creativity. Tiffany, Louboutin, and Glossier are all fashion companies that use and have registered well-known single-color marks for their products or packaging. Other designers are working to convert recognition of their use of certain colors into secondary meaning to trademark other colors and effectively gain monopoly rights over their use.

Inherent Distinctiveness and Design

In some cases, courts will determine that a design is "inherently distinctive," and thus no evidence of secondary meaning is required for its registration as a trademark. In 1995, in *Two Pesos*, the Supreme Court held that the trade dress of a Mexican restaurant was inherently distinctive and could be registered as a trademark on the Principal Register, even without a showing of secondary meaning. In a unanimous decision, the Court held that the trade dress (which consisted of the restaurant decor) was inherently distinctive, and proof of secondary meaning was not needed.

In this case, the Supreme Court had the chance to put right the lower courts' expansion of the subject matter eligible for trademark protection on the Principal Register in the *Qualitex* decision and others. However, it used the broad ordinary-language meaning of the phrase "symbol or device" to justify the judicial recognition of trade dress protection, not just traditional trademarks, on the Principal Register. In doing so, it was interpreting the trademark terminology not merely incorrectly but in precisely the opposite manner from the one Congress had intended. Congress had specifically added the technical trademark language "word, name, symbol or device" to foreclose trade dress protection. Since the decision in *Two Pesos*, trade dress protection has continued to be strengthened so that "simply copying a popular and successful product can establish a triable claim of actionable trade dress infringement" (Lunney 2019, 226–7).

In 2000, the Supreme Court addressed trade dress protection in respect of fashion in *Wal-Mart v. Samara* and limited the broad holding in *Two Pesos*. Wal-Mart had asked its supplier to manufacture children's clothes based on photographs of Samara's outfits. A unanimous Supreme Court held that "to prevail on a trade dress infringement claim, the plaintiff must prove that its trade dress is distinctive" by showing that it has acquired distinctiveness through "secondary meaning."

The Court held that "design, like color, is not inherently distinctive," and that the design of children's clothing was not entitled to protection as trade dress, unless it could be shown to have gained secondary meaning. Scalia, delivering the court's opinion, noted that many Courts of Appeal had expanded trade dress to "encompass the design of a product." He perpetuated the broad reading of the Lanham Act that trade dress constitutes a "symbol" or "device," stating that: "The text of § 43(a) provides little guidance as to the circumstances under which unregistered trade dress may be protected." In fact, the text of the section makes clear that the claimant must prove false statements or misrepresentation that leads to a likelihood of confusion as to the source of origin of the product.

Scalia made a somewhat artificial distinction between the trade dress at issue in the *Two Pesos* and *Samara* cases by saying that *Two Pesos* was about product packaging and *Samara* was about product design. Without any additional explanation he said: "Consumers are aware that the purpose of product design is not to identify the source, but to render the product itself more useful or more appealing." For this reason, he held that to be registrable as trade dress Samara's clothing designs would have needed to acquire secondary meaning as source indicators, while product packaging could be inherently distinctive and registrable without the need to show that it had acquired secondary meaning.

It is difficult to reconcile the reasoning in *Two Pesos* with that in the *Samara* case. In *Samara*, Scalia said: "Consumers should not be deprived of the benefits of competition with regard to the utilitarian and esthetic purposes that product design ordinarily serves" because "where product design is concerned we have little confidence that a reasonably clear test can be devised."

Scalia raised the same problem that had concerned Congress when it limited protection to technical trademarks (and had decided not to protect trade dress on the Principal Register), namely that, "[c]ompetition is deterred ... not merely by successful suit but by the plausible threat of successful suit." However, he still held that a product design could be registered as a trademark if it was shown to have secondary meaning. Scalia cautioned in this case: "To the extent there are close cases, we believe that courts should err on the side of caution and classify ambiguous trade dress as product design, thereby requiring secondary meaning." However, in *Two Pesos*, the court did not discuss how it determined that the trade dress in that case was packaging and not design and so did not require any proof of secondary meaning.

The distinction between product and packaging design is important because, while packaging might be used as a source identifier, design is less often used in this way. Product design may also be protected by a design patent or by copyright, which would render protection by trademark law unnecessary. Samara had, in fact, obtained a design patent for certain elements of its designs.

Courts tend to believe that "each IP right provides a separate and distinct protection, and they are not part of a scheme of potentially complementary protections." Thus, they may avoid protecting rights under IP schemes that they believe are for a different purpose.

Fair Use and Non-Trademark Use

Clothing brands are often used for the purpose of expression. As Schechter pointed out more than 100 years ago, trademarks have a broader purpose than just providing information to consumers. They are powerful because of their selling power. They are used by brands and consumers to express themselves. Luxury and fashion brands are well aware that brands, and their legal protection trademarks, are recognizable global symbols and containers of meaning.

This means that, when these expressive symbols are used in a way that is a satire or social commentary, they are not being used to provide information about the product to consumers. They are used because they are an expression of meaning, and such use should be permissible. The doctrine of fair use should limit the reach of trademark protection. One of the most recent creators to test the limits of fair use for well-known trademarks is Mason Rothschild who has created 100 NFTs he calls MetaBirkins. These are small digital images in the shape of the iconic Hermès Birkin bag that look like they are covered in fur. Hermès has sued Mason for trademark infringement. Mason argues "the First Amendment gives me every right to create art based on my interpretations of the world around me." He also argues that the MetaBirkins (from which he has made $1.1 million) are "also a commentary on fashion's history of animal cruelty, and its current embrace of fur-free initiatives and alternative textiles." Hermès argues that the bag images infringe on its trademark rights and are an example of fake Hermès products in the metaverse.

Hermès argues that the MetaBirkins infringe its trademark rights because Rothschild is using the name as a trademark rather than as an artistic fair use under the First Amendment. It points to the language Rothschild uses to promote his sales which, it says, confuses customers either by implying the bags are associated with Hermès or by suggesting that they are a tribute to the iconic bag. It lists numerous comments from social media to show that consumers have also been confused as to whether Hermès is involved in creating and/or offering up the MetaBirkin NFTs. It asserts that it may start selling its own NFTs in the metaverse, and that Rothschild is stealing its valuable and famous goodwill in its trademark (TFL 2021a). In October 2022 Rothschild's Motion to Dismiss was denied and a trial date set for January 2023.

Whether a court agrees with Hermès that Rothschild is using the name MetaBirkin in a trademark capacity rather than as artistic expression remains to be seen. The case is one of the first that will answer the question of how far trademark rights extend into the virtual world. Simply because Rothschild appears to be making a profit should not be sufficient to enable Hermès to argue that Rothschild's use of its mark is not fair. However, if consumers are confused, and Hermès can show that Rothschild is using the Birkin name in a trademark sense in the metaverse, this may enable it to prevent Rothschild from selling the MetaBirkins.

Trademarks' Disadvantages for Fashion Design

Since the purpose of trademark law is not to encourage design creativity and innovation but to protect customers from confusion, enabling a designer to obtain indefinite protection of a particular design can easily lead to anticompetitive effects. Well-established and famous designers will find it significantly easier to protect designs as trade dress than newer designers with less access to big marketing and legal budgets. This is illustrated by adidas's several lawsuits against Target for selling shoes with design elements including stripes, shell toes, and flat soles. In a 2002 case, the district judge held that the design elements of adidas's shoes were strictly ornamental and therefore part of its trade dress. The court agreed with adidas that evidence of significant advertising, sales since 1969, and famous basketball stars and hip-hop and rap stars wearing the shoes were sufficient to establish secondary meaning. adidas was able to obtain legal protection because its design was so well known. The designer of a newer shoe would not have been able to do this.

Trademarks, especially trade dress marks, tend to overprotect well-known designers. Courts should refocus on the informational value of trademarks for consumers in assessing color and design marks to avoid the risk of imposing these kinds of limits on fashion designers' creativity. When trademark law is used to protect design features that do not specifically convey information about the brand to the consumer, but are perhaps pleasing and attractive to the eye, the removal of these features from possible use by other designers is anticompetitive because it reduces the variety of products available to the consumer.

Trademarks are a particularly powerful legal protection because, unlike either copyrights or design patents, trademark protection lasts indefinitely, assuming payment of renewal fees. There is also a clear mismatch between the purpose of trademark protection and the purpose of design protection. The job of a trademark is not to promote creative and original design but to indicate the source of origin of goods. Design, as far as it can be protected by trademark law, is protected as a symbol referencing those who created that design. Trademarks applied to design will have the effect of preventing others from using that design for their product. It takes particular designs out of circulation.

When designs are protected as trademarks, we prevent competition using design, and the price of the product goes up. According to Lemley, US courts seem to be replacing the traditional rationale for trademark law with a conception of trademarks as property rights, in which trademark owners are given strong rights over the marks without much regard for the social costs of such rights (Lemley 2005, 1065). We can see this in some of the recent trademark cases on design.

To avoid the possibility of anticompetitive trademarks, courts should focus on the protection of consumers from confusion rather than the protection of well-known designers from competition. The recent history of trademark law has unfortunately led in the opposite direction. The Supreme Court has protected product design and packaging as trademarks and enabled more famous designers to use trade dress as a weapon to prohibit new entrants to the market.

In "Non-Traditional Trademarks: The Error Costs of Making an Exception the Rule," Glynn Lunney explained that courts must be willing to allow some unfair behavior: "[T]he law must draw the line between fair and unfair competition, not at the exact place where competition becomes unfair. Rather, the law must draw the line between lawful and unlawful competition to leave room for some unfair behavior" (Lunney 2019, 233). The reason for this is because well-known designers' propensity to sue will automatically cause their rights to have broader protection than the law provides. Arguably, although they have become increasingly important, trademarks are not the appropriate legal tool for the protection of design.

Design Patents

Design patents are a uniquely American IPR. They are intended to fill the gap between copyrights and patents and protect new and original ornamental design. Design patents may be used to protect the "visual ornamental characteristics embodied in, or applied to, an article." They cover "any new, original and ornamental design for an article of manufacture." As in copyright law, there is a demarcation between functional and ornamental features of an article. A design patent will not be issued for a design form that is dictated primarily by the function of the article (Monseau 2011).

History of Design Patent Law's Purpose and Protection of Designs

Congress has protected industrial designs through patent law in the US since 1842. Apparently, this came about not for any clear doctrinal reason that patent protection was preferable to copyright protection, but because of the personal influence of the first commissioner of the Patent Office, Henry Ellsworth. At the time, patent law was seen as the stronger branch of intellectual property, and there was no central registry for copyrights. Thus, Ellsworth encouraged Congress to choose patent law as the appropriate place for the protection of industrial design rather than copyright (Thomas 1948). Copyright is, arguably, now the stronger branch of IP law, having been significantly extended in terms of both duration and subject matter, but patent law remains the main law for the protection of industrial design in the US.

The 1842 Design Patents Act provides protection for "[w]hoever invents any new, original and ornamental design for an article of manufacture." Design patents are subject to the same criteria as utility patents—novelty and nonobviousness. Unlike copyrights, in order to register a design patent there is a substantive review of the design to see if it meets the criteria for protection as a design patent. The term of a design patent is 14 years from the date of its grant.

In *Gorham Co. v. White*, the Supreme Court stated that the purpose of design patent law was to "give encouragement to the decorative arts." The Court suggested that the reason for providing legal protection was that "giving certain new and original appearances to a manufactured article may enhance its saleable value, may enlarge the demand for it and may be a meritorious service to the public." The law could protect those creators who created new and original designs.

Design patents have, for years, been an underutilized IPR for all types of design. In a 1981 case, the Eighth Circuit Court was able to say that "this is only the second design patent case we have heard since 1926." A 2021 article in *IPWatchdog* stated that not nearly enough designers sought design patent protection for the visual appearance of their creations. It stated that there was some evidence that this was changing. Since the turn of the twenty-first century, "design patents have enjoyed a renaissance, with soaring application numbers and high profile infringement suits" (Quinn 2021).

This may demonstrate a new interest in design patents. The number of design patent applications has certainly increased in recent years, but so has the number of patent applications. The proportion of design patents to patents remains fairly steady. Design patents currently make up about 7% of all patent applications.

In the fashion business, the time and expense of making an application mean that design patents tend to be most heavily used for more enduring fashion items such as footwear and handbags. Brands such as Nike, adidas, Lululemon, Louis Vuitton Malletier, and Hermès hold a lot of design patents and utilize this IP type to protect their brands.

Design patents and trademarks can be used together as part of a legal strategy to prolong the IP protection of iconic design. For example, Apple Inc. used design patents to protect the design of its products. Once Apple had been granted design patents, the company focused on advertising to firmly implant the designs as signifiers of the Apple brand in the minds of its consumers. When the design patents expired, it would apply to register the shapes that had acquired distinctiveness as trade dress marks (Orozco and Conley 2008). In 2016, Apple won a $399 million damages award against Samsung for infringing on the trade dress of the "black rectangular front face with rounded corners" of the iPhone, which had also been originally registered as a design patent. A jury awarded Apple another $140 million in damages (Reuters 2018). Large fashion companies, particularly luxury brands, use design patents and trademarks for their iconic and long-lasting designs in a similar manner.

Doctrines in Design Patent Law Limiting Protection for Design

There are two types of limitations on design patents that restrict their application in fashion designs to very long-lived designs. The first is not a doctrinal standard. It is the cost, length, and scrutiny of the application process. This deters the designers of many fashion items which have a relatively short shelf life from seeking the protection of a design patent. The second limitation is the familiar functionality requirement which prohibits the functional aspects of design from obtaining design patent protection.

The Application Process

A design patent application undergoes a review by a patent examiner to determine if it is eligible for protection. The review takes approximately two years or, if an expedited review is sought, closer to a year. Protection begins only on the date of grant and is not retroactive. The publication of the design in the patent application can aid and even spur copyists. In any event, the majority of fashion designs are obsolete too quickly for this lengthy application process to be worthwhile.

The review process involves a substantive evaluation of the novelty and nonobviousness of the design which adds to its cost. The standard of innovation required is a higher standard than that of originality required for copyright protection. Copyrights are, of course, also not subject to examination, although lack of originality may become an issue if a copyright is later challenged.

Functionality

Design patents cannot be used to protect any features of a design that are dictated solely by function. This may act as a hurdle for garments, given that they must be designed to fit the human form. The functionality doctrine in design patent law is narrower than functionality in trademark or copyright. Only the non-functional, ornamental features of the design are protectable using a design patent.

The examiner considers whether the design is ornamental. The word "ornamental" first appeared as a requirement for design patents in 1902. Congress changed the word "artistic" suggested by the Patent Office to "ornamental." It is well established that one of the elements of ornamentality is that the design is non-functional (an inventor of a new functional design could apply for utility patent protection). However, it is not clear how far "ornamental" requires a determination of the aesthetics of a design. In other words, does a design have to be attractive to obtain protection? In *Contico v. Rubbermaid*, a case about dollies for the transport of trash cans, the plaintiff, Contico, argued that the dolly could not be the subject of a valid design patent because such a product could not be ornamental. The court did not spend long on the subject of ornamentality and aesthetics but stated that "design patents are concerned with the industrial arts, not the fine arts," and, although it might be "too much to expect that a trash-can dolly be beautiful[, i]t is enough for present purposes that it is not ugly, especially when compared to prior designs."

An earlier Ninth Circuit Court (*Bliss v. Gotham Industries*) applied a standard which requires that the design "be the product of aesthetic skill and artistic conception." The problem with the seemingly higher standard is that, while it gives more meaning to the word "ornamental," it enables courts or patent examiners to insert their own subjective judgments about the aesthetics of a design.

Novelty and Nonobviousness

Assuming ornamental is simply that the design is not ugly, obtaining a design patent requires the article to reach the novelty and nonobviousness standards of a patent. This high standard is not in respect of its inventiveness, but in respect of its distinctive appearance. Patent examiners measure novelty by the impact of the design on an ordinary observer. If the "average observer takes the new design for a different, and not a modified already existing design," then the design is novel. A design patent is obvious if the differences between the design patent and the prior art at the time the design was made are so minimal that they would have been obvious to a designer with "ordinary skill in the art."

Obviousness makes sense as a standard for functional inventions applying for patent protection. It is harder to see when visual appearance or the ornamental aspects of a design qualify as novel and nonobvious.

Many fashion designs that are original works in the copyright sense of being created by an author and distinguishable from the prior art will nevertheless not be sufficiently different from the prior art to meet the higher design patent standard of novelty and nonobviousness.

Unfortunately, various circuits have added more confusion to this standard by applying other tests along with the "ordinary observer" test. In *Egyptian Goddess v. Swisa, Inc.*, the Federal Circuit sought to eliminate confusion about the various tests for design patent infringement by creating "the modified ordinary observer" test. It held that the standard of novelty for a design patent is "that a purchaser familiar with the prior art would be deceived by the similarity between the claimed and accused designs." This test, relying on the confusion of a consumer, appears more like the test for trade dress infringement, suggesting that a design patent may protect the consumer from confusion, as well as protecting the innovation of the designer. This simplified test might encourage more use of design patents by fashion and other designers, but it does nothing to eliminate the more serious problems for fashion designers of the lengthy and costly patent application process during which the design is on display to potential copyists.

Design Patents Disadvantages for Fashion Design

Unless the designer has a highly innovative design and wishes to protect a significant investment in R&D, the lengthy design patent application process, substantive review, and higher standard of innovation are strong deterrents to using the design patent system. But, for lasting and particularly innovative fashion items, design patents have several attractions. Protection lasts for 14 years from the grant of the application and prohibits any unauthorized use of the protected design by a third party. During this period of exclusivity, a designer is free to use Apple's strategy and focus on developing "secondary meaning" in order to protect the designed article through registration as trade dress at the expiration of the design patent. For shoe and handbag manufacturers, and for other designers of more enduring fashion items, design patents provide an attractive legal right.

Patents

Patents provide the strongest monopoly right in intellectual property law. The first to patent an invention is protected even against others who independently create the same invention. Few fashion items reach the level of innovation necessary for a utility patent application. And, for fashion designers, the patent application process suffers from the same defects as the design patent application process. It is even longer and more costly to obtain a utility patent than it is to obtain a design patent.

However, there are some highly innovative fashion designs where a patent application is worthwhile. Again, patent protection is more common for the creators of footwear and other accessories than for clothing. Generally, patent protection is appropriate for new materials or textiles rather than for original design. This reflects the difference between originality and innovation.

Nike is the largest holder of patents in the fashion industry. In the early 2000s, it filed a series of patents and design patents for a new shoe that would be knit in one piece and so reduce the waste from manufacturing sneakers with component parts, but would still provide peak athletic performance. The Flyknit sneaker is protected by 300 utility and design patents. Nike has been embroiled in litigation about the validity of some of these patents for almost 20 years. These sneakers made more than $1 billion for Nike in their first five years, demonstrating the value of patents to protect innovation. Nike has been willing to protect those patents aggressively and has spent millions in legal costs with patent battles against German company adidas and US-based Skechers.

In 2021, Nike beat adidas's long-running attempts to invalidate its Flyknit patents in the US (see Figure 3.4) and has asked the International Trade Commission

‖‖‖‖‖‖‖‖‖‖‖‖‖‖‖‖‖‖‖‖‖‖
US00D696853S

(12) **United States Design Patent**　(10) **Patent No.:**　**US D696,853 S**
Martin　　　　　　　　　　　　　　　(45) **Date of Patent:**　**　**Jan. 7, 2014**

(54)　**SHOE UPPER**

(71)　Applicant:　**NIKE, Inc.**, Beaverton, OR (US)

(72)　Inventor:　**Angela N. Martin**, Lake Oswego, OR (US)

(73)　Assignee:　**NIKE, Inc.**, Beaverton, OR (US)

(**)　Term:　**14 Years**

(21)　Appl. No.:　**29/465,825**

(22)　Filed:　**Aug. 30, 2013**

(51)　**LOC (10) Cl.** **02-99**
(52)　**U.S. Cl.**
　　　USPC **D2/972**
(58)　**Field of Classification Search**
　　　USPC D2/902, 906–908, 944, 946, 947, 962,
　　　　　　D2/969, 972–974; 36/45, 50.1, 77 M, 77 R,
　　　　　　36/83, 88, 113, 114, 126–131, 134
　　　See application file for complete search history.

(56)　　　　　**References Cited**

U.S. PATENT DOCUMENTS

D293,964 S	2/1988	Baumgratz	
D413,721 S *	9/1999	Roth	D2/972
D498,912 S	11/2004	Knobis	
D583,141 S	12/2008	Mermet	
D595,950 S	7/2009	Mayden	
D596,389 S	7/2009	Avar	
D610,339 S *	2/2010	Mermet	D2/972
D610,341 S	2/2010	Cooper	
D651,391 S	1/2012	Mokos	
D666,405 S *	9/2012	Shaffer	D2/972
D667,211 S	9/2012	Shaffer	
D667,625 S *	9/2012	Shaffer	D2/972
D667,626 S	9/2012	Shaffer	
D667,627 S *	9/2012	Shaffer	D2/972
D668,031 S	10/2012	Shaffer	
D668,032 S	10/2012	Shaffer	
D668,033 S	10/2012	Shaffer	
D668,034 S	10/2012	Shaffer	
D668,035 S	10/2012	Shaffer	
D671,730 S	12/2012	Shaffer	
D675,419 S	2/2013	Miner	
D676,227 S *	2/2013	Lee	D2/972
D676,647 S	2/2013	O'Connor	
D676,648 S *	2/2013	O'Connor	D2/972
D683,126 S	5/2013	Parrett	
D683,127 S	5/2013	Parrett	

OTHER PUBLICATIONS

Nike Footwear Catalog, 1997 Holiday Footwear, p. 9, published Mar. 1997, NIKE, Inc., USA.
Nike Footwear Catalog, 2005 Fall Footwear, p. 22, published Nov. 2004, NIKE, Inc., USA.

(Continued)

Primary Examiner — Domaine Santone
(74) *Attorney, Agent, or Firm* — Banner & Witcoff, Ltd.

(57)　　　　　　**CLAIM**

The ornamental design for a shoe upper, as shown and described.

DESCRIPTION

FIG. 1 is a front perspective view of a shoe upper showing my new design;

FIG. 2 is a side view thereof;

FIG. 3 is a rear perspective view thereof; and,

FIG. 4 is an enlarged view containing the claimed region of FIG. 2.

The three bold lines, including the curved upper loop segments and the interrupted lower segments, represent elements forming part of the claimed design. The uneven-length broken lines immediately adjacent to and fully surrounding the shaded area represent unclaimed boundaries of the design. The uneven-length broken lines showing the remainder of the shoe are for environmental purposes only and form no part of the claimed design.

1 Claim, 4 Drawing Sheets

Figure 3.4　One of Nike's Flyknit design patents

(ITC) to block the import of adidas's Primeknit footwear because it infringes a number of Nike's Flyknit utility patents.

Nike has also claimed that Skechers has a pattern of copying its innovative design patents and patents for sneakers. Nike's claims are that Skechers uses "innovative technologies developed by others to gain market share instead of innovating its own designs and technologies," (TFL 2021b). In this suit, Nike demonstrates its strong IP approach to its products and includes claims based on a variety of rights in its shoes including trademarks, design patents, and patents. This shows how it uses a blend of IP protections depending on the level of ingenuity in the design.

Nike alleged that, over a period of five years from October 2014, Skechers had committed trade dress infringement of the look of its Converse shoes. In 2016, it filed another infringement suit against Skechers concerning the Flyknit design patents. Skechers retaliated by attempting to invalidate several of Nike's design patents on the basis that they were not novel and nonobvious. Like adidas's attempts to invalidate Nike's patents, these petitions were denied by the Patent Office.

In 2019, Nike filed yet another lawsuit against Skechers arguing that it had infringed two other Nike utility patents, one that protects "an article of footwear" with a cushioning cavity that exists in the midsole of the shoe, and another that covers the "sole component, and a method of manufacturing the sole component" (TFL 2021b).

In these lawsuits, Nike has consistently argued that its patents and design patents are fundamental to its business model, stating that

> if companies cannot defend their innovation—and companies like Skechers are permitted to build multi-billion dollar businesses on the backs of creators and innovators by copying designs and technologies year-after-year—it stifles innovation and competition for businesses both big and small.
>
> (TFL 2019)

Nike has a huge patent and design patent portfolio and it aggressively protects this IP. However, for most designers, patents are the least useful of the IP rights because of their focus on inventiveness and the cost and time necessary to obtain them.

Notes

1 A specific design law has been proposed many times under US law (70 times since 1914; it almost became part of the Copyright Act 1976, Title II).
2 Orit Afori notes in "Reconceptualizing Property in Designs," 2008, "Under the orthodox interpretation of originality for purposes of copyright law, there are four different families of standards, speaking broadly, which, ranged from most restrictive to most generous, are the European Union's (E.U.) personal intellectual creation, the United States's *Feist* minimal degree of creativity, Canada's CCH standard of non-mechanical and non-trivial exercise of skill and judgment, and the United Kingdom's skill and labour standard."

3 This bill was to provide a five-year protection (renewable for up to one additional term) against unauthorized copying of an original design if registered. The issue of a design patent would terminate protection.

4 These decisions were made (in order) in the following cases: *Kieselstein-Cord v. Accessories by Pearl, Inc.*, 632 F.2d 989 (1980); *Pivot Point Int'l, Inc. v. Charlene Prods.*, 372 F.3d 913 (7th Cir. 2004) granted copyright protection to the designs. In *Carol Barnhart Inc. v. Economy Cover Corp.*, 594 F. Supp. 364 (E.D.N.Y. 1984), *Brandir International, Inc., v. Cascade Pacific Lumber Co.*, 834 F.2d 1142 (2d Cir 1987), and *Galiano v. Harrah's Operating Co., Inc.*, 416 F. 3d 411 (5th Cir. 2005), courts refused to grant copyright protection to the designs.

References

Afori, Orit. 2008. "Reconceptualizing Property in Designs." *Cardozo Arts & Entertainment Law Journal* 25 (3): 1105–78.

Buccafusco, Christopher, and Jeanne Fromer. 2017. "Fashion's Function in Intellectual Property Law." *Notre Dame Law Review* 93 (1): 51–108.

Burdick, Samantha. 2019. "Star Athletica Tells the Fashion Industry to Knock-It-Off with the Knockoffs." *Pepperdine School of Law* 46: 367–404.

Chatterjee, Mala. 2018. "Conceptual Separability as Conceivability: A Philosophical Analysis of the Useful Articles Doctrine." *NYU Law Review* 93: 558–88.

Chon, Margaret. 2014. "Slow Logo: Brand Citizenship in Global Value Networks." *University of California, Davis Law Review* 47 (3): 935–68.

Denicola, Robert. 1983. "Applied Art & Industrial Design: A Suggested Approach to CR in Useful Articles." *Minnesota Law Review* 67: 707–48.

Donahue, Sally M. 1990. "The Copyrightability of Useful Articles: The Second Circuit's Resistance to Conceptual Separability." *Touro Law Review* 6 (2): 327–57.

Fashion United. 2021. "Global Fashion Industry Statistics-International Apparel." Fashion United. 2021. https://fashionunited.com/global-fashion-industry-statistics.

Ginsburg, Jane. 2018. US Copyright Protection for Applied Art after *Star Athletica*. In Estelle Derclaye (Ed.), *The Copyright/Design Interface Past, Present and Future* (pp. 304–350). Cambridge University Press.

Lemley, Mark A. 1999. "The Modern Lanham Act and the Death of Common Sense." *Yale Law Journal* 108 (7): 1687–1716.

———. 2005. "Property, Intellectual Property, and Free Riding." *Texas Law Review* 83 (4): 1031–76.

Lunney, Glynn. 2000. "The Trade Dress Emperor's New Clothes: Why Trade Dress Does Not Belong on the Principal Register." *Hastings Law Journal* 51 (August): 1131–98.

———. 2018. "Non-Traditional Trademarks: The Error Costs of Making an Exception the Rule." In Irene Calboli and Martin Senftleben (Eds.), *The Protection of Non-Traditional Trademarks: Critical Perspectives*, 217. Oxford University Press.

Mann, Ronald. 2016. "Argument Analysis: Justices Worry about 'Killing Knockoffs with Copyright.'" SCOTUSblog. November 1, 2016. https://www.scotusblog.com/2016/11/argument-analysis-justices-worry-about-killing-knockoffs-with-copyright/.

Monseau, Susanna. 2011. "European Design Rights: A Model for the Protection of All Designers from Piracy." *American Business Law Journal* 48(1): 27–76.

Orozco, David, and James Conley. 2008. "Shape of Things to Come." *Wall Street Journal*, May 12, 2008. https://www.wsj.com/articles/SB121018802603674487.

Pouillard, Veronique, and Tereza Kuldova. 2017. "Interrogating Intellectual Property Rights in Post-War Fashion and Design." *Journal of Design History* 30 (4): 343–55.

Quinn, Gene. 2021. "Design Patents: Under Utilized and Overlooked." IPWatchdog.Com | Patents & Patent Law. March 4, 2021. https://www.ipwatchdog.com/2021/03/04/design-patents-utilized-overlooked/id=130540/.

Reuters. 2018. "Jury Awards Apple $539 Million in Samsung Patent Case." The New York Times, May 25, 2018, sec. Business. https://www.nytimes.com/2018/05/24/business/apple-samsung-patent-trial.html.

Schechter, Frank. 1925. *The Historical Foundations of the Law Relating to Trademarks.* Columbia University Press.

Schroeder, Jared, and Camille Kraeplin. 2019. "Give Me A ©: Refashioning the Supreme Court's Decision in Star Athletica v. Varsity Into an Art-First Approach to Copyright Protection for Fashion Designers." *UCLA Entertainment Law Review* 26 (1): 19–57. https://doi.org/10.5070/LR8261044051.

Suk, Jeannie. 2012. "Opinion | Little Red (Litigious) Shoes." The New York Times, January 21, 2012, sec. Opinion. https://www.nytimes.com/2012/01/22/opinion/sunday/louboutin-and-the-little-red-litigious-shoes.html.

TFL. 2019. "Nike Responds to Skechers' Open Letter with Another Infringement Lawsuit." The Fashion Law. October 29, 2019. https://www.thefashionlaw.com/nike-responds-to-skechers-open-letter-with-a-brand-new-infringement-lawsuit/.

———. 2021a. "From Baby Birkins to MetaBirkins, Brands Are Facing Issues in the Metaverse." The Fashion Law. December 13, 2021. https://www.thefashionlaw.com/from-baby-birkins-to-metabirkins-brands-are-being-plagued-in-the-metaverse.

———. 2021b. "Four Lawsuits, Corporate "Bullying" & Allegations of Rampant Copying: Nike v. Skechers." *The Fashion Law.* December 20, 2021. https://www.thefashionlaw.com/four-lawsuits-bullying-and-an-alleged-pattern-of-rampant-copying-the-history-of-nike-v-skechers.

———. 2022. "Hermès v. Rothschild: A Timeline of Developments in a Case Over Trademarks, NFTs" *The Fashion Law.* December 2, 2022 https://www.thefashionlaw.com/hermes-v-rothschild-a-timeline-of-developments-in-a-case-over-trademarks-nfts/.

Thomas, Hudson. 1948. "A Brief History of the Development of Design Patent Protection in the United States." *J. Pat. & Trademark Off. Soc'y* 30: 380–99.

4 European Design Rights
The Perfect Solution?

Introduction

The focus of this chapter is on how the EU design rights system protects fashion designers. The Community Design Directive (more properly the EU Design Directive, referred to as EUDD) and the Community Design Regulation (more properly the EU Design Regulation, referred to as the EUDR) created totally new pan-European design rights which have been in force for the last two decades. These relatively new legal rights have no counterpart in US IP law. Case law on design rights from both the CJEU and the national courts of member states provides some clarity on the protection of fashion design and the overlap between this system and other IP rights in the EU.

The History and Development of the New EU Design Rights

The over 100 years of international harmonization of IP law are reviewed in Chapter 2. In the 1990s, when the Uruguay Round of GATT talks created the WTO and the TRIPS agreement to provide some global harmonization of IP protections for design, the EU was embarking on a more ambitious project: The complete harmonization of design protection across its member states and the creation of a new legal right (see Figure 4.1).

Before the creation of the pan-European design rights system, the laws of the EU member states were characterized by confusion, overlapping rights, and the variety of different legal schemes of protection that have typified design law since its inception. All schools of design protection theory were represented, from the French *unité de l'art* (unity of art), where all art was treated in the same manner by the law, to the Italian *scindibilità* (separability doctrine), where legal protection differed depending upon whether the art was fine or applied art. Many EU member states (including Italy, the UK, and Denmark) had changed their approach to design protection not once but several times. The members of the European Union were also all long-standing members of the Berne and Paris Conventions and thus were part of the discussions and messy compromises created by those treaties.

In 1977, a subcommittee of the European Community's Coordinating Committee for Harmonizing the Law of Industrial Property had met to consider

DOI: 10.4324/9781003091400-5

EU Design Rights Events Timeline

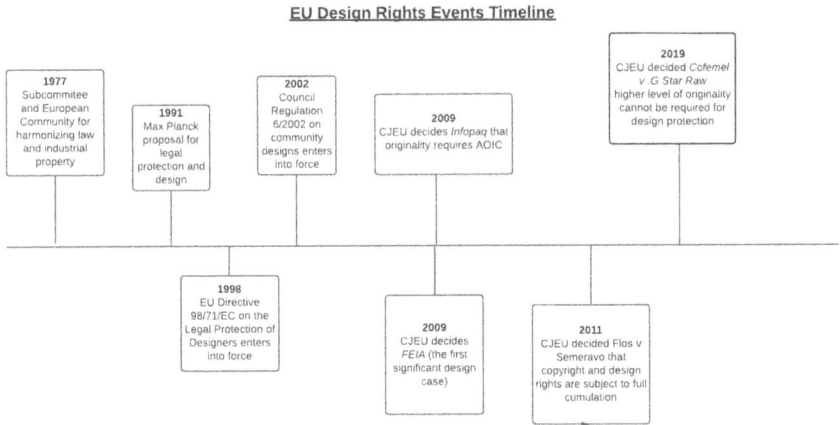

1977
Subcommitee and European Community for harmonizing law and industrial property

1991
Max Planck proposal for legal protection and design

2002
Council Regulation 6/2002 on community designs enters into force

2009
CJEU decides *Infopaq* that originality requires AOIC

2019
CJEU decided *Cofemel v .G Star Raw* higher level of originality cannot be required for design protection

1998
EU Directive 98/71/EC on the Legal Protection of Designers enters into force

2009
CJEU decides *FEIA* (the first significant design case)

2011
CJEU decided *Flos v Semeravo* that copyright and design rights are subject to full cumulation

Figure 4.1 EU design rights timeline

reforming design protection at the European level; however, no further action was taken on the report produced by the subcommittee until the 1990s, when the European Commission once again turned its attention to the process of harmonizing the protection provided to industrial design and tasked a small group of academic lawyers from the Max Planck Institute with determining the best way to protect industrial design (see Figure 4.1).

The group decided that designers would benefit from a clear focus on the subject matter for protection—industrial design—rather than an attempt to harmonize the complicated patchwork of existing design legislation, some based on copyright and some based on patents, in different EU member states.

Importantly, the academic reformers did not want to base any new EU-wide rights in design on the prior rights available in any specific legal system. They felt that squeezing design into either a copyright- or patent-like system was at the heart of the problems in protecting design. They wanted to create a legal right specifically for design and hoped to avoid entirely the difficult division between copyright and patent approaches that had plagued attempts to protect design for so long. Their stated aim was to encourage creativity in design "to an extent that would render supplementary protection under other legal regimes largely superfluous" (Kur, Levin and Schovsbo 2018).

Their market-oriented approach was largely accepted by the EU Commission, and a directive to harmonize the existing design laws of member states, Directive 98/71/EC of the European Parliament and of the Council of October 13, 1998, on the legal protection of designs (EUDD), entered into force on November 17, 1998. It was implemented into the national legal systems of all member states by October 28, 2001. It required each member state to provide a registered right to the exclusive use of a design renewable in 5-year increments for up to 25 years. Although some differences between national laws on the protection of design remain, this directive largely harmonized the law of the EU member states on industrial design.

The more far-reaching reform came in 2002 with the passage of Council Regulation (EC) No 6/2002 on Community Designs (EUDR). It created two new pan-European design rights administered at the European level. The first, the registered community design (RCD), was essentially the same as the right created by the earlier directive in member states' own laws. The second, the unregistered community design (UCD), provided a short-term (three-year) copyright-like right prohibiting the copying of a design. These two protections allowed European designers to bypass the remaining messy and confusing national laws on design and protect their designs across the whole region through either a Europe-wide registration or an unregistered, short-term, copyright-like right attached to a design from its first marketing in an EU member state (see Figure 4.1).

The European Union Design Directive

The EUDD, like most directives, was intended to harmonize existing EU national laws, in its case in the area of design. It provided for "the establishment of an internal market characterized by the abolition of obstacles to the free movement of goods and also for the institution of a system ensuring that competition in the internal market is not distorted." The EUDD immediately cleared up several differences in the laws of European countries by determining that design law should not protect "features dictated solely by a technical function," thus hampering technological innovation. It defined a protectable design as one that produced on "the informed user" "a different overall impression" to other designs, thus providing some guidance on the standard of originality required for the protection of a design. It established the important principle of cumulation of different IP protections, meaning that, in countries that provided copyright protection for industrial designs, designers did not have to choose between the two different legal protections. Design could be protected by both copyright and design rights. Thus, although the directive still left European countries with several types and levels of design protection and purposely avoided difficult issues such as whether to prohibit the copying of spare parts, it made several important contributions to the harmonization of design law in Europe. Some of the few remaining differences in how the UK, France, and Italy treat the legal protection of design are discussed in the next chapter.

The European Union Design Regulation

The EUDR went much further. EU Regulations create new legal rights directly applicable to individuals across the EU member states. It introduced a totally new "unified system" where "uniform protection is given uniform effect throughout the entire territory of the Community." According to the preamble to the EUDR, its rights are "directly applicable in each Member State" because this is the best way to "encourage [] innovation and development of new products and invest-ments in their production."

The EUDR provides two forms of Europe-wide protection: The registered right (RCD) and the unregistered design right (UCD). The regulation preamble explains that the RCD is appropriate "for sectors of industry which value the advantages of registration for the greater legal certainty it provides and which require the possibility of a longer term of protection corresponding to the foresee-able market life of their products." The UCD is appropriate for sectors that "pro-duce large numbers of designs for products frequently having a short market life where protection without the burden of registration formalities is an advantage and the duration of protection is of lesser significance."

Simply disclosing a design to the public gives rise to a UCD, which lasts for three years. The RCD requires registration at the European Union Intellectual Property Office (EUIPO), formerly the Office for Harmonization in the Internal Market (OHIM). It is valid for an initial term of 5 years which is renewable for up to 25 years. The UCD is cheap and easy to obtain (since no registration is required) and is meant to be attractive to industries where trends change quickly, like the fashion industry. A designer can convert a UCD to an RCD by applying for registration during the first 12 months of UCD protection since his own sales will not be counted as "prior art" and prevent him from registering the design.

On November 28, 2022, the EU Commission adopted proposals for a revised EUDD and EUDR. The revisions (which have not yet become law) are intended to improve design protection in a digital age by reducing complexity and cost, and increasing speed, predictability, and legal certainty. Where the new proposals may make a difference to the existing provisions of the design protection scheme this is noted.

The Interpretation of Design Concepts in EU Design Law

The design protection system set up by the EUDD and EUDR has been function-ing for most of the twenty-first century. The CJEU has now interpreted several important areas of the law and how it intersects with other areas of IP law. The EU Commission has also commissioned legal and economic reviews of the European industrial design protection system published in 2015 and 2016, respectively. The UK Intellectual Property Office (UKIPO) has published its own research on design infringement and the law. Thus, it is possible to describe how European design rights protect the fashion industry, as well as to note key areas that are still unclear, and where guidance for designers as to the interpretation of concepts in the legislation is still needed.

The Role of the CJEU

The role of the Court of Justice of the European Union (CJEU) under the Treaty on the Functioning of the European Community (TFEU) is twofold: To interpret EU law to ensure it is applied consistently in all member states, and to settle legal disputes between national governments and EU institutions. In cases involving design, the CJEU plays this role in two ways: It hears requests from national courts on the interpretation of EU design law under Article 267 of the TFEU. These requests are framed as preliminary questions for the CJEU to answer before the referring national court makes a final decision in the case. The national court must seek a preliminary ruling if it is the court of last instance in a case where there is no further appeal under national law. Second, the CJEU also hears appeals from decisions of the EUIPO to register (or not to register) designs.

The CJEU consists of a total of 27 judges but generally hears cases as a smaller chamber of three to five judges. The advocate general, in a role unfamiliar to US courts, prepares the case for the Court. The judges make the decision, but the advocate general's opinion is sought in every case tried by the Court. As well as providing the judges with the legal points presented and research on case law, the advocate general's opinions often provide solutions and reasoning. Quite often they are adopted by the court, and so the advocate general is an important part of the EU court system.

In recent years, the CJEU has been particularly active in defining the parameters of EU design law and in harmonizing EU copyright law in such a way that many commentators now argue that there is a body of EU-wide copyright law in its precedents (some of its most important decisions are set out in Figure 4.1).

EU Precedent

The concept of binding precedent (judgments of higher courts that lower courts are bound to follow in similar legal situations) and the doctrine of *stare decisis* are concepts strongly linked with Anglo-American legal systems. EU law does not have these concepts. EU law states that, when the CJEU decides an Article 267 preliminary reference, that decision does bind the referring national court as well as courts in other member states facing an identical question. The TFEU does not mandate that the CJEU or other EU courts follow their own prior decisions. However, in a series of copyright and design law decisions, the CJEU seems to be creating EU-wide case law by referring to and following its prior decisions in the majority of cases.

The Courts of the Member States

National courts' decisions are also important in EU jurisprudence as these courts are often called upon to interpret EU laws and, while they can make referrals to the CJEU on questions of EU law, they are not required to refer preliminary questions to the CJEU if they believe the law is clear. In addition, if the same or a similar question has already been dealt with by the higher court, they can apply that. The obligation of national courts is merely to seek to be consistent with other EU member states in similar situations. EU law does not require them to be bound by precedents from other member states by EU law. Language and other cultural and legal barriers probably somewhat limit the impact of decisions made by national courts on others within the union, but member states are supposed to attempt to harmonize their laws, and so these decisions have some persuasive value. If a national court believes a legal point is not clear, then it can seek to refer a question to the CJEU. The reference procedure is useful if there is an inconsistency in the application of an EU law by another member state or if there are conflicting decisions in different member states.

Key Issues in EU Design Law for Fashion Designers

What Is a Design?

What can be legally protected as a design is vitally important to any designer intending to use design right protection in the EU. Article 3 of the EUDR defines a design "as the appearance in whole or part of the product resulting from the features of, in particular, the lines, contours, colours, shape, texture and/or materials of the product itself and/or its ornamentation." It defines a product as "any industrial or handicraft item" while specifically excluding computer programs.

The 2016 *Legal Review on Industrial Design Protection in Europe* (the Legal Review) found some differences in the member states on which senses had to be used to perceive a design. In Poland, the Supreme Administrative Court held that a design must be perceived by the sense of sight, while a judgment of the Lisbon Court of Appeals in Portugal held that the design relates to visible or palpable perception. The Legal Review stated that this "seems to indicate that the sense of touch can be relied upon." The Portuguese approach seemed to be an outlier, as the Patent County Court of England and Wales also held that EU design law is only concerned with the "visual appearance of products" (Dumortier et al. 2016, 55).

In 2011, in *PepsiCo, Inc. v. Grupo Promer Mon Graphic SA*, a case about what the CJEU called "a circular promotional item," the advocate general stated that the protection of designs under the Design Regulation "considers only the visual impression which the designs produce on the informed user." In 2017, the CJEU finally clarified that design had to be perceptible by sight in *Easy Sanitary Solutions v. Group Nivelles and EUIPO*, declaring that "appearance is the decisive factor of a design" and thus visibility "is an essential feature" for protection. It now seems clear that to be protectable a design must be visually perceptible during the normal use of a product.

A more pertinent and unresolved issue for fashion designers is whether a design can consist of a color, a visibly distinctive texture, or a material. The Legal Review described how national offices in member states and the EUIPO have different interpretations on whether colors, textures, and materials can be registered as designs. Colors are registrable at the EUIPO and in about half the member states, while textures are registrable at the EUIPO and in most member states except Bulgaria, Denmark, Czech Republic, and Sweden. Ornamentation and patterns are registrable everywhere except the Czech Republic, graphic symbols are not registrable in Estonia, and interior décor is not registrable in Bulgaria.

Presumably, the application of case law from the CJEU will gradually eliminate inconsistencies, and colors, textures, materials, ornamentation, graphic symbols, and interior décor should be considered as registrable subject matter for
design rights throughout the EU.

The proposed new versions of the EUDD and EUDR expand the definitions
of "design" and "product." The broader definition of design now includes "the
movement, transition or any other sort of animation" of the design. Product also
includes designs in physical and digital form. In its explanatory memorandum
accompanying the proposals the Commission says that the "update, clarifica-
tion and broadening of the current definitions aim to future-proof the proposal
for a recast Directive against technological advances and provide greater legal
certainty and transparency as to the eligible subject matter of design protection"
(European Commission 2022). These changes will enable the registration of 3D
CAD files and virtual designs.

Novelty and Individual Character

There is no substantive examination of applications for RCD (and UCDs are not
registered), and so interpretations of the meanings of the terms "individual character," "overall impression," and "informed user" have come from case law on
infringement. In the last decade, the CJEU and national courts have made several
decisions which help us interpret these terms.

Article 4 of the EUDR provides that the design must be "new" and have "individual character" to be protectable. The requirement for "individual character" is
supposed to avoid protecting merely incremental designs that differ in insignificant ways from the prior art. The meaning of these two requirements is developed
in Articles 5–7 of the regulation.

Novelty is defined in Article 5. "A design shall be considered to be new if no
identical design has been made available to the public." Although the EUIPO reg-
isters designs without a substantive examination to keep the procedural burdens
on applicants to a minimum, lack of novelty is often used later to challenge the
validity of a design by those accused of infringing it.

In 2014, in an Irish referral concerning the sale by Irish department store
Dunnes of identical clothing to that of UK fashion designer Karen Millen, the
CJEU made clear that the assessment of novelty should be made in relation to one
or more specific earlier designs. That is, in determining novelty, the design was
not to be compared with a composite of common features that appeared in prior
designs but to a specific earlier design. The test of novelty is simply whether the
design is identical to a design already on the market. A design is not required to
be entirely new in the patent sense of innovative, but in the sense that it is not a
copy of an earlier design. The fact that novelty must be assessed in relation to one
or more specific earlier designs focuses design protection on prohibiting direct
copying while still enabling designers to reference or draw inspiration from prior
designs, something which is common in the fashion industry.

Article 6 (1-2) states that a

design shall be considered to have individual character if the overall impression it produces on the informed user differs from the overall impression produced on such a user by any design which has been made available to the public … In assessing individual character, the degree of freedom of the designer in developing the design shall be taken into consideration.

In *Karen Millen Ltd. v. Dunnes Stores*, the CJEU stated that, for a design to have individual character,

the overall impression which that design produces on the informed user must be different from that produced on such a user not by a combination of features taken in isolation and drawn from a number of earlier designs, but by one or more earlier designs, taken individually.

In *Group Nivelles*, the CJEU held that any identical earlier design, whatever the industry, destroys novelty. But there is no assumption that in assessing individual character an informed user would necessarily know of similar designs in a different industry. The Court essentially held that if the design is identical to another then it will lack novelty, and it will not matter that the designer did not know of the earlier design in a different industry. However, the product's nature and the industrial sector to which it belongs are relevant to an assessment of individual character. An informed user may well be unaware of similar designs in an unrelated industry, and so a design will not necessarily lack individual character simply because it is similar to a design in a different industrial sector.

The Legal Review noted that this is an area where design law lacks clarity and suggested that the EUDD should be amended to clarify that, when determining individual character, "national offices and courts should refer to the nature of the product, the manner of the use of the product, the purpose for which the product is intended, and the industrial sector to which it belongs." Surprisingly, the proposals for new EUDD and EUDR do not codify the definition of the "informed user."

Overall Impression

In 2007, the UK Court of Appeal became the first court in an EU member state to hear a case concerning the infringement of an RCD and to consider the overall impression requirement. In the case, *Proctor & Gamble v. Reckitt Benckiser*, the UK appellate court held that overall impression should be assessed with the two designs in hand, rather than merely recollected (which is the way that "likelihood of confusion" is assessed in trademark cases). The Court said that the test of overall impression is going to be inherently imprecise in its subjectivity because the purpose of design is to influence the customer to buy the product. Trademarks have a different purpose: To influence the customer by reminding him of a previous experience with a particular product which he takes to indicate its origin or quality. This is why, if a customer is merely reminded of a trademark, likelihood of confusion may result.

The court held that the comparison of two designs should be carried out with a reasonable degree of care and attention to detail of the important features of the product, characterizing in each case the impression they provide. A strikingly novel product is likely to create a substantially different overall impression than a less distinctive product. The court held, after looking at line drawings of the two designs, that the overall impression created by the plastic sprayers in the case was different (overturning the trial judge). The trial judge had characterized Procter & Gamble's (P&G) design as elegant, while he characterized the second, allegedly infringing, design as poor quality and cheap. The appellate court held that this meant that the two products created a different overall impression.

This decision could be criticized on the basis that an imitation would escape liability as an infringing design simply because it was of a poor quality. However, arguably, if the role of design is to influence a customer to buy the product, then a poor-quality copy of a design should not be able to achieve this. Whether this case was correctly decided or not, it also raises the question of what courts should compare in deciding whether a design is infringed. Is it more important to look at the actual products, or is simply reviewing the line drawing submitted with the registered design sufficient? Should the test simply be whether the later product looks like it's been copied from the earlier design? Lawyers suggest that applicants for registered designs make sure they submit several different illustrations of the design in their registrations, including both line drawings and colored photographs. This means any court will have plenty of ways to compare allegedly infringing designs with the original.

In a 2008 fashion industry case in the UK, *J Choo (Jersey) Limited v. Towerstone Limited & Others*, the infringer tried to rely on the poorer quality of his handbag to argue that it provided a different overall impression. In this case, the High Court used the design drawing to compare with the defendant's bag. It held that a comparison of the drawing with the infringer's bag did not give rise to a different impression on quality. The overall impression of the two bags was the same, and the second bag was an infringement of the first design. Whether the quality of the infringing design comes into play in determining its overall impression appears to depend somewhat on whether the Court compares two designs by looking at line drawings or at the actual products.

In the *Karen Millen* case, the CJEU did not compare line drawings of the designs with the allegedly infringing copies. It compared the infringing blouses directly with the actual Karen Millen designs to determine if they were similar as a whole to the Millen designs, holding that overall impression required a careful, direct comparison between the actual designs as a whole. "The imperfect recollection of several different earlier designs should be avoided because this might lead to the consideration of an amalgam of specific features or parts of earlier designs."

The UK Court of Appeal considered overall impression again in *Dyson v. Vax*. It decided that Dyson's RCD in a vacuum cleaner was not infringed by Chinese competitor Vax. Dyson argued for a high degree of protection for a design that it said was a major departure from earlier designs. The Court agreed that protection is greater for strikingly novel products but still agreed with the trial judge that the overall impression of each vacuum cleaner was different. It said "the list of nine features relied upon by Dyson is far too general." Thus, although Dyson compared the two vacuum cleaners by saying "both have transparent bins through which the cyclone shroud is visible," the reality was that both the bins and shrouds in the two designs were very different in shape. The Court stated that a designer could not "take features of a design, turn them into general words and then treat those words like a patent claim." It held that the two vacuum cleaners produced different overall impressions.

In decrying the UK decision, Dyson noted in its press release that it had won a design case against the same Chinese company in France. As the Legal Review noted, the overall impression assessment is different in each member state. Another demonstration that it can be an imprecise test is found in Procter & Gamble's attempts to enforce its RCD for its air freshener sprayers in several different member states. P&G won in France, Belgium, Germany, and Italy, while courts in Austria and the UK decided in favor of the defendant on the same RCD.

In its analysis of case law in infringement decisions in the different member states, the Legal Review found that the assessment of overall impression is the category that gives courts the most difficulty. Some member states are very generous in finding that the overall impression created by two designs is similar (and thus the later design infringes the earlier). Courts in Sweden found 85% of infringing designs created a similar overall impression. Other courts are much more reluctant. In Hungarian courts, only 16% of designs were found to create a similar overall impression.

The Informed User

Someone must decide if the overall impression of two designs is the same. Courts have devoted much analysis to this person called the "informed user" in design law. In *Proctor & Gamble*, the UK Court of Appeal described an informed user as someone who is not only aware of the body of existing designs but is also "fairly familiar" with design issues. He is not quite as much of an expert as the "person skilled in the art" in patent law. The informed user possesses some knowledge regarding which elements of design are dictated solely by function and has experience of the kind of products in question. He is thus positioned between the technical expert of patent law and the "average consumer" of trademark law. He is more discriminating than the "average consumer" but less knowledgeable than the "person skilled in the art to which the invention pertains."

In 2011, the CJEU essentially agreed with the UK Court of Appeal's definition of the informed user in the *PepsiCo* case, clearly linking this fictional being to the design sector concerned, but stating that he was not a technical expert or specialist capable of observing minute differences in the design. According to the Court, the informed user is someone who

> knows the various designs which exist in the sector concerned, possesses a certain degree of knowledge with regard to the features which those designs

normally include, and, as a result of his interest in the products concerned, shows a relatively high degree of attention when he uses them.

In a 2017 French case about shoes, *Einstein Shoes BV v. Ferro Footwear BV*, the Paris Court of Appeal tried to widen the scope of the informed user, defining him or her as being "any person likely to usually buy shoes, paying attention to their soles and thus possessing a good knowledge of shoe soles." On the basis of this test, the Court found that the shoes at issue provided a different overall impression to this attentive customer and thus did not infringe the registered design. The French Supreme Court overturned this judgment, stating, "the informed user is the professional of the sector concerned."

Although it is possible to find differences in the application of these concepts by national courts and by the CJEU, the Legal Review found that the concepts of informed user, individual character, and overall impression have largely been satisfactorily harmonized across the community, counting this as a major achievement of EU design law (Dumortier et al. 2016, 154). This is perhaps why the Commission felt no need to codify the definition of an "informed user" in the proposals for the new EUDD and EUDR.

Freedom of the Designer

Article 6(2) states: "In assessing individual character, the degree of freedom of the designer in developing the design shall be taken into consideration." The General Court of the EU (GCEU) discussed the degree of freedom of the designer in relation to handbags at length in *H&M v. OHIM – Yves Saint Laurent*. It held that the degree of freedom of the designer is part of the analysis of the perception of the informed user. The greater the designer's freedom in developing the design, the less likely that minor differences will create a different overall impression. Conversely, where the designer is restricted in design choices, minor differences might well produce a different overall impression on the informed user.

H&M attempted to have an RCD filed by Yves Saint Laurent declared invalid on the basis that it had no individual character. The OHIM dismissed the appeal, holding that the designer of a handbag had a high degree of freedom, and the differences between the designs at issue were significant enough to create a different overall impression. The GCEU agreed that the OHIM was correct in stating that the degree of freedom for designers of fashion items such as handbags was high. It held that the assessment of the designer's degree of freedom did not "constitute a preliminary and abstract step in the comparison of the overall impression produced by each of the designs at issue," and that this decision "does not on its own determine the assessment of the individual character of a design." The freedom of the designer is simply a factor which must be taken into consideration as part of the whole assessment of the individual character of a design. If the designer's freedom is high, then similar designs with minor differences may well lack individual character.

In 2019, in an ongoing battle between Barbie and Bratz, the EUIPO declared invalid an RCD for dolls' heads owned by Jieyand Defa Industry Co. The EUIPO held that the designer was limited by the fact that the heads had to resemble human heads, but that it was not limited by any requirement that the dolls' heads had to resemble Caucasian facial features, or be similar to the proportions of human heads. Thus, the designer had a reasonable degree of freedom. The dolls' heads in question were very similar. They seemed to be modeled after the same person and wearing almost identical make-up. The EUIPO held that the heads could not be registered as an RCD as the designer had a degree of freedom but had not differentiated the design from the earlier one.

Disclosure to the Public

Article 7 of the EUDR states

> a design shall be deemed to have been made available to the public if it has been published following registration or otherwise, or exhibited, used in trade or otherwise disclosed … except where these events could not reasonably have become known in the normal course of business to the circles specialised in the sector concerned, operating within the Community.

Once a design is disclosed, novelty is destroyed (although there is a grace period of 12 months for a designer to market their design protected by a UCD before their sales count as prior art and prevent them from registering the design).

In *Group Nivelles*, the CJEU clarified that novelty is lost with any disclosure to the public in the EU, even if the disclosure is in a different industrial sector. In an application for an RCD the designer must indicate a class of product in which they are using the design; however, this does not limit protection of the design to that industrial sector. A design is protected in all sectors, and thus novelty is not limited to novelty in a particular sector. The breadth of disclosure makes any search for prior designs challenging. In fashion design, the materials or ornamentation of products outside of the clothing and apparel industry could infringe on an existing fashion design or, if earlier, be used to invalidate a later fashion design. And a designer may not know of the existence of similar designs in different industries.

In 2013, in *H. Gautzsch Großhandel GmbH & Co. KG v. Münchener Boulevard Möbel Joseph Duna GmbH*, the German Supreme Court (Bundesgerichtshof or BGH) referred three questions about the meaning of disclosure to the public to the CJEU. The case was about who had prior rights to a gazebo design. The BGH wanted to know who, where, and what counted as disclosure "to the circles specialised in the sector concerned, operating within the Community." It asked whether disclosure to traders was sufficient disclosure of a design, or must specialized circles consist of designers, whether disclosure in China provided knowledge for those "operating within the community," and finally was disclosure to one EU undertaking sufficient disclosure?

The CJEU answered these questions in a frustratingly vague way. It stated that they were all questions of fact for national courts, and that all of these circumstances could count as disclosure in the right circumstances. However, it did provide some guidance on the issue of how disclosure might occur.

It held that disclosure to specialized circles did not just include disclosure to designers. It said that, depending on the circumstances, specialized circles might also include traders. The Court also said that it was not "absolutely necessary" for the disclosure to have taken place within the EU for the design to "have been made available to the public." But again, the CJEU noted that, "[t]he question whether events taking place outside the European Union could reasonably have become known to persons forming part of those circles was a question of fact" for the national court to determine. The Court made the same point about whether disclosure to a single undertaking in the sector concerned in the EU was sufficient to count as disclosure, saying: "it is quite possible that, in certain circumstances, a disclosure of that kind may indeed be sufficient."

What constitutes disclosure of a UCD and whether a design first disclosed geographically outside the EU can still qualify for protection as a UCD have become important questions for British designers, or any designer wishing to obtain design rights in the UK and EU markets after Brexit. In *Beverly Hills Teddy v. PMS*, a UK court referred this question to the CJEU. The court asked whether, for a UCD to come into being, the disclosure must take place within the EU or whether it is sufficient that, wherever it took place, "the event could reasonably have become known to the circles specialised in the sector concerned, operating within the Community." It also asked whether the date for assessing the novelty of a UCD is "the date on which the unregistered Community design protection for the design came into being" or "the date on which the relevant event of disclosure of the design ... could reasonably have become known." Unfortunately, the referral was later withdrawn, and so the CJEU has not yet ruled on these important questions.

An EU Commission Staff Working Document, *Evaluation of EU Legislation on Design Protection*, published in 2020 (the Evaluation Document) noted that the EUIPO takes the position that disclosure must take place within the territory of the EU in order to create a UCD, but there is legal uncertainty on this issue since the CJEU has not yet opined on the matter. Those favoring the narrow approach of only protecting designs first disclosed in the EU (sometimes called the "Fortress Europe approach") argue that foreign companies and designers not doing business in the EU should not be able to profit from design protection in the EU. It would undermine the EU design protection system if they could obtain a UCD based on a disclosure outside Europe. Others suggest a broad approach is preferable to allow EU designers to obtain the earliest possible protection even when they first disclose their designs at international trade fairs outside the EU. The Evaluation Document clearly prefers the narrower Fortress Europe approach, stating that

> allowing for the creation of a UCD on the basis of disclosure occurring everywhere outside the EU would imply nothing less than giving automatic rights

to the rest of the world without any reciprocity or possibility of monitoring to the clear detriment of EU industries. The argument that EU industries might also wish to profit from disclosures outside the EU dwarfs in comparison.

(European Commission 2020, 29)

So, it appears that in some circumstances disclosure of an RCD can take place outside the EU but that, for now, it is not clear where disclosure of the design must occur to obtain a UCD.

Functionality

Article 8 states that a design right "shall not subsist in features of appearance of a product which are solely dictated by its technical function." Two theories developed on what type of functionality excluded designs from protection. In Germany, and initially at the EUIPO, the "multiplicity of forms" theory developed: If there was an alternative design possible, then a design could not be said to be "solely dictated by function." The other approach, based on an earlier English design law, is called the "causality theory" or "no-aesthetic-consideration" theory. It holds that if *only* technical considerations, and no-aesthetic considerations, are used in creating the design then it is a design "solely dictated by function." This second theory has latterly become the approach used by the EUIPO.

In the 2018 case *Doceram GmbH v. CeramTec GmbH* (which dealt with weld centering pins used in various types of manufacture), the CJEU decisively rejected the view that "one design alternative is sufficient for determining that the characteristic of a product is caused exclusively by the technical function." The court held that, if "function is the *only* factor that determines" the features of a design, then the design is solely dictated by function and cannot be registered.

The Court was obviously seeking to avoid the use of design law to patent functional products by a backdoor route without any evaluation of the claims. It specifically considered the danger of a single economic operator obtaining several design registrations for different possible forms of a product and then benefitting from exclusive protection, equivalent to that offered by a patent, without being subject to the conditions applicable for obtaining a patent.

According to the CJEU, a design holder needs only to prove that its design was not solely based on technical considerations to prevail. However, it will be a question for national courts as to what type of evidence is relevant to this determination. The CJEU said only "the national court must take account of all the objective circumstances relevant to each individual case." Rules of evidence differ between member states, and there is no clear set of criteria to be taken into account in determining if other considerations, "particularly those related to the visual aspect," have played a role in the choice of features, and so the decision does not provide much clarity on how the court should determine if design features are functional. The decision also leaves unanswered the question of whether, in assessing the individual character of a design, features dictated solely by function are to be ignored.

In fashion, it is clearly going to be rare for a design feature to be based solely on technical considerations. This decision means that a design which is functional and protected by a patent might later be able to obtain further protection, probably through copyright law, as long as function is not the only factor determining its features.

Who Owns a Design Right?

All EU design rights are property rights and can be licensed or assigned to others for their duration. Article 14 states: "The right to the Community design shall vest in the designer or his successor in title." In Section (3) it states that

> where a design is developed by an employee in the execution of his duties or following the instructions given by his employer, the right to the Community design shall vest in the employer, unless otherwise agreed or specified under national law.

In the first significant design case to reach the CJEU in 2009, the Court made clear that ownership of a design right vests first in the designer. The case, *Fundación Española para la Innovación de la Artesanía (FEIA) v. Cul de Sac Espacio Creativo SL*, concerned the ownership of designs for cuckoo clocks. The FEIA (Spanish Foundation for the Innovation of Craftsmanship) created a design project for skilled artisans and then argued that it owned unregistered design rights in a cuckoo clock designed as part of the project. The Spanish court referred several questions to the CJEU, essentially on whether the cuckoo clock designer should be considered an employee of the FEIA.

The CJEU decided that a commission is not the same as an employment contract, and so the provision of the EUDR vesting ownership in a design created by an employee in the employer (subject to national law) "does not apply to Community designs that have been produced as a result of a commission." If the designer is an employee, then the owner of the design is the employer where the design is created by the employee as part of his or her job, unless the employee and employer have made a different agreement, or the member state's national law has different provisions about employment contracts. The CJEU rejected the idea that Article 14(3) applies to a commissioned design. Rights to the design do not automatically belong to the commissioner of the design but remain vested in the designer. A specific contractual provision is required to transfer the ownership of such a design to an entity other than the designer, unless the designer is an employee of that entity.

Differences between UCDs and RCDs

One of the most useful features of the UCD is that designers can use it as a stepping stone to applying for an RCD. Article 7(2) provides a grace period of 12 months for a designer to market his product without this counting as prior art.

If sales go well for a product protected by a UCD, the designer can apply for an RCD during the 12-month period, and his own prior sales will not count against him as the publication of prior art.

Article 19 sets out the differences between the rights granted by an RCD and those granted by a UCD. An RCD gives its holder "the exclusive right to use it and to prevent any third party not having his consent from using it." A UCD only protects its holder from third-party use if such "use results from copying the protected design."

Case law makes clear that RCD rights are protected against "use by any third party" on any type of product, not just a product that competes with those of the design right holder. In a Spanish case, *Celaya Emparanza y Galdos Internacional SA v. Proyectos Integrales de Balizamientos SL*, in 2012, the CJEU said that the rights of an RCD "extend [] to any third party who uses a design that does not produce on informed users a different overall impression."

Exceptions and Limitations to Design Rights

Article 20 provides six exceptions to the rights conferred by the EUDR. The important ones for fashion design are the exceptions in 1(a) for private and non-commercial acts and 1(c) for

> acts of reproduction for the purpose of making citations or of teaching, provided that such acts are compatible with fair trade practice and do not unduly prejudice the normal exploitation of the design, and that mention is made of the source.

The private and non-commercial copying exemption can obviously apply to home sewists who copy a design. The activities of home sewists have long been tolerated by fashion designers because their effect on clothing markets is minimal. New technologies such as 3D printing could change that. Some fear that the private use limitation would lead to immunity for in-home 3D printing activities and have suggested that this limitation needs to be modified by requiring that any acts of 3D printing are compatible with "fair trade practice" and "do not unduly prejudice the normal exploitation of the design." Certainly, if 3D printing develops so that commercial entities can offer fashion items as digital files to be downloaded and created on home 3D printers, then this particular exception might need to be significantly revised. The proposed new EUDD and EUDR include a new right protecting the owners of designs against illegitimate 3D printing.

In 2017, the CJEU decided in a referral from a regional German court, *Nintendo Co. Ltd v. BigBen Interactive GmbH and BigBen Interactive SA*, that "making citations" in 1(c) included the depiction of a 2D image of a design used to sell accessory items for the right holder's goods corresponding to this design. The Court said that a third party may, without the consent of the design rights holder, include images of the design goods on its website to "explain or demonstrate the joint use of the goods thus offered for sale." This means that fashion designers may potentially use images of designs owned by others in marketing materials for their own design goods.

The exceptions for design rights are not as broad as the exceptions for other IP rights such as copyright which, in the EU, generally include artistic freedom of expression.

This initially caused problems for activist and artist Nadia Plesner. In 2008, Plesner designed a t-shirt to raise money for the crisis in Darfur. She used a picture of Paris Hilton carrying a Louis Vuitton bag and transformed it into a picture of a starving Sudanese child toting the same Louis Vuitton bag. Louis Vuitton objected and brought suit against the artist in the Tribunal de Grande Instance in Paris for infringing its RCD in her artwork. It got an *ex parte* injunction against the artist, although this was clearly not a usual case of counterfeit design. The court awarded nominal damages but prohibited the presentation, offering for sale, and exploitation of the products infringing the Community design on pain of a penalty of €5000 per day. In June 2008, Plesner stopped selling the picture stating she couldn't afford to appeal. However, she continued to make works highlighting the situation in Darfur and, in 2010, she completed the painting *Darfurnica* (Figure 4.2).

In 2011, Louis Vuitton objected once again to the use of its RCD, this time in *Darfunica*. The Hague District Court granted *ex parte* relief to Louis Vuitton and, like the French court, prohibited Plesner from using the RCD owned by Louis Vuitton in her art. Plesner, assisted by two Dutch attorneys working *pro bono*, appealed to annul the preliminary ruling. She asked the court to hold that an artist is entitled to use an RCD to make a statement or to satirize. The Hague Civil Court reversed the earlier injunction against Plesner and her gallery for infringement of the design, holding that her right of artistic freedom of expression overrode Louis Vuitton's exclusive rights in the Community design ("Simple Living & Darfunica" n.d.)

The court clearly felt that Plesner's use should be an exception to the rights granted by a design right—as it likely would have been had she used a

Figure 4.2 Nadia Plesner's *Darfurnica* painting

trademark- or copyright-protected work in her art. Her right to express her artistic opinion outweighed Louis Vuitton's right to peaceful enjoyment of its property in the form of its design right. The court noted that the fundamental right to express an opinion is important in a democratic society, and artists enjoy considerable protection. It emphasized this by ordering Louis Vuitton to pay part of Plesner's legal costs. This case confirms that using another's design right in a satirical or other expressive way does not infringe the design right holder's property rights. Perhaps in response to this case, the proposed new EUDD and EUDR include specific exceptions for referential use and for "acts carried out for the purposes of comment, critique, or parody."

Deferral of Publication

Article 50 provides a useful right in respect of an RCD in a field where there is a lot of counterfeiting such as fashion. It enables an applicant for an RCD to request that the EUIPO defer publishing the design for up to 30 months from the date of filing. This could be used by a company to register a design while avoiding giving advance notice of it to copyists before it reaches stores.

Jurisdiction

If an EU design right is infringed, Articles 82 and 83 set out jurisdiction rules on where the case is to be heard to avoid forum shopping.

Litigation should generally be heard in a Community design court where the defendant has his domicile or a business establishment. If the defendant lacks a domicile or business establishment in the EU, then the case should be heard where the plaintiff is domiciled or has a business establishment. If neither has a domicile or establishment in the EU, then the case should be heard in the Spanish Community design courts as the EUIPO is based in Spain. Action can also be taken in the jurisdiction where the "act of infringement" occurred.

If there are multiple defendants in a design case, then the suit can be brought where one of them is domiciled, and sanctions such as damages can be sought in one proceeding instead of in multiple proceedings (to avoid conflicting judgments). The *Nintendo v. BigBen* decision clarified that the Community design court where the lawsuit is brought is not expected to apply the law of each individual country where infringement has occurred to determine relief. The CJEU said the court must "identify the law applicable by using a single connecting factor linked to the place where the act of infringement at the origin of several acts alleged against a defendant was committed or threatened." It can then apply this law to all the acts of infringement. This has also helped avoid forum shopping and made enforcement easier.

In good news for fashion designers, in 2018, a Milan court determined that it could provide EU-wide relief for infringement of design rights. Diesel and Marni complained that fast fashion retailer Zara had infringed their design rights in jeans and shoes, respectively. They claimed compensation in the Italian case for the entire amount of damages they had suffered across the EU, and the Milan court held it had EU-wide jurisdiction to rule on the infringement and the remedies, including damages. This decision will make it easier to sue in one court and gain EU-wide relief against a company which sells throughout the EU, such as Zara.

Under Article 91, to avoid the risk of multiple or irreconcilable judgments, actions should be stayed if an action over the same RCD is already taking place in another member state. However, declarations of non-infringement (DNIs) are excluded from this rule. Although DNIs and infringement actions are clearly related, a DNI is a relatively quick action, and important, because it can potentially affect third parties who may be selling the design. Requiring such actions to be stayed could enable a design right owner to bring action for infringement against a small seller of its product in a member state with a slow legal process and so prevent any actions for a DNI by others with an interest in selling the design elsewhere in the EU.

Since the validity of an RCD cannot be challenged in a DNI, allowing DNIs to proceed should not result in conflicting judgments. Under EU Regulation (EU) No 1215/2012 on jurisdiction and the recognition and enforcement of judgments in civil and commercial matters (the Brussels Regulation), DNI actions can be stayed if both actions have the same parties, the same cause of action, and the same object. The English version of Article 29 only requires that proceedings involve the same cause of action and the same parties. It does not contain the requirement that the object of the litigation is the same. Article 30 provides a judge with the discretion to stay the action in the second court if the actions are related. It is possible that this discrepancy could lead to conflicting decisions in different member states on whether to stay DNI proceedings, but it does not appear to have happened yet.

Enforcement and Costs

One of the main objectives of a pan-European registration system was to "improve access to a simple and affordable design protection system and to reduce transactional and litigation costs." Having a parallel national registration scheme means that designers can choose to register in one country or across the EU, depending upon their needs. The EUDR provides some rules on sanctions for infringement, to ensure that infringement proceedings are harmonized across member states, but not a detailed list.

EU Directive EC/2004/48 on the Enforcement of Intellectual Property Rights (the Enforcement Directive) is supposed to ensure the harmonization of sanctions and enforcement in IP law throughout the EU. Under the Enforcement Directive, all member states must provide the following for intellectual property cases: Injunctions, damages, removal and destruction of infringing goods, the award of legal costs, and the publication of judgments. An EU report in 2010 noted that the Enforcement Directive has been implemented by all member states but some differences in law and practice between different jurisdictions remained (European Commission 2010). The biggest difference was in how damages were calculated.

The majority of member states require a showing of fault to grant damages, while a few will grant damages regardless of fault.

Across member states, court fees, the cost of legal representation, and the obligations for legal representation differ depending upon the jurisdiction and type of court. Respondents to the EU's 2020 Evaluation Document indicated that they believed that the best type of legal protection for winning an infringement action was a national registered design followed by an RCD. Respondents to the survey also considered the type of court important, with the chances of success for rights' holders perceived as highest in specialized IP courts. They felt their chances of winning against an infringer were lowest when they relied on a UCD, mainly because of the burden of proving copying (European Commission 2020, 59).

Criminal Penalties

Criminal penalties for IP infringement are not harmonized across the EU. There are also national differences in substantive criminal law and evidence requirements. Whether or not a member state's court will grant criminal penalties for design infringement is a matter for the member state's own laws. The Enforcement Directive specifically does not affect any national provision related to criminal enforcement. Most member states provide for criminal liability for infringing a design right, but penalties vary considerably. In the majority, only minor criminal sanctions are available for design infringement and rarely include prison time. Fines are generally low and are the main criminal sanction. In cases where criminal organizations have committed major intellectual property infringement, it is very difficult to pursue a criminal case based on design infringement alone and better to combine any IPR enforcement with claims for money laundering, tax evasion, and fraud.

The Intersection of EU Design Law and other IPRs

As discussed in Chapter 2, intellectual property rights have developed as separate and distinct protections. Each protects a specific category of work. Copyrights protect artistic works, trademarks protect the source of origin of goods, and patents protect innovation in industry. Design has always straddled the artistic/industrial divide and often falls within the subject matter of all three IPRs—copyright, patents, and trademarks. Although the EU design rights system is supposed to create a distinct legal right that is not based on or part of either copyright, patent, or trademark rights, the expansion of the subject matter of all IPRs means that overlaps between design rights and these other IPRs are now increasingly common.

EU law permits the cumulation of IPRs to protect the same subject matter with different rights. Article 96 of the EUDR sets out the cumulative relationship of EU design rights with copyright stating:

> A design protected by a Community design shall also be eligible for protection under the law of copyright of member states as from the date on which

the design was created or fixed in any form. The extent to which, and the conditions under which, such a protection is conferred, including the level of originality required, shall be determined by each Member State.

The provisions with respect to trademarks, national designs, and other IPRs are almost identical.

Design Rights and EU Copyright Law

Although the EU provided for the cumulation of rights between copyright and design, it did not include any provisions in either the EUDD or EUDR on the harmonization of design and copyright law across the EU. Since the legislation did not attempt to harmonize copyright and design laws, the CJEU has taken up the challenge.

In 2001, the EU passed Directive 2001/29 on the harmonization of certain aspects of copyright and related rights in the information society (the Infosoc Directive). Article 2 of the Infosoc Directive grants authors "the exclusive right to authorise or prohibit direct or indirect, temporary or permanent reproduction by any means and in any form, in whole or in part." Article 2 of the Infosoc Directive has become the main legal vehicle that the CJEU has used to harmonize EU design and copyright law throughout the EU.

The CJEU Creates EU Copyright Law

In a series of four important decisions, starting in 2009, the CJEU harmonized the subject matter of copyright and defined the important terms "copyright work" and "originality" (see Figure 4.1). It has also determined how copyright and design rights intersect and apply to artistic commercial goods such as fashion designs.

In 2009, in *Infopaq International A/S v. Danske Dagblades Forening*, the CJEU first considered the standard of originality under EU copyright law. It decided that originality required that a work must simply be the author's own intellectual creation (AOIC) for copyright protection to arise. The dispute was over Infopaq's use of extracts from newspaper articles in its news feed database. The extracts in the database were just 11 words long. The CJEU held that the data capture process, where 11 words are stored on a computer memory and abstracts are printed, can constitute partial reproductions of works that are protected by exclusive copyrights as set out in Article 2 of the Infosoc Directive, "provided that the eleven words in themselves are works that are products of the authors' own intellectual creations." Infopaq could not take and publish those 11-word summaries without the author's consent. The judgment made clear the CJEU considered that the AOIC standard for originality was the same for all types of copyright works. The case highlights the problems of copyright infringement for digital business models, especially involving the collection and dissemination of data. However, it also makes clear that the originality required for a copyright to subsist in a work is simply that it involves some intellectual creativity by the author (AOIC), and that the requirement is the same regardless of the type of copyright work.

In 2011, in *Flos SpA v. Semeraro Casa e Famiglia SpA*, the CJEU heard a case that directly concerned design law and copyright and in it held that design and copyright rights were subject to full cumulation. Both rights could apply to one design; the designer had no need to choose between the rights. In the case, Flos's design right for its arco lamp had expired, but the company wanted to prohibit Semeraro from importing an imitation of the lamp from China by relying on its recently reactivated copyright protection. When Italy implemented the EUDD into its law, it meant that some copyrights for artistic articles (which had a shorter term than other copyrights under the old law) were resurrected by the change in the law.

Flos argued that, as its lamp was once again protected by Italian copyright law, it could use this copyright to sue the importer, Semeraro, for infringement. Flos argued that it did not matter that its design right for the lamp had now expired. The Italian court referred the question to the CJEU as to whether a member state that has introduced copyright protection for designs into its law to comply with the EUDD can now

> preclude such protection in the case of designs which—albeit meeting the requirements for protection laid down in copyright law—fell to be regarded as having entered the public domain before the date on which the statutory provisions introducing copyright protection for designs into the domestic legal order entered into force?

The CJEU held that, if a work met the requirements for copyright protection, a court could not exclude that work from protection because it had fallen out of design right protection. This means that, if a design meets the originality requirements for copyright protection, then there is full cumulation between the design protection and the (much longer) copyright protection for the work. This is the French principle of unity of art. In this case, the work had once been in the public domain, but that did not mean that when a new law entered into force that position could not change. Reinstated copyright protection for the designed object was possible, and the change in the lamp's legal status meant that the company importing the infringing lamp from China had to change its actions. The CJEU said: "it is settled case-law that the principle of the protection of legitimate expectations cannot be extended to the point of generally preventing new rules from applying to the future consequences of situations which arose under the earlier rules." Here, the new rule was that copyright protection applied anew, and that the fact that a design was protected by a design right did not prevent it from also being protected by a copyright. Under EU design law, the two legal protections were cumulated. This means that a designer could rely either on a design right or copyright protection for a designed object that was its author's own intellectual creation.

In *Levola Hengelo BV v. Smilde Foods BV*, the CJEU again considered the nature of a copyright work in a 2017 referral from a Dutch district court about a processed cheese product. The CJEU was asked whether the taste of a food product may be eligible for copyright protection. The referring court wanted to know whether

> copyright protection [is] precluded by the fact that the expression "literary and artistic works" in Article 2(1) of the Berne Convention ... includes "every production in the literary, scientific and artistic domain, whatever may be the mode or form of its expression," since the examples cited in that provision related only to creations which "can be perceived by sight and/or by hearing?"

The court also asked whether the instability of a food product and the subjective elements of taste would preclude a food product from copyright protection.

The CJEU restated that copyright protection required a work to be original and the AOIC. It held that copyright could not subsist in a flavor or taste, because it was too subjective. For a work to exist, "the subject matter protected by copyright must be expressed in a manner which makes it identifiable with sufficient precision and objectivity, even though that expression is not necessarily in permanent form."

There are two important parts of this judgment. First, the subject matter of copyright must be clear and precise, with "no element of subjectivity." The Court reasoned that, since the taste of a food product cannot (yet) be identified with precision and objectivity, it cannot be a "work" in the copyright sense. Second, as long as the subject matter is capable of clear and precise definition, it does not matter if the work lacks permanent form. Particularly because of this second factor, the *Levola* decision has important implications for UK copyright law, which are discussed in the next chapter.

Most fashion design is identifiable with sufficient precision and also expressed in a permanent form. However, this judgment provides a way for fashion designers to use copyright to protect common fashion activities that do not necessarily exist in a permanent form such as fashion shows, make-up, store displays, and possibly also perfumes. Currently, only Dutch law protects perfume via copyright. The Dutch Copyright Act's definition of a work is broad. It states that "anything can qualify for protection as long as it is perceptible and original" (Koelman, 2006). *Levola* suggests that EU law is headed in the same direction as Dutch law, since a copyright work simply has to be identifiable with sufficient precision but does not have to be permanently fixed or fit in a particular artistic category for protection.

These three CJEU decisions create a body of harmonized EU copyright law on the definition of an original work. To be protectable by copyright, a work must be its author's own original creation and it must also be capable of being objectively identified, although it does not have to be expressed in a permanent form. A work can also be protected by both copyright law and design rights as long as it meets the requirements for both legal protections.

The Overlap between Copyright and Design Rights

The case of *Cofemel – Sociedade de Vestuário SA v. G-Star Raw CV* in 2019 brought all these concepts together in a case concerning designs for jeans and t-shirts. The Portuguese Supreme Court asked the CJEU to rule on whether member states have the freedom to choose a higher level of originality for works of applied art and industrial designs under copyright law, or whether they must apply the CJEU standard of "the author's own intellectual creation" to all works, whether they consist of industrial designs or fine art.

Essentially, the question that the Portuguese Court asked was whether a member state can require that a design reach a higher level of artistic value before it can be protected by copyright. This would enable member states to continue to separate copyright protection for industrial objects from copyright protection for fine art. For example, in the UK, the law restricted the term of copyright protection to 25 years when more than 50 copies of a design were created. This was the same term as that for a registered design.

The advocate general was clearly cognizant that, if the relatively low level of originality of the AOIC test was applied to industrial design, it could lead to the overextension of copyright into industrial design. Under this standard, many quite banal designs would be eligible for copyright protection with its long term and lack of registration requirement. The advocate general suggested a "rigorous application" of the copyright principles by the national courts to deal with that risk, and stated that the protection of design and the protection of copyright pursue "fundamentally different objectives." Whereas the protection of design rights aims to compensate the designer for his/her investments, copyright protection is limited to subject matter which deserves to be qualified as an original work.

The CJEU adopted the advocate general's opinion. This opinion essentially overruled Article 96 of the EUDD that on copyright "the level of originality required, shall be determined by each Member State." The CJEU had used case law to create an EU-wide harmonization of copyright law to one standard of originality.

For any industrial design, including fashion design, copyright protection will arise as long as the design is the product of the AOIC. Nothing else is required for copyright to arise and protect a design. Copyright schemes which require the permanent fixation of a work, state that only specific types of work are eligible for protection, or have different rules of eligibility depending on the nature of the work to be protected are no longer compatible with EU copyright law. *Cofemel* makes clear that EU law provides full cumulation of copyright and design law, and that the standard of originality for copyright to subsist in a work is the same whatever the type of work.

Critics have pointed out that the endorsement of the low level of originality standard in *Cofemel* and the essential adoption of the unity of art doctrine from French law mean that trivial differences in manufactured utilitarian articles can be protected for almost a century under copyright law, and this might make design protection redundant (Schovsbo 2020, 12).

The European Commissionn proposal for the new EUDD and EUDR clearly states that "a design protected by a design right" is entitled to copyright protection as long as the requirements of copyright law are met. The intent of this position is to codify *Cofemel*. However, the wording is a little confusing. The usual point at which copyright protection is raised is once the design right no longer protects the design. Can the design right holder still assert copyright protection at this time?

Design Rights and EU Trademark Law

As in the US, trademark protection has become increasingly important to fashion designers in the EU. Trademarks have the significant benefit of lasting indefinitely (subject to continued use). Like other IPRs in both the US and EU, trademarks have expanded in scope and protection over the last 30 years. In the EU, trademark law has also been harmonized across the member states during that time.

TRIPS Article 15 required that countries protect "any sign, or any combination of signs, capable of distinguishing the goods or services of one undertaking from those of other undertakings." EU trademark law, like US law, currently goes well beyond the protection of symbols that provide information on the origin of products.

The current EU Trade Mark Directive (EUTMD) and EU Trade Mark Regulation (EUTMR) date to 2016. These laws provide some amendments to the EU-wide trademark introduced in Council Regulation No. 40/94/EC on the Community Trade Mark (CTM), probably the most important being that trademarks are no longer required to be able to be graphically represented for registration. This will make it easier to register sound and other non-graphic marks. EU trademark law already provided for the protection of non-traditional marks such as two- and three-dimensional shapes (or designs) in addition to traditional word marks.

In the US, the philosophy underpinning trademark law has received far less attention than the philosophy underpinning other IPRs. In Europe, the justification for the extension of trademark law protections never seems to have been discussed at all. Trademarks do not have the same purpose as other IPRs such as copyright, design, and patents of encouraging creativity and innovation. Their utility lies in their ability to protect rights in signs, provide consumers with source identifiers, and enable producers to build reputations. Unfair competition law also protects reputations against misrepresentation by competitors.

EU Trademark Protection for Designs

EU trademark law also provides protection for the advertising function of trademarks and thus protects the rights of mark owners beyond the simple indication of the source of origin of a product. The advocate general outlined in *Dior v. Evora* how origin is an "appropriate starting point" but that a trademark owner may protect his reputation to his "exclusivity and luxurious image" with a trademark (Neuwirth 2017, 466).

Trademarks are not simply used to convey messages about the source of origin of a product. Modern trademarks are often used to create distinctions between products and also to send messages to and about consumers. When a design can be linked to a marketing message, registering it as a trademark makes economic sense, as trademark protection is potentially indefinite. To be registered as a trademark, a shape does have to be recognized by consumers in that territory to denote a particular product origin.

National unfair competition rules can also be used to protect designs or shapes of products. Unfair competition law as a concept is somewhat elusive, and unfair competition laws in member states are not harmonized in the same way as most other IPRs. Unfair competition is generally meant to prohibit unfair trade practices. Some EU countries do this with specific legislation to protect consumers, competitors, and the public. Other countries protect competition as a tort concept. In the UK, there is no specific unfair competition law, but the tort of passing off can be used to protect against competitors who cause confusion as to the source of goods.

While EU design rights are relatively easy and cheap to register (RCDs) or can be obtained without formalities (UCDs), trademarks are more expensive and complicated to register. However, once registered, they can last indefinitely (and the EU does not require that a trademark is used in commerce at registration—although a trademark owner may be required to show use within five years to avoid successful opposition proceedings and cancellation).

Some of the most successful designs have been registered as trademarks rather than, or in addition to, obtaining design protection. Fashion examples of trademarks include the iconic shape of the Hermès Birkin bag and the red soles of Christian Louboutin's shoes. The main concern with using trademarks and unfair competition law to protect design is the anticompetitive effect on creativity of the indefinite duration of protection which undermines the limited term of design law.

As with copyright, the EUDR provides that design rights coexist and can be cumulated with trademarks and unfair competition rights.

The Overlap between Trademarks and Design Rights

There is a clear difference in the purpose of trademark and design protection: If a trademark is distinctive to one producer, unauthorized use by another is likely to lead to confusion, and the mark should be protected as long as it remains in use by the original producer. If a design is creative, it may need limited protection to compensate the producer for his or her creativity and innovation, but imitation of the design should eventually be permitted to benefit the public. Classic word trademarks do not overlap with design but, because shapes, colors, and other forms can now be registered as trademarks, there is an overlap between the subjects of trademark and design law. Trademarks can be used to protect design, and, because trademark protection has the potential to last until the mark is no longer used by the trademark owner in commerce, its protection can have the effect of removing a design from use by others for a long time. The overlap is not as wide as copyright because it is limited by several doctrines in trademark law.

Functionality and Substantial Value

Functional signs are excluded from trademark protection. The EU Trademark Regulation (in Article 4(1)(e)) excludes three types of functional signs, shapes, or designs from trademark protection. A trademark registration will not be granted:

- If the sign consists exclusively of the shape or "another characteristic" which results from the nature of the goods (natural signs).
- Is necessary to achieve a technical result (technical signs).
- Gives substantial value to the goods (ornamental signs).

The first ground is more relevant to natural phenomena. The second ground prohibits the protection of shapes that are more properly protected by a patent monopoly. The substantial value ground for refusal seems to have become the main provision in the EUTMR used to challenge applications for the protection of designs as trademarks.

The seminal CJEU case on the meaning of substantial value is *Hauck GmbH & Co. KG v. Stokke A/S* (which relates to the design of a children's highchair).

In *Hauck*, the CJEU considered what substantial value meant from three viewpoints: Commercial, aesthetic, and economic. These viewpoints overlap. In the case, Stokke argued that Hauck had infringed the shape trademark for its Tripp Trapp highchair. The CJEU held that it was grounds for a refusal or invalidation of a registration if the "sign [which] consists exclusively of the shape of a product with one or more essential characteristics which are inherent to the generic function or functions of that product and which consumers may be looking for in the products of competitors." This seems to mean that a shape necessary for its generic function cannot be registered as a trademark if consumers look for the same shape in competitors' products.

The *Hauck* Court guidance on how to determine whether a shape gives substantial value to a product was based on considering why a product is purchased. The Court held that value for the trademark owner may derive from the fact that a product is purchased primarily because of its shape. It would encourage monopolistic behavior and limit competition to let one owner register that shape as a trademark. The Court held that the perception of the target public as to the value of a particular shape for the product is one way of considering what is valuable. This is a relevant inquiry but not decisive on the question of value.

As in the US, Christian Louboutin spent time and money on protecting the red soles of his shoes as a trademark. The CJEU considered Louboutin's trademark in *Louboutin v. Van Haren Schoenen BV* in June 2018. The CJEU decided that Louboutin's red color mark for the outer sole of high-heeled shoes did not constitute a "shape" within the meaning of the EUTMD, and at the time that meant that no inquiry into whether the color added substantial value to the shoes was required. The CJEU's narrow interpretation of Louboutin's mark as a non-shape mark automatically prevented it having to consider if the Louboutin mark added substantial value to the shoes that would limit the ability of rivals to meet consumer demand for competing products in the women's shoes market (Ramirez-Montes 2019, 40).

The advocate general accepted Louboutin's assertion that there was no need to keep aesthetic characteristics that give substantial value to the goods available on a permanent basis because public preferences may change in line with fashion trends. This "evolutionary interpretation" of aesthetic functionality was a clear decision that aesthetic features of a product do not necessarily have sufficient economic effect over a long period to justify their permanent exclusion from trademark protection (Ramirez-Montes 2019, 59). This means that, even if a fashion design such as color or shape adds substantial value to a fashion product, the design can still be protected as a trademark.

Whether the aesthetics of the red sole gives substantial value to the shoes or the reputation of Louboutin (as demonstrated by the red sole) gives substantial value to the goods is a hard question. It seems that the CJEU and the Second Circuit Court of Appeals in the US both decided that the purpose of the sole is to associate the shoes with the famous designer, and that association is what gives value to the shoes. Louboutin admitted choosing the color red because it made the sole "pop." It was an aesthetic choice, at least initially (as most choices related to color are, particularly in fashion). Louboutin then spent time advertising the shoes and building the association of the red color with his brand. As a result, he was able to trademark red as a contrasting color on the soles of women's shoes. This design choice is probably no longer available for other footwear designers unless they want to face a lawsuit for infringement from Louboutin.

So, the effect of this decision is that other designers will lose the ability to use the feature in their designs for similar items. Since the CJEU decided *Louboutin*, the EUTMR has been updated. All types of marks can now be refused registration if they are considered to be functional, not just shape marks. It seems that the legislative intent of the new provision was to expand the criteria for refusing to register a mark. However, in the *Louboutin* decision, the CJEU took a narrow approach to the definition of functionality.

In a 2020 Hungarian case, *Gömböc Kft. V. Szellemi*, concerning a mathematical 3D shape, the Gömböc, the CJEU provided some clarity on several questions, including the substantial value ground, and another question of importance to designers: Can a design be protected using both design rights and trademark law?

Hungarian mathematicians had created a shape known as a Gömböc. Initially, they sought legal protection through an RCD. The designers then attempted to register a 3D shape mark in relation to goods in classes 14 (decorative items), 21 (decorative crystalware and chinaware), and 28 (toys). The Hungarian Intellectual Property Office (HIPO) refused the application to protect the shape of the Gömböc as a trademark in classes 14 and 21 on the grounds that it consisted exclusively of a shape that gave substantial value to the goods and, in respect of class 28 (for toys), it rejected the application on the grounds that the shape was necessary to achieve a technical result.

The Hungarian Supreme Court asked the CJEU three multi-part questions on its two grounds for refusal of the Gömböc trademark (technical result and substantial value), and on whether the earlier design registration had an effect on the later trademark application.

On the question of whether the shape gave substantial value to the goods, the Court asked whether the perception or knowledge of the buyer can establish the substantial value? The CJEU said that the perception of the buying public may be taken into account, but that such perception is not "a decisive element when applying the ground for refusal." However, "if it is apparent from objective and reliable evidence that the consumer's decision to purchase the product in question is to a large extent determined by that characteristic," then it is relevant in showing that the shape adds substantial value to the goods and should be denied registration as a trademark.

Even with the *Gömböc* decision, there is still little clarity as to the tests to be applied to determine the substantial value of a shape. How both the role/perception of the average consumer and the relevance of reputation are to be assessed remains uncertain. According to the CJEU, the relevant public's perception of the sign matters, though it may matter differently depending upon whether this perception relates to technical functionality or aesthetic functionality. The court did agree—substantially in line with the advocate general in the *Louboutin* case—that account must not be taken of the attractiveness of the goods as flowing from the reputation of the mark or its proprietor.

The third question in *Gömböc* related to whether the fact that the shape was already protected by a design right was relevant to subsequent attempts to obtain trademark protection. The CJEU confirmed the cumulation principle that a trademark and design right could coexist in the same shape, "provided that the conditions for registration of that sign as a trademark are satisfied." It also reiterated that the legal regimes concerning the registration of designs and trademarks "are independent, without any hierarchy existing as between [them]."

The London Taxi Corporation v. Frazer-Nash case confirms that to be registered as a trademark a sign must function as an indicator of origin. The English Court of Appeal held that the black cab was undoubtedly a recognizable and iconic shape, but its shape had not "come to identify the [taxis] as originating from a particular undertaking and so to distinguish those goods from those of other undertakings." The fact that its shape might add value to the goods was not the deciding factor for rejecting registration as a trademark. Trademark registration was denied because the shape did not indicate the product's source.

Distinctiveness

In addition to the prohibition against the registration of trademarks in respect of shapes or designs that are in some way functional, shapes or designs that are registered as trademarks must also be distinctive. "[T]he more closely the shape for which registration as a mark is sought resembles the shape most likely to be taken by the product in question, the greater the likelihood of the shape being devoid of any distinctive character" (Ramirez-Montes 2019, 45). Product shapes that are commonplace are likely to be refused registration because they lack this quality of being distinctive.

Time works in favor of trademarks, which can become more distinctive and therefore more registrable the longer they exist in the marketplace without registration, while time generally works against design applications. This means that a designer is better off applying for a design right while the design is novel. It can protect the design before it has become distinctive. Once the design is protected, the owner should advertise to create brand awareness (or acquired distinctiveness). This can be used next to apply for trademark protection, an approach pioneered by Apple.

Evidence

One important issue for a shape mark protected by a CTM is how widely must it be recognized across the member states to reach the level of acquired distinctiveness. In a long-running dispute between Nestlé and Cadbury over Nestlé's attempts to register a shape mark for the KitKat bar, *EUIPO v. Mondelez UK Holdings*, the GCEU had to decide what percentage of the general public across the whole territory of the EU must recognize a shape as having acquired distinctiveness for it to be registered as a trademark. The EUIPO had agreed to register the shape of the KitKat as a trademark on the basis of Nestlé's evidence that

> the contested mark has been used in almost the totality of the EU's territory, covering the market of fourteen of the fifteen member states that formed the EU at the relevant point in time; that as a consequence of such use, it can be determined that almost 50 percent of the general public of the EU taken as a whole [identified] Nestlé as the business origin of a product with the shape of the contested mark.

The GCEU held that the question is not whether

> a substantial proportion of the public in the European Union, merging all the member states and regions, perceived a mark as an indication of the commercial origin of the goods designated by that mark, but whether, throughout the European Union, it was proved that a significant proportion of the relevant public perceived a mark as an indication of the commercial origin of the goods designated by that mark.

The Court held that greater recognition of the mark in one part of the territory could not be used to offset a lower level of awareness in another part. Just because the mark has acquired distinctiveness in the largest member states did not mean that evidence was not needed from the public "in all, or most Member States."

Nestlé had submitted survey evidence of mark recognition for Germany, France, the UK, Italy, and Spain (the largest member states, with approximately

80% of the EU's population), as well as a table showing its significant market shares for all member states. When the General Court considered the evidence provided by Nestlé, it concluded that the shape of the KitKat bar had acquired distinctive character through use in these five big member states as well as in Denmark, the Netherlands, Austria, Finland, and Sweden. But, even though those states represented almost 90% of the population of the European Union, the evidence did not prove that the mark had acquired distinctiveness in other member states. The evidence did not provide the perception of the mark by the relevant public in, inter alia, Belgium, Ireland, Greece, and Portugal. The Court therefore annulled the decision of the board.

It is a major undertaking for any company to show that a shape has acquired distinctiveness across all of the member states. Chanel was recently denied trademark registration for the shape of its Chanel No. 5 perfume bottle in Lithuania. The Court decided that the shape of the perfume bottle was not distinctive and had not acquired distinctiveness in Lithuania. Chanel had submitted evidence to the Court, but it was based on consumer perception in France, not Lithuania. Unsurprisingly, this was considered insufficient to prove acquired distinctiveness in Lithuania (Wilkof 2022).

Conflicts

When there are conflicts between the protection of a design by a trademark and by a design right, the prior registration of either a design right or a trademark by a third party is capable of destroying the second registration. However, the test for whether the prior right conflicts with the new right depends on which right is being assessed. The test for whether a trademark is infringed is whether the average consumer is likely to be confused. The test for whether a design right is infringed focuses on the impression of the design on the informed user. The question of which of these tests the court should apply in determining whether infringement has occurred is not settled. Should the court focus on consumer confusion or the impression of the design? Should the test applied depend on which is the first right registered—the design right or the trademark—or should the court somehow apply both tests? This issue could be raised in a fashion context if one company held a design right for a shape which another attempted to register as a trademark.

Design Rights and EU Patent Law

Since design law is intended to encourage innovation in appearance, not in the way a product works or its materials, there is less likelihood of overlap between design and patent law than there is between design and copyright or trademark law, especially in the field of fashion, which focuses so much on appearance.

The Overlap between Patents and Design Rights

Fashion designs must fit the human body, but they are rarely, if ever, entirely functional in the sense that function is the only factor that determines the way the design looks. The *Doceram* judgment drew a clear line limiting the protection of design law for totally functional designs, but fashion designers will rarely be applying for a patent for a design without any aesthetic elements. Nike, for example, holds many patents in respect of its innovative materials, but those designs likely also include some non-functional or aesthetic elements.

After the patent has expired, a designer might apply for protection of the design under copyright law (design rights do not last long enough) for a design that has some aesthetic element.

In 2020 the *SI and Brompton Bicycle Ltd v. Chedech/Get2Get* case held that the functional shape of a folding bike, once protected by a patent, can be eligible for copyright protection after the patent has expired if its design is the author's own intellectual contribution (AOIC). The advocate general's opinion advised that, if the shape of an object is exclusively dictated by a technical result, then no copyright can subsist in it. He clearly wanted to limit the concurrent protection of a design by both copyright and patent law and said that the existence of an earlier patent might serve to identify technical constraints which dictate the shape of the product. Copyright protection should not generally be available to protect a functional design after the expiration of patent protection. Brompton submitted that its folding bike design was the AOIC of its designer and thus should also be entitled to copyright protection.

The CJEU decided

> that, in order to assess whether the folding bicycle at issue in the main proceedings is an original creation and is thus protected by copyright, it is for the referring court to take account of all the relevant aspects ... as they existed when that subject matter was designed, irrespective of the factors external to and subsequent to the creation of the product.

To avoid introducing any subjective elements into the consideration of whether the patented subject matter could be protected as a copyright, the court made a list of the factors which were *not relevant* to whether or not the design could be protected by a copyright. The irrelevant factors were the intention of the author, the external recognition of the design as innovative, the existence of other possible shapes for the design, and the intention of the alleged infringer. All of these factors introduced subjective considerations. The relevant factors that "should be taken into account only in so far as those factors make it possible to reveal what was taken into consideration [initially] in choosing the shape of the product concerned" included the effectiveness of the shape in achieving the result and the expired patent. If there was evidence of any creativity by the designer, at the time of creation, then the design could be protectable by copyright in addition to patent law. The much longer copyright protection would then outlast the patent protection.

Applying *Brompton Bicycle* to fashion designs could allow the owners of patents in new materials or innovative products in the fashion industry, such as Nike, to extend the IPR protection of their innovative textiles, shapes, or construction methods. To obtain copyright protection, it would simply be necessary to show that, at the time of creation of the subject matter, the designer had introduced their own artistic contribution into the innovation and the design was not just a matter of achieving a specific technical result.

Concerns and Criticisms of the EU Design Right System

Cumulation of Rights and Other Protections

The CJEU has made clear that copyrights, trademarks, patents, and design rights can all benefit from cumulative protection under EU law. There is no need to choose between different IP rights, and an object protected by one IPR is not systematically disqualified from obtaining the subsequent protection of another IPR. Even an innovative design once protected by a patent may obtain copyright protection after the patent has expired if it includes some aesthetic as well as functional considerations and is the AOIC of its creator. This sets up the possibility of designs being protected for long periods under consecutive rights.

The cumulation of design rights and copyright created by *Cofemel* has changed the calculus for fashion designers since they may be able to obtain lengthy copyright protection for quite commonplace designs without any formalities as long as the designs are the AOIC. *Cofemel* has significantly expanded copyright law, and it remains to be seen whether it makes the design system redundant and designers will now choose to ignore it in favor of copyright with its lack of formalities.

Since designs can so easily be simultaneously protected by design rights and copyright, the fact that there are differences between the two systems in ownership and the creation of moral rights could also cause problems, primarily between fashion designers working as employees or subcontractors or on commissions for a design house. Different entities could own the copyright and design right in a design. If a designer owns the copyright, he or she will have moral rights which could cause problems for the design house.

The cumulation of design rights with trademarks raises the public policy concern of everlasting IP protection. This conflicts with the balance IP protection is supposed to achieve between public and private property. A Norwegian attempt to use EU trademark law to prolong the copyright protection of artistic objects illustrates this concern, although it was unsuccessful. The city of Oslo owned the copyright in several statues by Norwegian artist Gustav Vigeland that were about to enter the public domain. It attempted to register a number of Vigeland's artworks as trademarks. The Norwegian Industrial Property Office (NIPO) rejected these applications on the basis, inter alia, that the artworks consisted of shapes that added "substantial value to the goods" (Rosati 2017). Without a rich public domain, the creation of new artistic work becomes less likely.

Courts need to be alert to the anticompetitive effect of attempts like this to protect earlier artistic objects and designs with a potentially everlasting trademark protection. They should rigorously apply the requirements that a trademark should identify the source of origin of goods, that it must consist of a sign that has acquired distinctiveness to act as a trademark, and that it must not add substantial value to the goods.

There is a strong case that it is the rare design that should be protected as a trademark because of the anticompetitive effects of such protection. Even if a product shape points to a particular source of origin, has acquired distinctiveness, and does not add substantial value to the goods, it will rarely if ever be the only way for a designer to indicate the source of origin of her product. From Christian Louboutin to Coca Cola, although customers may recognize distinctive shapes and colors, the purveyors of these products generally have many other ways to indicate source. The purchaser of a pair of Christian Louboutin shoes is going to look for the word trademark on the shoes and their packaging as well as the red color. The protection of shapes through trademark law provides a virtual monopoly on the use of the shape or color in a similar design context, which means that other designers are deprived of this shape or color for their designs.

The default IPR protection for aesthetic shapes that add substantial value to a product should be design, or perhaps copyright law. The expansion of copyright under *Cofemel* means that copyright protection now co-exists with design protection. In light of this development, trademark protections should not be expanded. Otherwise, it is likely that large design houses with access to lawyers will be able to increasingly remove designs from the public domain by using design rights and copyright protection followed by trademark applications once a design has acquired distinctiveness.

Future Concerns about the Design Right System

The EU system of design rights has been very successful for design. It provides high levels of protection for all kinds of designers. It includes the benefit of two types of rights—UCDs and RCDs. A UCD can be obtained without any cost or formalities, and even an RCD is not particularly onerous to obtain since there is no substantive review. As a result, the design rights system has become important to the protection of fashion design over the last 20 years although, since *Cofemel*, copyright law is now going to play an increasingly important role.

The Evaluation Document notes that some digital technologies might create new challenges for design protection. It identifies software development, AI, and 3D printing as some of the digital technologies that may have unforeseen and unintended consequences for design protection.

According to a 2020 European Commission Report on the Intellectual Property Implications of the Development of Industrial 3D Printing, stakeholders in the design industry were undecided whether the current EU design law framework provided sufficient protection against third parties copying a protected design by means of 3D printing (Mendis et al. 2020). The effect of AI, 3D printing, and other digital technologies on the protection of fashion design is discussed in Chapter 6.

References

Dumortier, Jos, Davide Parilli, Uma Suthersanen, David Musker et al. 2016. "Legal Review on Industrial Design Protection in Europe." MARKT2014/083/D. European Commission.

European Commission. 2010. "Application of Directive 2004/48 EC on the Enforcement of Intellectual Property Rights." COM/2010/0779. European Commission.

———. 2020. *Commission Staff Working Document Evaluation of EU Legislation on Design Protection*. 264 Final. Brussels.

———. 2022. "Proposal for a Directive of the European Parliament and Council on the Legal Protection of Designs (recast)." COM/2022/667 final.

Koelman, Kamiel. 2006. "Copyright in the Courts: Perfume as Artistic Expression?" WIPO Magazine, September 2006. https://www.wipo.int/wipo_magazine/en/2006/05 /article_0001.html.

Kur, Annette, Marianne Levin, and Jens Schovsbo. 2018. *The EU Design Approach: A Global Appraisal*. Edward Elgar.

Mendis, Dinusha, Jan Bernd Nordemann, Rosa Maria Ballardini, Hans Brorsen, Maria del Carmen Caletrava Moreno, Julie Robson, and Phil Dickens. 2020. *The Intellectual Property Implications of the Development of Industrial 3D Printing*. European Commission.

"Nadia Plesner Simple Living and Darfunica." n.d. Accessed May 28, 2022. http://www .nadiaplesner.com/simple-living--darfurnica1.

Neuwirth, Rostam. 2017. "Counterfeiting and Piracy in International Trade: The Good, the Bad and the … Oxymoron of 'Real Fakes.'" *Queen Mary Journal of Intellectual Property* 7 (4): 444–67.

Ramirez-Montes, Cesar J. 2019. "Louboutin Heels and the Competition Goals of EU Trade Mark Law." *UIC Review of Intellectual Property Law* 19 (1): 38–63.

Rosati, Eleonora. 2017. "Can a Public Domain Artwork Be Registered as a Trade Mark or Would That Be Contrary to Public Policy and Morality?" The IPKat (blog). April 8, 2017. https://ipkitten.blogspot.com/2017/04/can-public-domain-artwork-be-registered .html.

Schovsbo, Jens. 2020. "Copyright and Design Law: What Is Left After All and Cofemel?-Or: Design Law in a 'Double Whammy.'" *Center for Information and Central Law (CIIR)*, 1–16.

Wilkof, Neil. 2022. "Chanel Is Reminded: Trademark Territoriality Still Matters." The IPKat (blog). January 27, 2022. https://ipkitten.blogspot.com/2022/01/chanel-is -reminded-trademark.html.

5 Harmonization and Its Opposite (Brexit)

Introduction

EU IP laws, especially copyright law, have been largely harmonized by the CJEU. It is the courts of the member states that must interpret and apply these decisions, and a few differences remain in the application of laws protecting design in some member states. The chapter considers French, Italian, and English law since these jurisdictions contain the three big European fashion capitals. English law retains the most differences, and the UK split from the EU, known as Brexit, is likely to mean bigger changes for those wishing to do business in the UK as well as mainland Europe.

Design-Friendly Courts

In its decisions over the last decade, the CJEU has defined the relationship between copyright and design rights in EU law and created the body of EU-wide copyright law described in the previous chapter. In the EU system, the courts of the member states are responsible for directly applying this law, and so it is important to look at the decisions of these courts on design law.

A 2011 study by the UKIPO found a perception among designers that French and German courts were more "design-right-friendly" than UK courts (Haskel and Pesole 2011). The study also found that most cases of design infringement in the UK were not litigated but settled by cease-and-desist letters which were often sufficient to stop infringers.

A 2019 empirical analysis of EU design case law compiled by Oliver Church, Estelle Derclaye, and Giles Stupfler confirmed that French and German (and Italian) courts do tend to find in favor of rights holders. However, the data failed to confirm that UK courts were unfriendly to design rights holders.

The analysis showed that, overall, courts across the member states found 77.7% of design rights (whether registered, unregistered, national, or EU) valid. The proportions were similar whether RDRs or UDRs or other design rights were used. Lower courts were as likely as higher courts to hold design rights valid.

Over a period of roughly 16 years (2001 to 2017), there were 1408 litigated cases involving design rights in the 28 member states. The most pro IPR countries

DOI: 10.4324/9781003091400-6

were Germany (where 87.3% of design rights were upheld) and Italy, Spain, and France, which all upheld around three-quarters of designs. In a surprise for those who believe UK courts are unfriendly to IPR holders, UK courts upheld 83.5% of designs (Church, Derclaye, and Stupfler 2019).

The Church data showed that, EU-wide, half of all 2D design litigation related to clothing and footwear. In the UK, 100% of 2D cases concerned clothing. In Italy, the proportion was 60%, and in France 38.4%. Italy had the most cases related to clothing proportionately. This is not surprising given the importance of fashion in the Italian economy. The member states with the most litigation were, unsurprisingly, the bigger states: France, Germany, and Italy. France is the most litigious member state (which underscores the importance of design in the French economy).

As had emerged from the UKIPO's earlier report, most litigation either involved national registered design rights (RDRs) or RCDs. The RDR is involved in most litigation in France, where it is involved in 67.6% of litigation, much more than RCDs, which are only involved in 18.8%. The position is the opposite in Italy, where the RCD is involved in almost twice as much litigation as the national RDR.

In the UK, unregistered design rights (UDRs) are important, particularly the UK UDR. It is involved in 53.2% of litigation, far more than any other right in the British market. This right is likely to become even more important to designers in the UK owing to Brexit (discussed later in the chapter).

Copyright remains important for designers across Europe. The Church study stated that "copyright retains its full role for 2D designs," with designers using it more often than UCDs for 2D designs. This is probably because copyright is easy to obtain. UCDs are also important, more so in countries such as the UK and Italy, which "only protects works of applied art if they display artistic merit" (at least prior to *Cofemel*). The effect of *Cofemel* on member states' laws is discussed later in this chapter.

UK Courts and Design Infringement

One of the main reasons for the belief that UK courts are not as designer-friendly as French and other continental courts is because, in the four best-known design cases in the UK over the last decade or so (*Proctor & Gamble v. Reckitt Benckiser, Dyson v. Vax, Samsung Electronics (UK) Ltd. v. Apple Inc.*, and *PMS International Limited v. Magmatic Limited*), the courts all held that the design rights in question were valid but had not been infringed. A review of the cases shows that, after careful analysis in each case, the various courts decided that the overall impression of the second design was different to the first design.

In the *Proctor & Gamble* and *Dyson* cases, both companies lost in the UK on the basis that the overall impressions created by the allegedly infringing designs were different to the companies' RCDs. In *Proctor & Gamble*, the court held that a registered design based on a line drawing was for the shape alone. Jacob LJ in the Court of Appeal stated: "[t]he registration is evidently for a shape. The proper comparison is with the shape of the alleged infringement. Graphics on that (or on the physical embodiment of the design) are irrelevant." When the shapes of the two sprayers, absent any surface decoration, were compared the court found that they did not create a similar overall impression.

In *Dyson*, the company focused its argument on a description of its design rather than an image or representation of the design. For example, Dyson claimed about its striking vacuum design and the Vax design that "both have transparent bins through which the cyclone shroud is visible." Although this statement was accurate, the bins and shrouds of the two vacuum cleaners were different in shape. While it could be said that the concept of the clear bin was the same, the interpretation on the Vax cleaner was different (see Figure 5.1). The court held that Dyson's RCD was valid, and its design was very innovative, but the Vax design did not infringe it.

Both *Proctor & Gamble* and *Dyson* were, however, successful in litigation in other EU member states.

When Apple and Samsung battled over the validity of Apple's RCD for its tablet design in the EU, Apple was also more successful in Germany than in the UK. In Germany, Apple got a pan-European injunction against Samsung (Korea) and Samsung (Germany), although this was later reduced to a Germany-only injunction on the basis of unfair competition law, and not the RCD. Samsung then sued Apple in the UK (then part of the EU) for a declaration of non-infringement (DNI) of Apple's RCD by the Samsung Galaxy tablet. The UK court agreed that it could hear the case with respect to Samsung (UK) and decided that the Samsung tablet did not infringe the iPad design—a result it required Apple to publish on

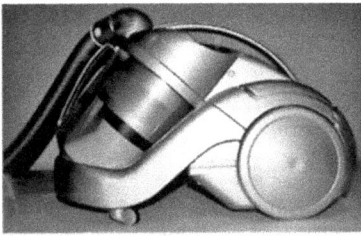

Registered Design

The Mach Zen

Figure 5.1 Dyson and Vax vacuum cleaner designs

its website. In the UK, the decision for Samsung was upheld on appeal, whereas, in Germany, Apple won most of its case and, in the US, Apple also won a similar case against Samsung using its design patents. The worldwide litigation was eventually settled out of court by the two huge companies without either taking their products off the market or changing their designs (Nicas 2018).

Of the well-known UK design cases where the designer lost, *PMS International Limited v. Magmatic Limited* (more commonly known as the *Trunki* case) was probably the closest call on infringement and copying. It is easy to see why it has been criticized by designers and others as bad for innovative design, given that the designer of the second Kiddee case had used the Trunki case as the basis for his idea. However, this case illustrates that creativity does not occur in a vacuum, and new ideas are derived from all kinds of pre-existing content. It would be anti-competitive to enable the first designer of a design, which while innovative had not reached the level of patent novelty, to prohibit others from using his ideas as the basis for their inspiration. The UK Supreme Court wanted to ensure that the RCD for the Trunki did not gain the status of a patent monopoly for children's suitcases.

The UK Supreme Court dismissed an appeal filed by Magmatic, owners of the RCD for the Trunki suitcase, and upheld the Court of Appeal's decision that PMS's Kiddee case did not infringe Magmatic's design. The trial judge had compared the shape of both cases to hold that PMS's case created a similar overall impression to Magmatic's Trunki case. The Court of Appeal held that this was an error. It stated that the comparison should be between the CAD drawing filed for the RCD (which was in two monochrome colors) and the (more decorated) Kiddee case (see Figure 5.2). The Court of Appeal did its own comparison of the CAD drawing of the Trunki case (which it said provided the overall impression of a horned animal) versus the Kiddee case, which had eyes, antennae, and other features but not the contrasting color wheels of the Trunki case. After completing this comparison, it held that the two children's cases did not produce similar overall impressions.

On appeal, the Supreme Court upheld the Court of Appeal's decision of non-infringement. Lord Neuberger did, however, note that he felt some regret for upholding the decision, as the conception of the Trunki was both original and clever, and "Mr Beverley of PMS conceived the idea of manufacturing a Kiddee Case as a result of seeing a Trunki." So, even though the Trunki had won prizes for its clever and innovative design, and the creator of the Kiddee case had essentially copied features of the Trunki, the second suitcase had enough differences that it did not infringe the Trunki. Magmatic had asked for a reference to the CJEU on the question of whether absence of decoration can be a feature of a design. The Supreme Court refused this request as it said that it was unnecessary to the decision in the case, and, in addition, the CJEU would likely say that the question was one of fact and so should be answered by the court reviewing the actual design.

As Lord Neuberger explained in his judgment, the design drawing is chosen and submitted by the applicant as a representation of the monopoly he wants to claim:

Figure 5.2 Magmatic's Trunki and PMS's Kiddee case

> an applicant for a design right is entitled, within very broad limits, to sub-
> mit any images which he chooses ... an applicant should appreciate that it
> will almost always be those images which exclusively identify the nature and
> extent of the monopoly which he is claiming.

In describing the applicant as the driver of the application for an RCD with freedom to choose what he wants to protect, he went on:

> an applicant is entitled to make any number of applications. More broadly, it
> is for an applicant to make clear what is included and what is excluded in a
> registered design, and he has wide freedom as to the means he uses. It is not
> the task of the court to advise the applicant how it is to be done.

This case demonstrates that designers should consider carefully with their legal
advisors how best to represent their designs in any legal claim or application.
They can improve their chances of success in an infringement claim for an RDR
if they follow Neuberger's advice and file several different types of representation of the design. A line drawing is likely to be conceived as covering the design
shape in any color, whereas a CAD drawing with shading will be taken to show
color contrasts. It is hard to determine, ahead of any infringement, whether a lot
of detail or surface decoration will help or hinder the applicant's case. On the one
hand, it may weaken the impression of a strong similarity between underlying

shapes or, on the other, it may reinforce similarities between slightly different shapes that have similar surface decoration.

Is There Still a Role for National IP Laws in Europe?

The harmonization of design law across the member states is very recent. As late as 2015, in an article, "Anatomy of a Design Regime," Kathryn Moore was able to describe the current EU system of protection for design as "an increasingly complex system of cumulative and overlapping intellectual property rights" (Moore, 2015).

Although the CJEU has to a great extent harmonized EU copyright law and eliminated national differences by its case law, courts in member states have at times failed to apply CJEU precedents fully. One of the most controversial EU copyright cases is *Cofemel* since it overrules previous case law in all of the member states that treated industrial designs differently to fine art. Unsurprisingly, some courts have not uniformly applied it to remove all considerations of aesthetic or artistic value in the evaluation of whether an industrial design can obtain copyright protection.

In the first national application of *Cofemel*, the UK Intellectual Property Enterprise Court (IPEC) court applied the decision to fashion in *Response Clothing Ltd. v. The Edinburgh Woolen Mill Ltd.* It held that Response Clothing's jacquard fabric design was a "work of artistic craftsmanship" in the UK closed system of copyright works as well as applying the AOIC standard. Stating that, under *Cofemel*, "national law could not impose a requirement of aesthetic or artistic value" for the design to be protected, the judge said he simply had to be "satisfied that the [fabric] was the author's own intellectual creation" as well as the result of "the author's free and creative choices." However, he still analyzed whether the fabric was protected under the higher UK aesthetic standard for designs of artistic craftsmanship, as well as whether it met the *Cofemel* standard.

This seemed to be a cautious way of avoiding conflict between English law and EU law. The judge decided that, although *Cofemel* has created a consistent copyright standard across Europe, which courts in all member states must apply, applying English law would still reach the same conclusion (at least in this case). It will be interesting to see if the *Cofemel* decision continues to be applied by UK courts in cases where the result might be different under English law, especially post-Brexit.

In Italy, another legal system which used to require a higher standard of originality for applied art, courts have not always clearly followed the *Cofemel* standard for copyright protection. In a case brought by Longchamp over the protection of its bestselling handbag design, the Italian court accepted that the bag could be protected by a 3D trademark but rejected Longchamp's copyright claim on the basis that the bag displayed no artistic value (Rosati 2022a). This should no longer be the test of whether copyright protection is available in Italy. Longchamp won its case using trademark rights, but it should probably also have done so on the basis of its copyright claim.

In another, earlier Italian case, however, the Italian Supreme Court applied *Cofemel* correctly. In *Kiko v. Wycon*, a dispute about the store layout for a make-up store, the court held that the store layout was protectable as an architectural work under Italian copyright law since it "results from an original combination, which is not imposed by choices of the author aimed at solving a technical-functional problem" (Rosati 2020). This decision applied *Cofemel* without caveats.

Several Danish decisions also show how its courts have struggled with originality in design.

Danish case law is the most liberal of the Nordic countries but, prior to *Cofemel*, it was a jurisdiction that required a higher standard of originality for applied art to obtain copyright protection. In 2012, it rejected a copyright for a t-shirt design on the basis that "Danish legal traditions have set up considerable requirements in regards to originality and artistic efforts before copyright protection can be awarded to articles of fashion" (Schovsbo 2020). This is now incompatible with the *Cofemel* originality standard which has explicitly removed any requirements for copyright protection other than that a work must be the AOIC.

In June 2020, the Danish Supreme Court again stuck with the higher originality standard, despite the existence of *Cofemel*, when it rejected a copyright claim for fashion boots. It held that the designer, Ilse Jacobsen, could not prohibit the import from China of very similar rubber boots to ones she had designed. The Court upheld a lower court judgment that Jacobsen's boots did not meet the criterion of AOIC originality and therefore did not qualify for copyright protection. The Court was ostensibly applying the *Cofemel* standard to the boot, but it stated that "it is not sufficient in order to qualify as a work that the said designs beside their technical purposes provide a specific and characteristic effect from an aesthetic view." In *Cofemel*, the determination of originality is not supposed to involve a consideration of aesthetic effects but simply whether the work is imbued with the AOIC. The Danish Court appeared to require additional aesthetic value for the boots to obtain copyright protection in Denmark (Woolgar 2020).

However, in two more recent cases concerning design, Danish courts have applied a standard of originality that is more clearly in line with *Cofemel*. In 2020, the Danish High Court confirmed a copyright in a very minimalist hanging flower pot, although it rejected the grant of copyright protection for an even more spare cylindrical vase and pot. In 2022, the Eastern High Court agreed that another minimalist Nordic design, this time for a plant box, was protected by copyright and had been infringed by the marketing of a similar, but not identical, box. These cases have reduced the threshold of originality under the Danish Copyright Act and seem to have brought it substantially into line with the *Cofemel* standard (Rosati 2022b).

In one indication of how courts in member states that previously required a higher standard of originality have found it hard to apply the *Cofemel* standard, the Swedish Society of Crafts and Design has established a new impartial expert body to help Swedish courts determine originality regarding works of applied art. It can also express opinions on infringement ("The Copyright Panel | Svensk Form" n.d.).

National IP Laws

Trademark and patent laws across the EU have been mostly harmonized by EU directives and regulations. This means that there are very few substantive areas of difference between IPRs under design, copyright, trademark, and patent laws across the EU member states.

The differences in IPR protections as far as fashion designers are concerned mainly consist of a stronger tradition of copyright protections in France than in other member states because of the unity of art doctrine and now also the effects of Brexit on design rights in the UK. These differences are described in more detail below.

French Law

France has probably been the member state that has had the biggest effect on CJEU jurisprudence through preliminary questions and briefs on cases, and the CJEU harmonized EU copyright law bears a strong resemblance to the characteristics of French law. In France, copyright does not require that the protected work display any particular type, form, artistic merit, or purpose. In the line of cases to *Cofemel*, the CJEU essentially applied the French unity of art principle across the member states of the EU.

When France harmonized its design law under the EUDD in 1998, the French legislature did not transpose the term "individual character" from the directive but used the term "own character" instead. This was done to avoid confusion between the objective requirement under design law of individual character and the more subjective character of copyright originality that the work is a reflection of the personality of the creator. French courts have held that the terms "individual character" and "own character" convey the same meaning—the objective meaning that a design is not copied from an earlier design so that its "overall visual impression on the informed observer differs from that produced by any [earlier] disclosed design." There is thus no difference between the French registered design right and the EU-wide right, the RCD.

There is no French unregistered design right, but in France copyright law has always specifically protected works of fashion, and unity of art is settled law, and so in a sense a French unregistered design right is unnecessary. In fact, the question since *Cofemel* is whether all unregistered design rights are obsolete. The Church data found that France was the largest user of national RDRs and had the most design right litigation in Europe, suggesting that design rights will remain useful.

Under French law, a specific transfer of copyright is necessary between the employee and employer. It is not part of the employment contract unless specifically stated. However, a clause in an employment contract assigning design rights to the employer is permitted. As long as there is no claim of ownership of the design by an employee, the corporate entity which markets the design is presumed to be the owner of the rights in such work.

This means that it is possible for an employer to own the design rights in a design, but for the employee who created the design to own the copyright. The employee copyright owner would also enjoy the moral rights. This split could lead to problems, and French contract law for works made by an employee needs to be updated.

Remedies for infringement of a design right in France can include criminal liability including fines up to €500,000 and imprisonment up to five years. Not all member states have criminal liability for infringement of IPRs, and there is no EU-wide requirement to adopt it. According to the 2020 EUIPO Report on the Status of IPR Infringement, the greatest costs of IPR infringement fall on the private sector, and it is particularly burdensome for small to medium sized enterprises (SMEs), but there are several ongoing global-scale law enforcement operations to combat intellectual property rights infringement.

Italian Law

After starting as a system of full cumulation of rights for design, Italian courts and legislatures have moved back and forth several times between a full cumulation unity of art approach and a separability approach (*scindibilità*) for the copyright protection of applied art and design. This made for high legal uncertainty for most of the last century. However, Italian design thrived and was often described as very innovative during this period. Some commentators argue that this was, in fact, owing to the short period of protection for applied art under Italian law, in contrast to the long period of protection available under French law by copyright. It showed that the separability doctrine worked well, encouraging better design and a speedy cycle of innovation. This is similar to the argument in favor of the so-called "piracy paradox" of the US fashion industry.

In 2001, Italy formally abandoned the doctrine of *scindibilità* in favor of the criterion of artistic value (*valore artistico*) which aimed to restrict copyright protection for design and created a two-tier system with copyright protection available for designs of higher artistic value. Less innovative designs were able to take advantage of design right protections only. This higher requirement for artistic value to obtain copyright protection for industrial designs lasted until the CJEU made clear in *Cofemel* that evidence of originality for copyright, whatever the type of work, is always that the design is the AOIC. Artistic value, or any higher standard, cannot be required for a design, or any other type of work, to obtain copyright protection, and, although Italian courts sometimes still refer to the higher standard, they have in general applied *Cofemel*.

Like France, Italy does not provide its own unregistered design protection.

UK Law

Even after over 100 years of harmonization between UK and continental law, via Berne and other international treaties, its 50-year membership of the EU, the creation of the EU design rights system, and CJEU case law, the UK retains several anomalous positions in its copyright law.

UK Design Rights

After the creation of the EU design rights system and before Brexit came into force at the end of 2020, five design rights coexisted in the UK. The EU rights (the RCD and UCD), UK unregistered and registered design rights (UK UDR and UK RDR), and copyright. Since Brexit, the UK government has created four new design rights in the UK to replace the EU design rights that were no longer valid in the UK from January 2021. These new rights are discussed in the section on Brexit below.

In 1988, the UK Parliament passed a new Copyright Designs and Patent Act (CDPA) creating the UK UDR. It was an attempt to redefine the relationship between copyrights and design. The UK UDR protects "the design of the shape or configuration (whether internal or external) of the whole or part of an article." It protects functional designs. However, it does not protect surface decorations (which may be protected by copyright). The UK UDR is useful for fashion designers because it arises automatically and gives its owner the right to prevent unauthorized copying. It lasts longer than the EU UDR (up to 15 years versus 3 years) and, unlike the EU right, it can also be used to protect functional designs. However, since it does not protect surface decorations, its usefulness for artistic designs such as fashion items is significantly reduced.

When the EUDD came into force at the beginning of the 2000s, it did not change the UK UDR, and so it continued to coexist with the EU right. However, the EUDD amended the existing UK RDR (created by the Registered Design Act 1949) to define design in the same terms as in the rest of the EU. The harmonized UK RDR is the same right as the national RDRs available to designers in all member states.

UK Copyright Law Conflicts with EU Laws

In the UK, three aspects of copyright law have endured notwithstanding that they appear to conflict with the CJEU decisions by which the UK is still bound, even post-Brexit; CJEU case law prior to Brexit day has become part of the British system of case law precedent. To change the current position, the UK would have to legislate, or its courts would have to overturn the CJEU precedents, neither of which has occurred.

The three major conflicts between UK and EU law are that copyright protection in the UK is available only to a closed list of works; protection for "works of artistic craftsmanship" (which is generally where fashion designs are protected) requires a higher and generally different standard of originality under UK law; and, to obtain protection in the UK, a copyright work must be fixed in a permanent form.

Closed list: Copyright protection in the UK is available only for works that fall into the specific closed list of categories that are set out in statute, currently the CDPA, as amended. The categories of work protected under UK law are original literary, dramatic, musical, or artistic works, sound recordings, films or broadcasts, and typographical arrangements. Further explanation expands the category of "artistic work" to include works of artistic craftsmanship. If fashion designs obtain copyright protection in the UK, they generally do so as works of artistic craftsmanship. There are several examples in English jurisprudence of cases where works that would likely have been able to obtain copyright protection in the EU and other jurisdictions were denied it in the UK because they did not fit into the closed list of copyright protected works. In 2011, in *Lucasfilm v. Ainsworth*, the design for a stormtrooper's helmet from *Star Wars* was held not to be eligible for copyright protection because it did not fit in the closed list of works. It was not a sculpture within the category of artistic work.

There are signs that UK courts are becoming uncomfortable with the closed list and its conflict with EU law. Justice Arnold noted in 2010 that:

> In the light of a number of recent judgments of the CJEU, it may be arguable that it is not a fatal objection to a claim that copyright subsists in a particular work that the work is not one of the kinds of work listed [in the CDPA].
> *(SAS Institute Inc v. World Programming Ltd.)*

Following *Cofemel*, the end of the closed list exceptions was raised again in the *Response Clothing* case discussed above. The judge held that Response Clothing's Wave fabric qualified as a work of artistic craftsmanship under UK law and was entitled to protection, although there was no need to fit it into this closed list. The judge stated that he was required to interpret the CDPA and subsequent UK case law as far as possible in line with EU law. So, after determining that the fabric in question was original under *Cofemel*, he also decided that it was a work of artistic craftmanship under UK law.

Standard of originality: The standard of originality under English law is ostensibly higher than the *Cofemel* AOIC standard. It requires that the creator of the work must have expended a degree of labor, skill, or judgment in creating the work.

From the 1976 case *George Hensher v. Restawile Upholstery (Lancs)* to *Response Clothing* in 2020, UK courts required this higher standard of originality for industrial designs or works of artistic craftsmanship. In 1976, *Hensher* held that an industrial design must be "artistic" before it can be protected by copyright. The case concerned sofa design. Hensher claimed that Restawile had infringed its copyright by making and selling several of its sofa designs. It won in the trial court, but the House of Lords upheld the Court of Appeal's reversal of the trial court decision. The Appeal Court said that Hensher's mass-produced furniture could not be considered to be artistic, and so could not be protected by copyright. This case is now clearly at odds with the position of the CJEU that there is only one test for whether a copyright work is original and that is whether it is its author's own intellectual contribution (AOIC). However, once again in *Reponse Clothing*, the judge felt bound to consider the artistic value of the fabric when determining if it was protectable as an original copyright work. UK courts need to clearly embrace *Cofemel* and dispense with other tests of artistic value or labor, skill, and judgment.

Permanent fixation of works: UK copyright law, unlike EU law, requires the permanent fixation of a work for it to obtain copyright protection. In the 1983 case of *Adam Ant, Merchandising Corporation of America v. Harpbond*, make-up was held to be unprotectable because "the marks would disappear when the artist would wash." However, a more recent UK case about designs embossed on foundation powder, *Islestarr Holdings Ltd. v. Aldi Stores Ltd.*, may have changed the law. It held that, despite the ephemeral nature of the design in the make-up, it could be protected by copyright. The court mentioned other works that might lack permanence—ice sculptures and wedding cakes—but could still be protected by copyright. It is clear from the CJEU decision in *Levola* that, as long as a work is "identifiable with sufficient precision and objectivity," it is protected under EU law without the need for permanent fixation. It is not clear whether the *Islestarr* case has brought UK law completely into line with *Levola* or not.

For fashion design, the requirement in UK law for permanent fixation is a potential problem. Designers create several types of art that lack permanent fixation. These include temporary designs on skin and hair with materials such as make-up or henna, as well as designs for store layouts and runway shows. It is not clear which types of impermanent displays UK law is willing to protect and which it might consider too transient and fleeting. Impermanent works are protected in other member states. Runway shows have been protected in France, store layouts in Italy, and perfume designs under Dutch law.

Changes to UK Law to Comply with EU Precedents

In 2016, the UK repealed part of its design law in response to an EU decision. Section 52 of the CDPA limited the period of copyright protection for any work that had been industrially manufactured (defined as more than 50 copies made) to 25 years to avoid the term of copyright being longer than registered design protection. After *Flos* made clear that there must be total cumulation between design protection and copyright protection, this provision was clearly incompatible with EU law, and the UK Parliament repealed it. However, there have been no legislative changes to the other areas where UK law diverges from EU law—the closed list of exceptions, the different standard of originality, and the requirement for permanent fixation of a work.

Just as the CJEU started to create a more unified EU copyright law and defined the overlap between design protection and other IPRs more clearly, the UK voted to leave the union. This has created more confusion between its copyright and design laws and those of its European neighbors.

UK Law and Brexit

The Status of CJEU Decisions

The UK government's White Paper on the effect of Brexit on the legal system issued in March 2020 stated that all CJEU decisions up to Brexit day (January

31, 2020) would have the same status as UK Supreme Court decisions, meaning they can only be departed from in limited circumstances. The White Paper did not make clear what the status of CJEU judgments would be post-Brexit. At a conference in New York, Mr. Justice Arnold of the UK High Court, said: "It is inevitable that future decisions of the CJEU will have persuasive value. The question is what persuasive weight they will have" ("Are You Braced for Brexit?" 2017). UK law, at least until it is updated in some way whether by legislative action or through court decisions, has been harmonized almost entirely with EU law over the last 50 years, so clearly EU law should continue to have persuasive value in UK courts. Design rights consist of the same rights, subject to the same legal provisions, whether in the UK or the member states that remain part of the EU.

Replacement Rights

From 2021, EU design rights (unregistered or registered) are no longer valid in the UK. EU rights owned before Brexit have been automatically replaced by UK rights without the need for any action on the part of existing rights holders. The UK IPO created approximately 700,000 registered designs in the UK from existing RCDs. These new rights will continue to protect the design in the UK for the same length of time that the original rights protected the design in the EU, so that a designer with an existing RCD will now have two identical rights, one valid in the EU and one in the UK.

After Brexit, the protection of a new design is available to designers in the UK in the following ways: They can still apply to the UK IPO for a national RDR or they can assert the old UK UDR. They will also have the choice of a new right which is the same as the existing UCD but for the UK only.

For a limited period, the new rights take the form of rights that continue previously owned EU design rights but for the UK market only. These will protect designs in the UK on the same basis as in the EU. These rights are called continuing rights. There is the continuing registered design right (CRDR) and continuing unregistered design right (CUDR). All CUDRs will cease to exist from January 1, 2024. CRDRs can exist for the same period as the original EU RCD, which means that they can last an initial 5 years but can be renewed, like the EU right, up to a maximum of 25 years.

Today, if a designer wants an unregistered design right for the protection of a new design, they have the choice of two rights in the UK and one in Europe. In the UK, the designer can assert the original UK UDR or a new right, which is the replacement of the UCD called the supplementary unregistered design right (SUD). Both of these rights provide protection for a design in the UK. The SUD exactly mirrors the UCD but it applies only in the UK. If a designer wants to protect unregistered rights in the EU member states, she can continue to use a UCD.

If a designer wants a registered design right in the two markets, she has two possibilities—a UK RDR for the UK or an RCD in the EU. The choice between EU and UK design rights is the biggest concern for fashion designers post-Brexit.

The difficulty with having a choice between two rights systems in Europe is that disclosing a design and obtaining protection under one regime may preclude a designer from seeking protection under the other regime.

If a design is first disclosed in the UK, then it would lack novelty in the EU and vice versa. It is unclear whether simultaneous disclosure in the UK and EU is possible and would enable a designer to obtain both an SUD (for the UK market) and a UCD (for the EU). The same question concerns registered rights. Would disclosure in the UK to obtain an RDR preclude the designer from obtaining an RCD?

Designers may need to think carefully where they first disclose a design. If a design is first disclosed in London, for example at London Fashion Week, it is protected in the UK market of 67 million people. But it is not clear whether this first disclosure in the UK loses the designer the right to the same design right in the EU—a much larger market. It is not clear if simultaneous disclosure will prevent a designer from obtaining rights in either territory based on the disclosure in the other territory.

Many fashion designers and brands rely on the UCD for seasonal collections because there are no registration requirements and it is a short-term right useful mainly against blatant copying. The UKIPO states in its post-Brexit IP information that "[f]irst disclosure in the EU will not establish a SUD right. It could destroy the novelty of the design should you later seek to establish UK unregistered rights" ("IP after 1 January 2021" 2020). Designers will need to consider carefully where to disclose their designs to make sure they are properly protected in their most important markets.

The original UK UDR provides up to 15 years' protection (longer than the UCD or the SUD) but, because it does not protect surface decorations or color—design features that are generally of great importance to fashion designers—it is not likely to take the place of the UCD. The scope of protection of the UK UDR is also narrower: It requires that the infringer has actual knowledge that the unauthorized dealing is infringement. Bridging these discrepancies poses a challenge for fashion designers after Brexit.

The Opportunity of Brexit

In some ways, Brexit could be seen as an opportunity for the UK to review and overhaul its law on the protection of designs. Currently, the design rights that have been created to provide a replacement for lost EU rights make the law more confusing, which is clearly unsatisfactory for the longer term. Any review should determine which protections the UK should retain from the existing regimes and how these design rights should fit with copyright protection.

Even without a broader review of design protection, clarity is lacking on how works of applied art are to be protected by copyright in the UK because of courts' unwillingness to wholeheartedly embrace CJEU precedents. If it was clearer that UK copyright law had followed CJEU precedents, from *Infopaq* to *Cofemel*, to protect all works of art, whether applied or not, if they were the AOIC, then UK designers could perhaps rely on copyright for wider protection in the whole article rather than just for graphic elements of any surface decoration. This could enable them to ignore the confusions of different unregistered design protections in the UK, and the problem of whether simultaneous protection of a design in the UK and EU is possible. However, it is unclear if UK courts will turn decisively away from English precedent cases such as *Hensher* and *Lucasfilms* to apply the unity of art standards clearly required in the CJEU precedents.

The UK Supreme Court may now depart from the CJEU precedents on the same basis that it overrules its own. Post-Brexit, CJEU case law will merely be persuasive, not binding, in the UK. Post-Brexit, the UK Parliament could also choose to modify UK copyright law without concerns about EU standards or CJEU case law, although global standards will still apply as the UK remains a party to the Berne, TRIPS, and WIPO conventions.

The UK is no longer required to use the exhaustive list of exceptions set out in the Infosoc Directive and it could, if it chose to, adopt a fair-use exception modeled on US law. The UK could also reinstate Section 52 of the CDPA to reduce a copyright's term to 25 years from first marketing in respect of industrial products. The UK could equally choose not to reinstate Section 52 and could finally clarify that all copyright works (whether fine or applied art) are protected by copyright if they are the AOIC. There are a number of choices to be made.

Initially post-Brexit, the overlap between design right protection in the UK and EU is unclear. The most important question for fashion designers is whether concurrent protection of EU and UK design rights is possible or whether they must choose either EU or UK protection. The UK courts' ambiguous attitude to originality, and the cumulation of copyrights and design rights are also going to concern designers until the law becomes clearer.

The EU design system has been very successful over its 20 plus years in existence, and it would be a shame for designers working in the UK to lose its valuable protections or have to choose between countries in which their designs could be protected.

Acknowledging that UK design law is currently overly complex and confusing the UK government ran a consultation in 2022 Calls for Views on Designs which received 57 responses, mainly from legal firms and trade bodies. In July 2022 the government published its own response to the issues. Other than suggesting that further consultations and legislative changes were likely on simplifying the UK design system the government response provided little detail on how this would occur or other concrete action. It stated that it would "investigate options to simplify the designs regime, in particular unregistered designs." It also promised to consider the relationship between copyright and design and provide more guidance for designers on using the design rights system. It acknowledged the problem, post-Brexit, of whether concurrent protection of a design in the EU and the UK is possible. However, in lieu of any concrete proposals or guidance, it stated that it would "seek additional stakeholder views and evidence on options to address the problems raised." Legislative improvements to the UK design rights system do not appear likely to be quick.

References

"Are You Braced for Brexit?" n.d. *Managing Intellectual Property*. Accessed May 15, 2022. https://www.managingip.com/article/b1kbpksfbn246h/are-you-braced-for-brexit.

Church, Olive, Estelle Derclaye, and Gilles Stupfler. 2019. "An Empirical Analysis of the Design Case Law of the EU Member States." *International Review of Intellectual Property and Competition Law* 50: 685–719. https://doi.org/10.1007/s40319-019-00813-0.

Consultation Outcome Call for Views on Design. 2022. GOV.UK. July 12, 2022. https://www.gov.uk/government/consultations/reviewing-the-designs-framework-call-for-views/outcome/call-for-views-on-designs-government-response#executive-summary.

Haskel, Jonathan, and Annarosa Pesole. 2011. "Design Services, Design Rights and Design Life Lengths in the UK." *SSRN Electronic Journal* pp. 36. http://doi.org/10.2139/ssrn.2707093.

"Intellectual Property after 1 January 2021." 2020. GOV.UK. October 28, 2020. https://www.gov.uk/government/news/intellectual-property-after-1-january-2021.

Moore, Kathryn. 2015. "Anatomy of a Design Regime." *Indiana Journal of Global Legal Issues* 22 (2): 789–808.

Nicas, Jack. 2018. "Apple and Samsung End Smartphone Patent Wars." The New York Times, June 27, 2018, sec. Technology. https://www.nytimes.com/2018/06/27/technology/apple-samsung-smartphone-patent.html.

Rosati, Eleonora. 2020. "Italian Supreme Court Applies CJEU Cofemel Decision to Makeup Store Layout." The IPKat (blog). May 10, 2020. https://ipkitten.blogspot.com/2020/05/italian-supreme-court-applies-cjeu.html.

———. 2022a. "How Do You Protect an Iconic Handbag? Milan Court Considers IP Rights Vesting in Longchamp's Le Pliage." The IPKat (blog). March 10, 2022. https://ipkitten.blogspot.com/2022/03/how-do-you-protect-iconic-handbag-milan.html.

———. 2022b. "[Guest Post] Second Time Is a Charm: Danish Design Company Wins Plant Box War." The IPKat (blog). May 8, 2022. https://ipkitten.blogspot.com/2022/05/guest-post-second-time-is-charm-danish.html.

Schovsbo, Jens. 2020. *Design Protection in the Nordic Countries: Welcome to the Smörgåsbord*. SSRN Scholarly Paper 3526173. Rochester, NY: Social Science Research Network. https://doi.org/10.2139/ssrn.3526173.

"The Copyright Panel | Svensk Form." n.d. Accessed May 16, 2022. https://svenskform.se/en/about-svensk-form/the-copyright-panel/.

Woolgar, Alex. 2020. "[Guest Post] These Boots Are Made for Walking...and Not for Copyright Protection." The IPKat (blog). June 28, 2020. https://ipkitten.blogspot.com/2020/06/guest-post-these-boots-are-made-for.html.

6 Beyond Intellectual Property

Other Dimensions of Protections for Fashion Design

Introduction

The three previous chapters have focused on how intellectual property laws in the US and EU protect creativity in fashion design. The US and Europe are where the modern fashion industry started and where the largest and best-known fashion companies are still based. They also remain the two largest fashion markets in the world (although Asia, and in particular China, is fast catching up). Thus, these jurisdictions are the places where the law is most developed in relation to design protection.

This chapter explores additional modes of protection for design and creativity beyond IP laws. It starts by considering who and what in the fashion business most require protection in the twenty-first century. Using this framework, it looks at four dimensions that protection and regulation of design and creativity might take beyond IPRs.

Creativity without Law

It is a truism that it is never just laws that regulate our actions and endeavors. The creativity, originality, and inventiveness that IP law has developed to protect have been protected in different times, places, and contexts by all kinds of regulators. Despite the IPRs available to designers in Europe and in the US, legislation is probably not the most important means of regulating behavior in the fashion industry in either location. We know that many well-known creative endeavors and industries rely less on laws for the encouragement and protection of creativity than on other methods (and fashion design is often noted as one of these "negative spaces" for law).

Yochai Benkler has argued for some time that strong intellectual property rights are becoming obsolete in a networked digital economy as they impede, rather than facilitate, innovation. In 2017, in "Law, Innovation, and Collaboration in Networked Economy and Society," he said that "knowledge flows in learning networks, mixing [...] market and nonmarket models and motivations," and innovation is better understood as a collaborative, networked activity (Benkler 2017, 231). The concept of authorship in intellectual property law which focuses

DOI: 10.4324/9781003091400-7

on a sole creator working alone has probably never been an accurate depiction of many creative endeavors. It is certainly not particularly accurate for fashion design. However, IP law relies heavily on this concept to allocate legal protection to individual authors for some endeavors and not others.

Activities with higher fixed costs (such as film and opera) seem to benefit more from IP protection than endeavors that rely more on collaboration (Sprigman 2017). For activities such as fashion design, where IP protections are available, but often not well suited to protecting creativity, other methods of controlling harmful behaviors such as blatant copying and free riding need careful examination. Much research remains to be done on the effects of IP protection on creativity in different activities.

What and Whom to Protect?

As simply stated as possible, the ideal protections of fashion design would ensure that innovation and creativity are encouraged, but that copying and free riding on the work of others are discouraged. For some time, there have been calls for more legal regulation of the fashion industry, mainly because of the development of fast fashion. Fast fashion, with its excess of cheap products (which are often fakes and knock-offs), has hugely detrimental environmental and social impacts on the planet. The goal of reducing the environmental and social impacts of fast fashion is consistent with the goal of ensuring that creative design flourishes while blatant copying, counterfeiting, and piracy are limited.

The Twenty-First-Century Fashion Industry

The structure of the fashion industry has already changed a great deal since its start in the eighteenth century. This evolution is described in Chapter 1. The hallmarks of the early industry were that fashionable clothing was available only to the very wealthy, that the center of the industry was in Paris, and that a small group of elite Parisian designers of haute couture dictated what was fashionable and what was not. This hierarchical organization made it simpler for norms to monitor the industry and protect creativity.

Today, the fashion industry is far less hierarchical and centralized. Good design does not just emanate from Paris and the other fashion capitals. It is created and available worldwide, beyond a small, wealthy elite. Sumptuary codes have largely been abolished, and a global middle class craves more and more luxury goods; one of the most popular luxuries is clothing. While this democratization of the fashion business has generally been a positive development, it has also led to a huge increase in the amount of clothing produced and purchased. The industry has continued to change rapidly in the twenty-first century; it has become more global, and it relies more and more on digital technology.

Globalization and Digital Technology

In the twenty-first century, the old hierarchy of fashion design continues to break down. Although designers, and certainly the luxury conglomerates that employ some of the best-known designers, remain disproportionately based in the four fashion capitals, there are fashion designers working all over the world. These designers create many types of fashion at a variety of price points.

Developments in transportation and the liberalization of trade through GATT and other free-trade agreements have enabled a severing of the geographic link between the designers and the production stages in the creation of fashion. Since 2000, the relocation of manufacturing to the Global South has led to a huge rise in cheaply manufactured clothing. Consumers in the industrialized world now buy almost twice as much clothing as they did at the end of the last century.

Beyond these developments in transportation, communications, and the liberalization of trade, a raft of newer digital technologies are poised to transform the industry, including the protection of design. Some of these developments have been discussed briefly in Chapter 1. Designers can use AI to analyze trends and create new fashion designs. Three-dimensional manufacturing is also likely to create other new business models for design (and manufacturing). Blockchain technologies are changing design (and retail). These digital developments all have the capacity to aid and promote the process of design and protect creativity.

Counterfeiting and Piracy: A Danger to Creativity?

Counterfeiting and piracy have existed for centuries, but the democratization of luxury and the huge increase in sales of branded luxury fashion items mourned by commentators such as Agins and Thomas have led to a parallel rise in counterfeiting and piracy. New, less well-off consumers want to satisfy their cravings for the branded luxury offerings they see everywhere by buying cheaper fakes as well as, or instead of, the real thing (McNeil and Riello 2016, 265).

Digital communications platforms have also provided counterfeiters and pirates with new ways to distribute their products globally and reach new customers. Their anonymity helps them evade tracking, and online marketplaces have provided limited assistance to law enforcement, brand owners, and designers attempting to combat the trade in fakes ("Social Media Influencers and Counterfeit Goods" 2021). This often makes protection of creativity harder to achieve.

Clearly, some trade is lost by designers because of the growth in counterfeit and pirated products. However, the analyses of the sale of counterfeit goods are both inaccurate and incomplete. First, there are a range of different stakeholders to consider in the real versus fake debate beyond IPR owners, consumers, and governments. Second, there are several types of products beyond the binary distinction of real or fake. Finally, there are both positive and negative externalities from the sale of counterfeits and fakes. These issues are discussed in more depth in Chapter 1. All of this makes it hard to untangle the many different effects on designers of the sales of counterfeit and fake goods.

The usual narrative on counterfeiting and piracy considers IPR owners such as designers to be victims of duplicitous customers and weak IP enforcement by governments. However, there are designers who have benefited from the sale of fakes and have even gone as far as faking their own product to suggest their exclusivity. Designers may even get new ideas from fakes that change some aspect of the copied product.

The fashion pyramid ranges from haute couture at the top to fast fashion at the bottom. The legal line between real and fake is drawn somewhat arbitrarily near the bottom of the pyramid. Some designers call any fast fashion copy of their goods a counterfeit or fake; others only focus on those products which copy trademarks. Some IPR owners, such as Rolex, consider any alteration of its products to render them fakes. Rolex timepieces that are repaired to include any non-authentic Rolex parts (or parts that are not approved by Rolex) are transformed in Rolex's view from genuine Rolex watches into fakes or counterfeits.

As discussed in Chapter 1, even within the fake category there are several different types of fake, from outright fakes to those that are barely distinguishable from the real products, made in the same factories as the real thing, perhaps on a third shift. Fakes could be further subdivided into two categories: Goods where everyone knows that they are not manufactured by the IPR owner (generally because of their poor materials and lower price point) and well-executed copies that deceive customers.

The variety of types of fakes requires us to be cautious about accepting all of the harms and financial losses ascribed in the reports of rampant counterfeiting and piracy and see a more nuanced picture. While some fakes will displace sales of originals, there are several other possibilities. Some consumers purchasing fakes may be encouraged to buy genuine products, and the sale of fakes may also speed up the fashion cycle as wealthy buyers shy away from products which are copied a lot. Protection for designers from "fakes" needs to take into account that some copying in the fashion business is how designers create.

Future Protections for Creative Fashion Design

The protection of creativity in fashion design should also encourage a reduction in the social and economic harms of the fast fashion model. While this model might be fleetingly financially beneficial to fast fashion purveyors, it should raise red flags for everyone else. Many fashion industry stakeholders, particularly in the EU, are starting to recognize that we need to reduce these harms and make fashion a more sustainable industry with a lower carbon footprint. This will require significant work by all stakeholders: Designers will have to design more sustainable clothing, which will require creativity. Manufacturers will have to avoid materials and processes that cause environmental damage and also pay their workers a fair wage. Retailers will need to embrace new business models beyond selling as much clothing as possible. Governments will need to monitor the activity of these stakeholders and pass and enforce laws to encourage more sustainable practices for the design, manufacture, and sale of clothing. Consumers will need to educate themselves about the harms caused by the purchase of disposable clothing and start to use other circular business models such as renting and resale.

Laws and regulations should help drive these positive changes, but social, technological, and economic drivers are likely to be just as, if not more, important.

Incentives in the future need to focus on rewarding designers who have succeeded in creating more sustainable and ethical textiles and clothing. Good design can help make the fashion industry more sustainable and reduce the harms caused by fast fashion. Designers are well placed to drive that creativity, but other stakeholders will also play a part in these changes. Consumers will need to develop new norms of behavior around purchasing fashion, including engaging in circular economy business models such as renting, resale, and recycling. Renting new looks or special occasion clothes instead of buying them, and accessing repair services to keep clothes in use for longer before disposal need to become new social norms. Manufacturers will also need to revolutionize their supply chains to reduce pollution and waste within the fashion industry. They could also use technology to replace humans for tedious or dangerous work while preserving creativity and roles for skilled artisans and craftspeople.

The Different Dimensions That Regulate Behavior

Binding versus Voluntary Regulations

A variety of drivers beyond intellectual property laws could assist in promoting a more creative fashion industry where there are strong incentives and protections for designers to create sustainable fashion. The drivers that act on and regulate behavior are often divided into binding forces, such as laws and regulation, and voluntary forces, such as social norms and ethics. Both are important. Writing about the phenomenon of cultural appropriation and the role of IP laws in "The Law and Ethics of Appropriation," Mathias Siems argued "that law's role should be limited, leaving space for the role of ethical considerations" (Siems 2019, 422).

As this book shows, fitting the protection of fashion design into IP law's division of creativity between applied and fine art over the last 200 years has often been problematic, whether under the US or EU legal systems. The limited amount of empirical research already shows that many creative people often do not rely on legal protection but use other means to protect their creativity. The fashion industry has a long history as an important part of society, and a variety of voluntary methods to regulate behavior have long played an important role in the regulation of the industry.

Existing Structures of Control

Commentators have discussed many other structures that control and protect creativity. Like law, these structures tend to benefit the dominant players in the industry; they include the role of institutions, assumptions, and the existing organization of society. All play a role in defining behavior and regulating creativity.

In *The Color of Creatorship*, Anjali Vats argues that the institutions of intellectual property law are deeply intertwined with racism and racial capitalism, and that the goal of intellectual property is the creation of private property and the ownership of ideas by the dominant group. IP law is shaped by culture, identity, and power and so it tends to protect White creativity while assigning traditional knowledge, music, shared cultural heritage, and customs (often created by indigenous people and people of color) to the public domain (Vats 2020, 207).

Martha Buskirk also focuses on the strength of the dominant group, although her dominant group is corporate interests. In *Is It Ours? Art, Copyright and Public Interest*, she calls authorship the central organizing principle both for copyright and for art and describes it as a "convenient fiction" and a "fundamentally arbitrary boundary." Her view is that current copyright "has much more to do with corporate interests than with protecting the rights of individual creators" (Buskirk 2021, 8). The Supreme Court decision in *Star Athletica*, for the dominant brand against the upstart, tends to back up her argument.

Florence Palpaceur explains in her chapter "Voluntary versus Binding Forms of Regulation," in the book *Unmaking the Global Sweatshop*, that the neoliberal and market-oriented values of corporations in a globally deregulated market have become structural impediments to attempts by state actors and NGOs to establish more ethical production systems (Prentice and Neve 2017, 60).

Few Turn to Laws

Jessica Sibley noted in "The Eureka Myth: Creators, Innovators, and Everyday Intellectual Property" that few creative people turn directly to the law even when copying or counterfeiting of their work occurs. In fact, many of the artists Sibley interviewed were not particularly concerned if others copied their work (Sibley 2015, 2). Almost every review of how EU design law is working seems to confirm Sibley's finding that many designers either do not know enough about their rights or think of them as theoretical and decline to pursue them in practice for a variety of reasons, often cost.

Kate Darling and Aaron Perzanowski also noted, in their work *Creativity without Law: Challenging the Assumptions of Intellectual Property*, that law is not central to most designers; it is generally something that is considered after other modes of protecting creativity have been used. They argue that legal scholarship demonstrates "the value of putting law on the edges, rather than the centre, of scholarly analysis." They describe the importance of non-legal factors such as "norms, community dynamics, emotions and market forces" which have far more effect on creativity and innovation and suggest that we should take these factors into account in crafting laws (Darling and Perzanowski 2017).

In "Copyright and Creative Incentives: What We Know and What We Don't," Christopher Sprigman described intellectual property ownership as not an end in itself but rather a means to an end. The law may sometimes shape behavior, but it does not define it. If we ask whether intellectual property law is itself an adequate or appropriate incentive to produce, we are asking the wrong question; virtually no one creates because they want a copyright, a trademark, a patent, or a trade secret. However, they may turn to the law to protect their creativity if they think that it will provide an adequate remedy (Sprigman 2017, 477).

Academic studies, reports, and reviews by national IP offices, the EU Commission, and the OECD clearly show that law generally works best for big players with deep pockets who can afford to hire attorneys and shape their businesses to protect their intellectual property rights. Certainly, IP litigation can seem like extortion for those with fewer financial resources. Many small designers do not have the same kind of sophisticated IP strategies that larger companies do, and recourse to the law to protect their creativity is the exception rather than the norm. For many creative designers, other methods of protecting creativity are as, if not more, important than IP law.

Expanding the Dimensions of Protection

Lawrence Lessig and Christian Katzenbach have both described four forces that play a role in regulating behavior in different areas of human activity and go beyond the binary division of binding versus voluntary. Their categorizations of the forces acting on cyberspace (Lessig 1999) and on the online gaming industry (Katzenbach 2018) focus not just on mandatory and binding regulation on the one hand and voluntary social and ethical norms on the other, but on a more complex set of interrelated forces that include technology and economics. Both Lessig and Katzenbach include law as important to the regulation of creativity but acknowledge that it is not the major regulator in the sectors that they discuss.

Lessig and Katzenbach each include law, social norms, and technology as regulatory forces. Lessig also includes the role of market forces in regulating cyberspace,[1] and Katzenbach uses the term "discursive dimension" to describe the ongoing debate in the online gaming industry about creativity, authorship, and originality. As discussed in Chapter 2, a similar debate about the concepts of creativity, authorship, and originality has taken place in the fashion and other design industries for over 200 years.

The Technology Experts Group of the EUIPO considers Lessig's framework of four regulators so important that it has adapted it to use to review all the impacts of new technologies on the EU intellectual property law framework. Its starting point is that each new technology can create both opportunities for IP in terms of new creativity and threats in terms of its ability to facilitate infringement of rights. The group therefore states that the impact of new technologies on IP should be reviewed from four angles, the market, the law, social context, and the technology itself ("Study on the Impact of AI" 2022).

Like Lessig, Katzenbach noted that each dimension of protection is distinct, but they are also interrelated and interdependent. The object of his study was to "understand [...] how different modes of governance frame and regulate imitation and innovation in game production." Katzenbach noted that, when interviewing video game creators, he was surprised by how unimportant laws were for the creators of the games: "In the interviews we conducted, we were confronted with a striking neglect of the regulative dimension both with regard to the tension between imitation and innovation as well as to legal aspects of game production in general" (Katzenbach 2018, 16). The game creators he spoke to would generally reach first for another method to protect their creative endeavors before considering the legal dimension.

Four Dimensions for the Protection of Creativity in Fashion Design

The rest of this chapter reviews protections for fashion design focusing on how they can provide an optimal balance between innovation and creativity, and public access (the supposed aim of IPRs) under the following four dimensions, which are similar to those defined by Lessig:

- **The legal and regulatory dimension:** As IPRs have been discussed in previous chapters, this chapter considers some non-IP laws that might assist fashion designers in the protection of their creativity.
- **The social and ethical dimension** describes how evolving social norms in the global fashion industry might be used to protect fashion design.
- **The technological dimension** considers some of the many developments in digital technology that might protect creativity in fashion design. Undoubtedly, there are and will be others.
- **The economic dimension** describes some of the aspects of the marketplace and its participants that might act as regulators for creativity in fashion design.

These dimensions all interact, co-evolve, and overlap.

The Legal and Regulatory Dimension

The fashion industry is a global industry, but laws are still mostly jurisdiction-specific. The previous three chapters have already shown that IPRs differ between the two big fashion markets of Europe and the US, and that this can create inconsistencies and difficulties in combating copying and protecting creativity for designers, although the differences in laws do not seem to have had a particularly large impact on the way in which European and American designers operate.

Although intellectual property contains the obvious legal rights for the protection of creativity, there are other laws that might assist designers attempting to prohibit copying and protect their creative work. Law that is used to limit a harm in one area can limit the party undertaking the harmful activity in such a way that they are prevented or restricted from causing other harmful effects through their actions. For example, a law to prohibit making products with child labor might also decrease the amount of counterfeiting since many counterfeit goods are produced in factories that use child labor.

Two areas where laws that regulate one activity might also control copying and protect creativity are labor and environmental laws. Often, those who flout legal protections in these areas are the same people who produce counterfeit and knock-off goods. In an era of fast fashion, there are added benefits to encouraging sustainable behavior. Regulators on both sides of the Atlantic seem to have recently decided that stricter regulation of the fashion industry is needed to drive it to adopt more sustainable behavior.

Expanding Labor Laws

Many of those violating labor law are also engaged in pirating others' designs. Kristin Sutor suggests, in "Fast-Fashion, One Day You're In, and the Next Day You're Out," that labor laws, in particular the Fair Labor Standards Act (FLSA), could be used to protect against both piracy and unfair labor practices. Fast fashion retailers who manufacture copies of original designs in sweatshop conditions overseas could be enjoined under a portion of the FLSA known as the "hot goods provision." This provision enables the secretary of labor to stop anyone from transporting or selling goods produced in unfair work conditions. If the hot goods provision applied internationally to fast fashion manufacturers and retailers who purchased or shipped goods produced in violation of fair labor standards, this would prevent both the unfair labor practices in the factories and the sale of pirated goods in the US marketplace.

Sutor argues that applying the hot goods provision to clothing manufactured overseas as well as to clothing manufactured in the US would incentivize brands to take greater control of their supply chains, producing the dual advantages of ensuring compliance with labor laws and of giving workers suffering from unfair labor conditions in overseas factories an entity to sue for relief (Sutor 2020, 889). The greater enforcement of labor laws might also decrease the manufacturing of counterfeit and knock-off goods since it would increase the costs of production for fast fashion retailers. If it was more costly to run an unethical company using cheap labor and copying designs, then it should become less difficult to compete using creative designers and avoiding copying designs.

Mandating Corporate Social Responsibility

The fashion industry has largely escaped regulation for the last quarter century, in spite of widespread concern about its labor and environmental abuses (Gamble 2022). However, calls for this to change are increasing from all quarters, including government, NGOs, consumers, and even industry players themselves.

There are a number of laws that mandate supply chain transparency with a view to enabling customers to understand where goods come from and whether they are harming either the environment or the workers in the supply chain (or both). Some are specific to the fashion industry; others apply to all companies.

In the UK, the Modern Slavery Act of 2015 requires companies that operate in the UK and have annual turnovers greater than £36 million to publish annual transparency statements, called Modern Slavery Statements, setting out what they are doing to stop slavery and forced labor practices in their business and supply chains. The law provides no private right of action, but a company disobeying it can be subject to a fine. As with the hot goods provision in the FLSA, the focus of this law is on poor labor practices overseas. While the law does not prohibit these labor practices, it does require companies to publish them and explain what they are doing to stop them.

In France, the Duty of Vigilance Law of 2017 applies to both human rights and environmental concerns. It requires French companies with over 5000 employees in France, or 10,000 worldwide, to establish and implement vigilance plans to identify and prevent abuses. Unlike the UK law, there is a private right of action to compel the publication of a report.

The Australian government is also considering similar legislation which would require all companies with revenue of over A$100 million to publish an annual statement of the steps that they are taking to address forced labor in their supply chains. Like the UK Modern Slavery Act, there is no individual cause of action.

The EU proposed a new Directive on Corporate Sustainability and Due Diligence (CSR Directive) in February 2022 (*Proposal for a Directive on Corporate Sustainability* 2022). It is the culmination of two or more years of work in the EU on a legal framework for sustainable corporate governance as part of the way to achieve the European Green Deal. It requires that companies investigate their suppliers to ensure that they are not using forced labor and/or child labor, and they must also create a plan to ensure that their strategy is compatible with limiting global warming in line with the Paris Agreement. The directive will add to the fiduciary duties of company directors that "when fulfilling their duty to act in the best interest of the company" they must take into account "the human rights, climate change and environmental consequences of their decisions." It also provides those harmed by abuses within the supply chain with a right of action against the company. It applies to all EU companies with 500 employees or more and over €150 million in turnover and to smaller companies which are in high-impact sectors, one of which is apparel and footwear.

If it is adopted, as is likely, this directive will require companies operating in the EU to focus much more attention on their supply chain and have a business strategy to limit their impact on global warming. It will also provide more protection of the human rights of workers in the supply chain. Authorities will be able to fine companies who do not identify and end adverse human rights and environmental impacts in their supply chains. After adoption by the EU Parliament, member states will have two years to transpose the CSR Directive into national law. Companies in the fashion business operating in the EU (a major world market) will need to integrate sustainability, and in particular human rights and environmental due diligence, into their corporate governance.

Two EU initiatives directed at achieving the goals of the European Green Deal and the EU Strategy for Sustainable and Circular Textiles are the Product Environmental Footprint (PEF) labeling scheme and the proposed Ecodesign for Sustainable Products regulation. The PEF scheme was first proposed by the European Commission in 2013 as part of the Building a Single Market for Green Products initiative. It will require manufacturers to include product labels that convey a product's environmental impact in simple language to help consumers make "greener" purchasing decisions. The French Agency for Ecological Transition (Ademe) is currently testing proposals for collecting the data and creating the labels. France intends to require a label detailing climate impact to be attached to clothing by 2023. The EU is also working on PEF labeling with representatives from the textile industry and plans to complete its work by 2024. The Ecodesign for Sustainable Products regulation is slated to require binding product-specific design requirements for textiles in terms of "durability, reusability, reparability, fibre-to-fibre recyclability and mandatory recycled fibre content."

In the US, New York is the first state to attempt to mandate social responsibility specifically for fashion businesses. The New York Fashion Act (BIAGGI 2021), introduced in 2021 and supported by a host of non-profits and many designers, would apply specifically to fashion companies with annual revenues over $100 million worldwide that do business in New York. It would require them to map out at least 50% of their supply chain, disclose their environmental and social impacts, and set up targets for improvements. The proposed law also contains sanctions. Those in violation risk fines of up to 2% of their annual revenues, with those fines to be used for environmental justice projects. The New York attorney general would also publish an annual list of companies found to be noncompliant.

As the first US legislation to focus specifically on the social and environmental accountability of the largely unregulated fashion industry, the New York Fashion Act has been lauded by many environmentally conscious designers and non-profits (Friedman 2022). The New Standards Institute praised the law, stating that: "Fashion retailers and manufacturers operate in a regulatory-free vacuum … [which] has led to a global race to the bottom, where the companies that have the least regard for the environment and for workers have the greatest competitive edge" (TFL 2020a).

The main benefit of these supply chain transparency laws is that they may make it easier for another regulator of the fashion industry—consumers—to regulate the industry using their economic power. If consumers refuse to buy products from companies with supply chains filled with abuses, this will discourage companies from racing to the bottom. It is companies that "have the least regard for the environment and for workers" that will be targeted by these laws on labeling and ecodesign. This could help indirectly promote creativity and decrease copying by targeting companies that often engage in copying.

However, these attempts to use laws to mandate good behavior have often been criticized as dishonest and ineffective. NGOs often complain that the laws only apply to a small group of very large undertakings, when much of the fashion supply chain involves much smaller companies. The CSR Directive applies only to a tiny fraction of companies in the EU. The non-profit coalition Make the Label Count says that the PEF methodology to measure a garment's sustainability "downplays or excludes critical environmental impacts and does not reflect the EU's own sustainability and circularity goals" (Chua 2021).

According to Indiana University law professor Karen E. Bravo, these efforts also ignore the other stakeholders in industry such as nation-states, and the structure of the global free trade system, which are both implicated in exploitation. She states that the "complexity of the origins and nature of the forms of contemporary exploitation" means that these laws "direct […] attention toward individual bad-guy perpetrators and away from state policies and structures that contribute to the exploitation [they] purport [...] to target" (Bravo 2019, 5).

Importantly, expecting this type of regulation to protect creativity in design is based on several assumptions: First, the somewhat untested assumption that consumers will react to supply chain abuses by withdrawing their support from companies that engage in them; second, that these abuses occur because corporations create these conditions; and third, that it is always fast fashion and companies producing a lot of knock-offs that treat workers and the environment most poorly. As discussed in the section on the social and ethical dimensions of protection, luxury brands seem just as likely to be in this group.

Measuring CSR Reporting and Compliance

An additional major problem with implementing this type of CSR regulation derives from the current lack of global uniform data standards, as well as the ability of companies to use voluntary schemes to comply with many reporting requirements.

Unlike for financial reporting, there is no internationally agreed-upon standard to measure or calculate environmental, social, and governance (ESG) factors, "nor a process for auditing to ensure compliance against such a common standard" (Fanarakis 2022). This means that "greenwashing" is common, and it is hard for the recipients of information such as investors and purchasers to understand what it means. Even where there are some measurement standards, the conflicting regulatory regimes between the US and EU harm the potential of these socially beneficial changes in behavior (Lashitew 2021).

The European Coalition for Corporate Justice director, Claudia Saller, commenting on the proposed CSR Directive, stated, "companies should not be allowed to shift their responsibilities on to their suppliers or to get away with harm by participating in voluntary industry schemes" ("Dangerous Gaps" 2022). These laws often allow companies to offload their obligations to perform due diligence and verification to third parties or the very suppliers committing the abuses.

According to the Brookings Report, the differences in approach between the US and the EU are that the US "is following a laissez-faire approach with sustainable investing and disclosure being guided by voluntary, private-sector-led processes, protocols, and guidelines." This is an approach that relies on peer pressure and image. The EU approach mandates measurement for businesses with regard to Paris Agreement goals of achieving climate neutrality by 2050. It includes stronger oversight and generally more transparency of business activities. This means that, although greenwashing is possible, it is much harder.

The approach that mandates clear, legally required standards is likely to lead to a "better public understanding of the positive and negative externalities that corporations create, allowing the market to reward 'good' ones and penalize 'bad' ones" (Lashitew 2021). If consumers can rely on corporate measurements to understand the fast fashion supply chain, it is more likely that stronger social norms will develop against poor business practices. This is likely to lead to more opportunities for creativity and ethical fashion designers. This currently looks more likely in the EU than in the US.

Certification Marks

Certification marks have some of the characteristics of trademarks. They can be used to signal information to consumers, but in this case about sustainability and other product attributes, rather than sources of origin. They are used in both the US and EU. An EU certification mark is defined as a mark

> capable of distinguishing goods or services which are certified by the proprietor of the mark in respect of material, mode of manufacture of goods, or performance of services, quality, accuracy, or other characteristics, with the exception of geographical origin, from goods and services which are not so certified.

The EU also has an Ecolabel mark for products that comply with rigorous ecological criteria.

In the US, certification marks can also include geographical indications. A certification mark is supposed to show that goods have met certain standards, but, like ESG reporting in the US, certification often requires self-certification rather than meeting mandatory measures.

Consumers are typically the driving force behind the demand for certification marks in the US marketplace (Barron 2007, 415). Trusted certification marks might provide a way to signal to consumers that clothing was made by a reputable company with a transparent supply chain. The EU PEF labeling scheme described above could achieve this and could assist ethical companies that wanted to protect and promote creative design and well-run supply chains by providing them with a way to communicate this to consumers.

However, currently, the sheer number of certification marks globally dilute their effect. Many of them mean little to consumers and thus do not affect their purchasing behavior (Bennett 2017).

The Social and Ethical Dimension

The social and ethical dimension consists of the unwritten assumptions, beliefs, and attitudes which guide our behavior. No attempt is made here as to an exhaustive study of the enormous variety of cultural, social, and ethical norms, attitudes, and assumptions that surround fashion. The discussion is on how developing norms for corporate social responsibility (CSR), and designers' use of social media might promote and protect creativity in the fashion business.

Developing CSR Norms in a Global Environment

The increasingly global and digital world is leading to changes in the norms of behavior in the fashion industry. In "Unmaking Global Sweatshops," Florence

Palpacuer discussed the rise in voluntary regulation by companies of the conditions of clothing workers (Prentice and Neve 2017, 59). There are many signs that some new norms are forming around the social responsibility of corporations and the need for them to engage in practices such as environmental sustainability, ensuring labor right protections, and restraining counterfeiting and piracy.

However, although almost all large companies now tell us that they measure their impact on sustainability (and the number of companies using the most comprehensive Global Reporting Initiative (GRI) standards has increased one hundredfold over the last two decades), it turns out that reporting does not necessarily signal progress. As discussed in the previous section, because of the lack of clear standards, ESG measurements and reporting are "often nonstandard, incomplete, imprecise, and misleading" (Pucker 2021).

While the fashion business has so far mostly avoided regulation, there have been increasing international efforts to expand the ethical duties of corporations in society. In 1999, the UN secretary-general at the time, Kofi Annan, announced a voluntary initiative that brought together businesses and UN agencies to encourage global businesses to play a part in tackling global social issues. The UN Global Compact set out ten voluntary principles derived from core international law sources in the areas of human rights, labor protections, the environment, and measures against corruption. Since 2000, around 8000 companies in 160 countries have endorsed the principles. The Global Compact supports the concept that private businesses have social and ethical duties that go beyond just obeying minimal legal requirements.

In 2003, Annan also appointed a UN special representative on business and human rights to put together a set of guiding principles for businesses on how they could protect human rights. The "Protect, Respect and Remedy" framework that was created is supposed to guide corporate action. It has led some governments to begin mandating a certain level of social responsibility for global corporations. As discussed above, these efforts could limit unfair copying and counterfeiting as many of the producers who ignore environmental and labor protections are also the ones creating knock-offs and counterfeit copies of fashion designs.

In 2015, the UN adopted a list of 17 Sustainable Development Goals (SDGs) to guide nations' economic policies until 2030. These goals are wide-ranging, including goals for more sustainable agriculture, energy, and consumption. The UN has integrated these SDGs into industry in partnerships. One of these, the Conscious Fashion Campaign, attempts to get fashion industry event leaders to integrate the SDGs in areas such as climate action, clean energy, and responsible production into their business models (UN Office for Partnerships n.d.).

The UN Climate Change Conference COP 21, in Paris in 2015, had governments agreeing to stronger and more ambitious policies on climate change. The resulting Paris Agreement determined that change had to come not just from governments but also from businesses and other stakeholders.

The Global Compact, Protect, Respect, and Remedy framework, SDG partnerships with industry, and the Paris Agreement all acknowledge that global businesses have a duty to help combat the world's environmental and social problems.

These initiatives are leading to changes in attitudes about corporate behavior and responsibility (Monseau 2017, 68).

The UN has focused on an industry partnership with the fashion industry, calling it the second most polluting industry in the world and stating that, in terms of carbon emissions, "the industry is responsible for more than all international flights and maritime shipping combined" (UN Office for Partnerships n.d.). The figures used by the UN and others to encourage action from the fashion industry are disputed (Wicker 2020), but the UN efforts have led to many fashion industry stakeholders at least starting to become more serious about their contributions to global social problems.

Fashion designers and other industry stakeholders have created at least two voluntary initiatives to reduce the negative environmental impacts of the global fashion industry. In 2018, over 100 fashion industry stakeholders, from individual designers to well-known brands such as Adidas, luxury conglomerates such as Kering, and even fast fashion retailers such as H&M, combined forces to create the Fashion Industry Charter for Climate Action (United Nations 2018). Its goal is to achieve net-zero greenhouse gas emissions in the global fashion industry by 2050. In 2019, a number of UN agencies, including the Global Compact, created the UN Alliance for Sustainable Fashion to help contribute to achieving some of the SDG through coordinated action in the fashion sector.

Many NGOs focused on human rights and the environment have also spotlighted the fashion industry and its impact on labor and the environment. The Ellen MacArthur Foundation's circular economy report, "A New Textiles Economy: Redesigning Fashion's Future," outlines how circular economy business principles could transform the fashion industry and end its role as a major source of pollution ("A New Textiles Economy" 2017). KnowTheChain, a collaborative partnership between several business and human rights non-profits, produces a report on the impact of forced labor on the supply chains of apparel and footwear companies so that companies can benchmark their progress in cleaning up their supply chains. Another industry stakeholder and non-profit partnership, the Sustainable Apparel Coalition (SAC), produces a tool called the Higgs Index so that apparel companies can standardize the measurement of value chain sustainability.

The UN spotlight on the pollution caused by fast fashion, its fashion industry alliances, and the various initiatives by human rights activists, non-profits, and industry stakeholders have undoubtedly encouraged the fashion industry to work toward cleaning up its supply chains, educating consumers about the environmental damage, and reducing labor abuses in the industry. This has led to some changes in business practices. However, the companies making the most voluntary changes to their supply chains are rarely the companies that engage in counterfeiting and piracy or the creation of fast fashion knock-offs. The lack of clear and standardized ways to measure corporate environmental and social impact means that even companies that try hard to change their practices are disappointed by their lack of progress on achieving real change. Patagonia founder and environmental pioneer Yvon Chouinard is no longer optimistic about corporate ability to change behavior. He lamented, "It's all growth, growth, growth—and that's what's destroying the planet" (Pucker 2021).

Achieving the goal of reducing fashion industry damage is of paramount importance to a vibrant and creative fashion industry. The fact that none of the major stakeholders in the industry can agree on the amount of environmental damage done by fashion, and the lack of coordination on the development of globally acceptable disclosure standards jeopardize these efforts.

As norms change in the industry, it may become less and less acceptable to be engaged in unethical labor and environmental practices, and voluntary corporate ESG reporting may gradually act to regulate fashion by enabling consumers to avoid less ethical companies. The impact of consumers as regulators is discussed further in the economic dimension section.

Social Media Norms

One of the biggest twenty-first-century changes to the relationships between stakeholders in the fashion industry is the use of social media. As well as enabling the consumer to achieve a greater say in the design of products and to purchase fashion in different ways, social media is also being used by new designers as a tool to publicly shame those who transgress social norms by engaging in unfair copying.

Designers are increasingly using social media sites such as Instagram to "call foul on big brands for allegedly hijacking their designs" (TFL 2020b). Most instances have involved a younger or lesser-known designer who has shown their work to a larger fashion brand, often in a job interview, and then seen the brand put out a design which they feel too closely copies their creative ideas. In other cases, a well-known brand copies a design from a lesser-known designer. Most designers would have a hard time pursuing a legal claim in these circumstances where the copy is rarely an exact replica of the original. Even in the EU, where the designer could theoretically use a UCD, the difficulty is still likely to be the cost of pursuing a legal claim. However, calling out a brand on social media is free.

Social media has instant effects and the "power to tarnish a brand's reputation and potentially even its bottom line." In fact, cancel culture has become so powerful that some designers have attempted to get ahead of social media shaming and used social media posts to point "to their own alleged sources of inspiration, a pattern that is noteworthy given that brands have traditionally remained silent when faced with allegations of copying" (TFL 2020b).

The Instagram account Diet Prada is a good example of the power of social media. The account was initially anonymous, but its creators identified themselves in 2017 as fashion industry professionals Tony Liu and Lindsey Schuyler. Liu and Schuyler have turned Diet Prada into a pioneer of social media shaming. The site is seen as something of a fashion industry watchdog as it flags cultural appropriation and copying by industry power players such as luxury conglomerates or fast fashion chains (Tashjian 2020). Companies targeted by Diet Prada's posts have had to cancel fashion shows, pull designs, and manage damage to their brand's reputation.

Diet Prada has almost 3 million followers, so its posts can quickly lead its targets to make changes, and its power acts to restrain blatant copying by major brands. However, in some cases, it has been forced to apologize for taking public shaming too far. For example, the site faced a lot of criticism for slamming Gap's collaboration with Kanye West's line Yeezy, since it failed to mention Mowalola Ogunlesi, the Black female designer at the helm of the collaboration. It is currently being sued by Dolce & Gabbana for defamation after it accused the brand of racism for its campaign called #DGLovesChina.

Some creators who have used social media to highlight unfair copying have not only stopped the copying but found that it has led to a creative partnership with the copier. Actor Ana Coto went viral on TikTok in early 2020 with a roller-skating routine to the song "Jenny from the Block." She then discovered that Fortnite had used a nearly identical dance for a game released that summer. Coto posted both videos side by side with the caption "Flattered but no dance credit?" A week later, Fortnite attributed the dance as having been "inspired by" Coto and then worked with her to create another skating-themed emote (Sung 2022).

Fast fashion company Shein is such a prolific user of others' creative work that #shameonshein is used by artists who have had their designs copied by the company (Das 2022). Social media certainly has the power to amplify the voices of less well-known designers and enable them to call out copying by those who are harder to hold accountable through laws because of the power imbalance.

The development of norms on social media has the power to be an important protector of creativity. It is often more "attention grabbing than court trials" (Palandri 2020, 16). It is a powerful way for smaller designers to balance their lack of economic power in fights with larger, better-established brands. However, giving everyone the power to "bring a brand to its knees in hours" (17) has its dangers. Mistakes, the lack of due process, and harsh judgments mean that using social media to regulate creativity can have major, often unforeseen consequences. It is an area for caution, and more research on the protection it can undoubtedly provide to designers is needed.

The Technological Dimension

The development of digital communications platforms in the late twentieth century greatly assisted in the globalization of the fashion business. It became easier for designers to share their designs globally. The next wave of technological change promises several new digital technologies that could be used to protect creativity and other aspects of fashion design, three of which are discussed below. Artificial intelligence (AI) is already being used for several purposes including to generate new design and to track and protect against copying and design infringement. Some worry that 3D printing has the potential to make copying and design infringement easier. Blockchain, familiar to the world from virtual currencies such as Bitcoin, has potential as a way to authenticate goods, protect designs, and distinguish them from "fakes."

Artificial Intelligence

It is hard to define AI, and it is already everywhere. Deep machine learning that can recognize patterns and learn from data is already in use to generate designs by industrial designers, architects, and (most recently) food designers. Sony's project to enhance gastronomy with artificial intelligence and augment "creativity and techniques of chefs around the world" ("Renowned Chef" 2021) shows that AI is entering the design space of creative endeavors. If AI can be used to create designs in industry, architecture, and food, there is no reason that AI could not be used to generate new fashion designs.

Deloitte has created an AI called Dupe Killer which it describes as a "copycat detection solution." The software uses AI to recognize key features of a design and investigates online marketplaces and social media platforms to identify copycat products. Because AI can learn from and manipulate large amounts of data, it is likely to find more design-infringing goods than a human could (Salerno-Garthwaite 2022).

Two former Amazon employees have created a virtual shopping assistant called Mona (Perez 2015). Mona learns your style preferences and then makes purchase suggestions. It can learn from feedback, so the more you use it, the more it learns. "It is entirely possible that in future Mona, or applications like Mona, will reach the stage where the customer can simply request a whole new wardrobe and Mona will select, order and deliver it" (*Managing Intellectual Property* 2017). This would radically alter the design and manufacturing processes by changing from a "shopping-then-shipping" to "shipping-then-shopping" model. Fashion designers might have to create more to please the AI rather than the consumer since it would be the initial point of contact between the designer and consumer. It could be set to alert the consumer to certain branded products, but also to particular styles. This would change the role of the consumer in the shopping process and elevate the AI to decision maker. In addition, if the AI purchased an infringing design, it is not clear who would be liable, the AI or the consumer?

There are pros and cons to these uses of AI. First, they are likely, at least initially, to be available to wealthier, more established designers. Applications such as Dupe Killer and Mona could both chill creativity as designers seek to avoid their designs being flagged as too similar to those of the dominant design companies that are likely to use Dupe Killer, or seek to fit their aesthetic to designs selected by Mona.

However, AI-assisted design could provide designers with new ideas and freedom to experiment and create new designs.

The protection of any design created entirely by an AI by copyright law is problematic because of the requirement of human authorship. The difficulties of AI creatorship are prefigured in the case of a famous photograph taken by a curious monkey with a wildlife photographer's camera, essentially a monkey selfie.

A California district court held that an animal could not own a copyright even though it had apparently taken the shot. The case was eventually settled with the wildlife photographer agreeing with PETA (who had sued on the monkey's behalf) to donate 25% of revenue from the photographs to groups that protect the monkeys and their habitat in Indonesia (Slotkin 2017). The US Copyright Office has recently confirmed that protection also does not extend to a design created by AI because of the lack of a human author. Susan Scafidi is concerned that: "Twentieth century formulations of legal doctrine that at present keep copyright from applying to algorithmic designs also nullify what might otherwise be the rights of designers, programmers, companies, and consumers who each make contributions to this creative enterprise" (Scafidi 2020, 396). It remains to be seen whether there will be calls for legal change if the use of AI in design increases.

Three-Dimensional Printing

Three-dimensional printing, or additive manufacturing, has been around since the 1980s. A computer-aided design (CAD) file provides the data to print a 2D or 3D model, usually by a process of joining materials layer upon layer. Older 3D printers used layers of plastic to build up designs, but newer printers have been designed to use a variety of printing materials including metals, foods, nylon, and linen pulp. The types of material that can be 3D printed are expanding.

Technologists have predicted for some time that 3D printing would completely revolutionize manufacturing and retailing, including the fashion business. In 2019, in *Fashionopolis*, Dana Thomas explored the possibility of 3D printing as another technology that could end retail. Rather than selling clothes, fashion brands would sell a digital file that you would use to print clothes at home in your size. She quoted Andrew Bolton, curator in charge of the Metropolitan Museum of Art's Costume Institute, as saying that 3D printing would be "as radical as the sewing machine in terms of its democracy" (Thomas 2019, 208). In 2016, Ray Kurzweil, director of engineering at Google, stated that "[a]s the variety of materials available to print in 3-D become more extensive and less expensive, both free open-source and proprietary clothing designs will be widely available online in as little as 10 years." He predicted that we would be 3D printing our own clothes by 2020 (Paton 2016). Most people have yet to print their own outfits, but that may change as new materials for printing are developed.

Some designers have embraced the technology because of the way it enables them to expand their creative range. Dutch designer Iris van Herpen has used 3D printing since 2009 to create a range of complex designs including a "sheer shift enveloped by a cloud of paper-thin metal bubbles the size of baseballs" (Thomas 2019, 210) and other striking and creative elements. The technology enables designers such as van Herpen to push creative boundaries beyond what could be achieved with old-fashioned materials and techniques. As such, it could lead to an explosion in creativity and innovation in fashion design.

Nike, New Balance, and other apparel and sportswear brands use 3D printing for components of their running shoes. UK-based software design company

Unmade collaborated with New Balance to build unique customizable sports clothing. The process could be used to translate customers' design additions into production data ready for manufacture anywhere in the world, although current materials somewhat limit what can be achieved.

The widespread use of 3D printing of clothes has implications for design protection. The 2020 EU Report on 3D Printing says that it is unclear whether a CAD file for a 3D design can be protected as a design (Mendis et al. 2020, 180). Under current EU law, a protected design needs to be a physical product, although there is no requirement for permanence. Computer programs are specifically exempt from protection under both the EUDD and EUDR, as programs are deemed not to be products. The computer program exception does not cover the "results of running a computer program," which means it is not clear if the exception applies to CAD files for 3D designs. However, under the proposal for the new EUDD and EUDR the definition of design is expanded to clearly include CAD files.

Another concern noted in the Report on 3D Printing is the use of scanning as a tool to copy and modify an existing design. Should scanning constitute the "use" of a design and therefore be regulated by the ownership of IPRs in the design? Designers often use the designs of others for inspiration. If they started this process by creating a 3D scan of another design in order to modify it, would the original designer be able to restrain this? The EU report noted that it may be that designers currently depend on the complexity of their design or the time needed to produce a duplicate to protect them. If 3D scanning and printing allow even complex designs to be reproduced easily and quickly, should the EU design law framework provide "protection against third parties copying a protected design by means of 3D printing?" (Mendis et al. 2020, 138).

Some designers are concerned about infringement by home copyists if 3D printing becomes ubiquitous. Currently, there is a private and non-commercial use exception in the EUDD and the EUDR that allows the copying of a design non-commercially, for example by a home sewist. The provisions of the proposed new EUDD and EUDR make copying protected designs using 3D printers illegal.

Blockchain

A blockchain is "a shared database or digital ledger that automatically updates information across an entire network, without the need for a central intermediary. When a user enters information in the ledger, that entry becomes linked to every other entry, or "block," and every other copy of the ledger is automatically synchronized via the internet. The distributed nature of the data makes it supposedly unhackable, although Bitcoin have been stolen.[2]

Blockchain is commonly associated with Bitcoin and other virtual currencies and therefore often discussed in relation to finance. However, it could also revolutionize supply chains, and this is where it is relevant to the control and regulation of creativity in the fashion business. Blockchain technology has been used to create NFTs, a kind of verifiable, unique digital asset. NFTs have even become a kind of luxury good themselves, selling for high prices online. They work as a kind of distributed electronic record that links to a physical or digital product and tracks its ownership history. This has raised interest in the luxury fashion business where the focus is on the ability of NFTs to certify authenticity and uniqueness. Luxury brands could use blockchain to link digital authenticators with real-life physical products, such as handbags or shoes. When placed onto products, these devices would "act as a link between the physical item and the digital ledger that contains data, such as the product's source and ownership history" (Yang et al. 2022).

Various companies have already started to use blockchain to track provenance. Walmart is now using IBM's blockchain platform to track food shipments to improve safety, and the diamond industry is using Everledger's blockchain to verify the source of its diamonds. In 2017, London designer Martine Jarlgaard

> produced the first garments with "smart labels" that the consumer could scan to see every step in the production process, from raw material to finished product, complete with time stamps and location mapping for every step—even identifying the source of a sweater's alpaca yarn.
>
> (TFL 2018)

And in May 2019, LVMH partnered with blockchain company ConsenSys and Microsoft to launch a platform that it said would "serve the entire luxury industry with powerful product tracking and tracing services" (TFL 2021).

Some brand owners believe that blockchain will revolutionize their ability to control and authenticate their products. If branded goods can be tracked through the supply chain, and even in second-hand sales, then blockchain will "enhance intellectual property protection for designers and brand owners." According to many commentators such as Birgit Clark and Ruth Burstall,

> Blockchain technology stands to play an important role within the context of unregistered IPR, such as copyright and unregistered design rights, since it can provide evidence of their conception, use, qualification requirements and whether the right is still in the period of protection.
>
> (Clark and Burstall 2019, 256)

A designer could upload an original design or copyright document with their details to a blockchain. This would create a time-stamped record that could be used as evidence of creation and ownership.

However, there is currently no regulation of blockchain technology, and any regulatory proposals are focused on the regulation of virtual currencies such as Bitcoin, and not NFTs or the role of blockchain in supply chains. Blockchains raise several concerns as protectors of authentic designs.

It is a major barrier to using blockchain as a way to authenticate a design that anyone can create an original certificate. As Adam Sulkowski states, "no matter how allegedly tamper-proof it may be, data verification is only useful if the original record is reliable" (Sulkowski 2019, 313).

Blockchain merely authenticates the ownership of a token. It does not mean that the token itself has not been stolen. It also does not mean that the purchaser has any right to the physical product to which the token is linked. NFTs "provide purchasers with a digital certificate of ownership that can be bought and sold online, yet generally do not give the purchaser rights to the physical product" (Beckett 2022). The asset that the NFT represents may not be authentic, and the asset and token are often not stored together.

In order to link the NFT token with an asset, the NFT carries unique information about the design within its smart contract, but, owing to the expense of data storage, it does not usually provide access to the entire file for the asset. It is possible to store the entire data for the creation within the actual NFT code, often called "on-chain storage." However, storing a blockchain in this manner "is impractical on most blockchains, since transfers on the chain incur a transaction fee based on the size of the token" (Mahmood 2021). The more common method is to store a link to the file in the NFT code. This runs the risk that it may not always be possible to access the design or creation if the link is modified in any way.

Sulkowski argues that, without law, any contract, including a smart contract such as an NFT, lacks a means of enforcement. "[T]he true potential of blockchain technology can only be realized when coupled with effective governance." While some argue that blockchain "can function in the absence of legal frameworks," Sulkowski argues that lawyers will retain their essential roles in a blockchain-enabled business environment (Sulkowski 2019, 306). Law is needed to clarify the rights under a smart contract and ensure that the original record is reliable. It is also needed to provide a means of enforcement of these rights. The possibility that NFTs can be stolen means there is also a need for criminal law enforcement just as there is for other types of property.

There have already been instances of artists creating NFTs for sale in the metaverse using the trademarks of well-known brands without permission. An example is artist Mason Rothschild, the creator of the virtual mini Birkin bag NFTs (which he calls MetaBirkins) described in Chapter 3. Rothschild also collaborated with artist Eric Ramirez to create the image of a Birkin bag adorned with the design of a 40-week-old fetus (Dafoe 2022). Hermès has sued Rothschild, arguing that these MetaBirkins infringe its trademark rights. Interestingly, Rothschild is not the only creator of digital Birkin bags. There have been other virtual Birkin NFTs which Rothschild says he did not produce. While Rothschild may have a First Amendment or fair use defense against a claim of trademark infringement, his actions illustrate that NFTS are not necessarily ideal as a protection of design.

The use of NFTs to authenticate design is certainly a form of preemptive self-help that should not be discouraged by legislatures or courts, but, as Rothschild's MetaBirkins show, the technology has vulnerabilities. Nothing stops anyone from creating an NFT: The creator does not have to own the underlying asset, and the NFT does not necessarily provide access to the underlying asset. All of these issues mean that an NFT is a type of contract that requires legal institutions to apply and enforce it in the real world.

The Economic Dimension

The Role of Consumers

The consumer is a major potential regulator in an industry as ruled by cultural trends as fashion. Consumer purchasing decisions create the profits of fashion businesses. If consumers decide to avoid buying from particular designers or types of clothing such as fast fashion and opt instead for sustainable clothing and circular economy business models, this behavior will have a major effect on fashion design.

Numerous studies suggest that consumers wish to avoid counterfeits and knock-offs and would prefer more sustainable clothing from brands they trust (Robinson 2021). When a 2020 report in the *Sunday Times* exposed that fast fashion company Boohoo operated a network of exploitation-ridden "dark factories" in Leicester, UK, and that these factories often failed to comply with employment law, workplace health and safety rules, and environmental regulations, consumers turned against the brand (TFL 2020a). Within days of the publication of the *Sunday Times*'s findings, the company saw its share price plunge. It lost approximately one-third of its value, or £1.5 billion. The company said it was investigating the claims about the poor working conditions (Butler and Davies 2020).

The more activist consumer who cares about and is actively engaged with the product, brand, and messaging of goods that she purchases is becoming common in fashion, enabled by consumer and activist organizations such as the Clean Clothes Campaign, which has been advocating and partnering with companies on topics such as transparency in the supply chain and a living wage for 30 years ("Clean Clothes Campaign" n.d.).

The role that consumers have in the fashion business has been limited thus far by the murkiness and complexity of fashion supply chains. Although it is relatively easy for a consumer to guess that they are buying an outright fake from the price, it is often hard for them to determine who makes their clothing, and if it is a knock-off. Consumers often lack the information that they need to make educated decisions about fashion purchases, and this prevents them from exercising their full economic power (Turunen and Halme 2021, 2).

The rise in both voluntary initiatives and mandatory reporting requirements that cause companies to make their supply chains more transparent is an important precursor to consumers using their economic power to discourage fashion designers from engaging in bad behavior, including blatant copying. While most fashion activists have focused on highlighting poor working conditions and environmental damage in supply chains, consumers can also assist designers trying to protect creativity if the companies who ignore labor and environmental issues are the same ones making fakes and knock-off goods. The assumption that it is fast fashion companies that are the worst offenders may not be entirely accurate. The 2021 KnowTheChain report on forced labor in the fashion supply chain found that luxury brands are among the companies that have the most labor and environmental violations. Prada, for example, scored an appalling 5 out of 100 on their efforts to fight forced labor, and LVMH only scored a low 19 ("Benchmark" 2020).

Consumers can act to promote creativity in fashion design by spending on companies that are ethical and avoiding those that are not. In a 2019 article on consumer market power to change the food system, Parker, Johnson, and Curll say "consumer choices send market signals through supply chains to the actors that influence where and how the supply chain functions, and under what conditions." They go on that consumer choice can be understood as "a regulatory regime based on voluntarism, market solutions and the state acting at a distance" (Parker, Johnson, and Curll 2019, 7).

Consumer Education

Consumer activist groups and other NGOs focus on educating ethical fashion consumers and providing them with information to use as they purchase fashion. As well as the Clean Clothes Campaign, there are numerous groups that seek to educate and empower fashion consumers to use their economic power to change the fashion industry. Two of the many groups are Re/make, a group seeking to get fashion industry workers properly paid and to change the fashion world by education, advocacy, and transparency ("Remake—Let's Turn Fashion into a Force for Good" n.d.); and the Wardrobe Crisis, a project by Clare Press that uses a book and podcast to push for a more sustainable fashion future ("Wardrobe Crisis" n.d.). Andrew Morgan's documentary *The True Cost* came out in 2015 with the aim of exposing the environmental and social damage done by the overproduction of disposable clothing. It showed the people who makes these clothes and the toxic environmental conditions in which they work to get consumers to rethink their fashion purchases (*The True Cost* 2015). Numerous other NGOs work to assist and educate consumers to choose more sustainable fashion. Creative designers who seek to embody sustainable ideals will benefit from this consumer movement.

The Consumer and Social Media

As described in the section on social norms above, social media has definite benefits for those trying to promote creativity in design and prevent the sale of fakes. It provides a revolutionary tool for the ethical consumer to interact directly with fashion designers and brands to ask questions and access information about goods. It can create pressure on companies to change their behavior when they are called out.

Unfortunately, some studies suggest social media has also led to the sale of more, not fewer, counterfeit goods since it can also be used by the sellers of fake goods to advertise and distribute their wares. The US Intellectual Property and Counterfeit Goods—Landscape Review of Existing/Emerging Research (Bharadwaj et al. 2020) noted that younger, female consumers are more likely than other consumers to buy counterfeit goods. Consumers with higher education levels were more resistant to the idea of buying counterfeits. Intentional buyers of counterfeits were also often heavy users of social media, especially sites such as Instagram. Overall, the report noted that social media has radically altered the way in which consumers buy, rent, and sell clothing and luxury goods, and "social media platforms have become the preferred online marketplaces for counterfeiters, due in part to the increased protections and regulations on e-commerce sites like Amazon and eBay."

A 2016 report by Ghost Data published on the *Washington Post*'s blog analyzed 750,000 Instagram posts that focused on top fashion brands and found 20% featured counterfeit and/or illicit products. The study's authors said their research "reveal[ed] that a big shift is taking place in the (online) world of counterfeiting." An update to the research in 2019 found that, while the number of posts by counterfeiters on Instagram had risen, the percentage of the total number of posts featuring counterfeit goods had dropped. However, counterfeiters' influence on Instagram remained a major concern, with these posts reaching an audience of at least 20 million people. The report noted, "these sellers are no longer hidden in some far-away 'souks' or confined in a rough neighbourhood market. They operate 'in the open,' posting a wide range of ads and images on social media and openly selling their goods worldwide" (Stroppa et al. 2019).

A report in the *World Trademark Review* in 2020 revealed that the newer social media platform TikTok, used extensively by young people, is hosting increasing numbers of influencers who push fake products to their followers. Counterfeit fashion items are very popular with younger audiences who are image conscious and have less money than older people (Lince 2020). For fashion brands, it is a major problem that popular influencers can shape the perception of counterfeits by young people as being trendy and cool.

Fashion designers face a significant challenge from social media influencers: While social media and the influencers it has created can be used to alert consumers to fakes or design copying, they can also be used to sell these products to a wide audience.

The Role of Financing in Promoting Creative Design

A major economic regulator of activity in the design industry, including creativity, is the fact that designers often need to secure financing to realize their creative visions. This means that any changes to materials, methods, or supply chains must get the backing of banks and those who finance the industry. Financial backers tend to focus on cost and immediate returns, which limits the ability of designers to move to using more sustainable materials even where they wish to do so. This is an area where laws that require companies to focus on sustainability such as the proposed CSR Directive, Ecodesign requirements for sustainable products, PEF labelling, or the New York Fashion Law may be useful to creative designers who want to change their supply chains to use more sustainable new materials but need to get their financial backers to agree to finance these changes. If these laws mandate the inclusion of ESG considerations in the supply chain, they will limit the ability of financial backers to refuse to countenance changes that cost money but may protect and boost creativity.

Conclusion and New Avenues for Research

Designers rarely think of law and legal rights as the reason they create, or the first place to turn to protect their creativity, but laws and the other dimensions of protection discussed in this chapter have evolved together and continue to do so. This chapter provides an overview of these other dimensions that protect fashion design and describes some examples within those dimensions.

There is insufficient research on how designers and other creative people work and what types of protection they use for their work.

More study is particularly needed to ensure that laws promoting CSR are clear, the measurement of ESGs is meaningful, and they are applied uniformly to fashion companies and beyond. We need to better understand the role of social media shaming in protecting creative work. New technologies such as AI, 3D printing, and blockchain also need to be studied to understand how they might be used to support design creativity, especially by limiting sales of fast fashion and fake or counterfeit goods.

Notes

1 In *"Code and Other Laws of Cyberspace"* Lessig argued that cyberspace could be effectively controlled by its software and hardware architecture (code). Although his book is mainly about the regulatability of cyberspace by code and laws, Lessig described four significant regulators that operate for any activity, whether in the real or virtual world: law, code, norms, and the market. Lessig identified several variables in the ability of each constraint to regulate. He explained that these regulators are interconnected. Changes in one type of constraint affect the regulation as a whole as each constraint imposes different types of costs or controls on behavior and these constraints are not fixed. Lessig used various examples of the different constraints and their effects to illustrate his argument that these regulators are similar for all endeavors. For example, smoking is regulated by law in certain places (airplanes), by norms in others (someone else's house or car), by the market (it is expensive), and by technology (the manipulation of nicotine creates more or less addictive cigarettes). Lessig's point is that all of these tools, not just laws, are available to regulators to control particular behaviors.

2 There have been several instances of Bitcoin theft. On March 23, 2022 hackers stole cryptocurrency now worth almost $615m from players of online game "Axie Infinity," in one of the largest cryptocurrency heists on record.

References

"A New Textiles Economy: Redesigning Fashion's Future." 2017. The Ellen MacArthur Foundation. http:www.ellenmacarthurfoundation.org/publications.

Barron, Mark R. 2007. "Creating Consumer Confidence or Confusion? The Role of Product Certification in the Market Today." *Marquette Intellectual Property Law Review* 11 (2): 414–42.

Beckett, Lois. 2022. ""Huge Mess of Theft and Fraud:" Artists Sound Alarm as NFT Crime Proliferates." The Guardian, January 29, 2022, sec. Technology. https://www.theguardian.com/global/2022/jan/29/huge-mess-of-theft-artists-sound-alarm-theft-nfts-proliferates.

"Benchmark." 2020. KnowTheChain (blog). June 17, 2020. https://knowthechain.org/benchmark/.

Benkler, Yochai. 2017. "Law, Innovation, and Collaboration in Networked Economy and Society." *Annual Review of Law and Social Science* 13: 231–50.

Bennett, Lydia. 2017. "Ethical Fashion Certifications and Standards: What Do the Labels Mean?" Good on You. October 6, 2017. https://goodonyou.eco/ethical-fashion-certifications-explained/.

Bharadwaj, Vega, Marieke Brock, Bridey Heing, Ramon Miro, and Noor Mukarram. 2020. "U.S. Intellectual Property and Counterfeit Goods—Landscape Review of Existing/Emerging Research." *SSRN Electronic Journal.* https://doi.org/10.2139/ssrn.3577710.

BIAGGI. 2021. "State of New York 7428 2021-2022 Regular Sessions in Senate," October, 4.

Bravo, Karen E. 2019. "Contemporary State Anti-'Slavery' Efforts: Dishonest and Ineffective." *N. Ky. L. Rev.* 46 (106): 1–37.

Buskirk, Martha. 2021. *Is It Ours? Art, Copyright, and the Public Interest.* University of California Press.

Butler, Sarah, and Rob Davies. 2020. "Boohoo Shareholders Demand Answers after Shares Plunge by a Third." The Guardian, July 7, 2020, sec. Business. https://www.theguardian.com/business/2020/jul/07/boohoo-shares-concern-factory-conditions.

Chua, Jasmin Malik. 2021. "Is Eco-Labeling Scheme Guilty of Greenwashing?" *Sourcing Journal (Online)*, October.

Clark, Birgit, and Ruth Burstall. 2019. "Crypto-Pie in the Sky? How Blockchain Technology Is Impacting Intellectual Property Law." *Stanford Journal of Blockchain Law & Policy* 2 (2): 252–62.

"Clean Clothes Campaign." n.d. Clean Clothes Campaign. Accessed May 17, 2022. https://cleanclothes.org/front-page.

Dafoe, Taylor. 2022. "Hermès Is Suing a Digital Artist for Selling Unauthorized Birkin Bag NFTs in the Metaverse for as Much as Six Figures." Artnet News. January 26, 2022. https://news.artnet.com/art-world/hermes-metabirkins-2063954.

"Dangerous Gaps Undermine EU Commission's New Legislation to Hold Corporations Accountable." 2022. European Coalition for Corporate Justice. February 23, 2022. https://corporatejustice.org/news/dangerous-gaps-undermine-eu-commissions-new-legislation-on-sustainable-supply-chains/.

Darling, Kate, and Aaron Perzanowski. 2017. *Creativity without Law: Challenging the Assumptions of Intellectual Property.* New York: New York University Press.

Das, Shanti. 2022. ""They Took My World": Fashion Giant Shein Accused of Art Theft." The Observer. March 6, 2022. https://www.theguardian.com/artanddesign/2022/mar/06/they-took-my-world-fashion-giant-shein-accused-of-art-theft.

Fanarakis, Kristen. 2022. "As New York Lawmakers Unveil the Fashion Act, Is Larger Reform on The Way?" The Fashion Law. January 12, 2022. https://www.thefashionlaw.com/as-lawmakers-unveil-sustainability-bill-needs-to-discuss-data/.

Friedman, Vanessa. 2022. "New York Could Make History with a Fashion Sustainability Act." The New York Times. January 7, 2022. https://www.nytimes.com/2022/01/07/style/new-york-fashion-sustainability-act.html.

Gamble, Melissa. 2022. "Is the Tide Changing for the Fashion Industry When It Comes to Regulations?" The Fashion Law. January 4, 2022. https://www.thefashionlaw.com/is-the-tide-changing-for-the-fashion-industry-regulations-environment-in-the-u-s/.

Katzenbach, Christian. 2018. "There Is Always More than Law: From Low IP Regimes to a Governance Perspective in Copyright Research." *Journal of Technology Law and Policy* 22.

Lashitew, Addisu. 2021. "The Risks of US-EU Divergence on Corporate Sustainability Disclosure." Brookings. September 28, 2021. https://www.brookings.edu/blog/future-development/2021/09/28/the-risks-of-us-eu-divergence-on-corporate-sustainability-disclosure/.

Lessig, Lawrence. 1999. *Code and Other Laws of Cyberspace*. Basic Books.

Lince, Tim. 2020. "'Dupe Culture' Grows on TikTok; Why This Helps Counterfeiters and Harms Brands." *World Trademark Review*. November 5, 2020. https://www.worldtrademarkreview.com/anti-counterfeiting/dupe-culture-grows-tiktok-why-helps-counterfeiters-and-harms-brands.

Mahmood, Ghaith. 2021. "NFTs: What Are You Buying and What Do You Actually Own?" The Fashion Law. March 18, 2021. https://www.thefashionlaw.com/nfts-what-are-you-buying-and-what-do-you-actually-own/.

Managing Intellectual Property. 2017. "AI Is Coming and It Will Change Trade Mark Law," 2017.

McNeil, Peter, and Giorgio Riello. 2016. *Luxury A Rich History*. Oxford University Press.

Mendis, Dinusha, Jan Bernd Nordemann, Rosa Maria Ballardini, Hans Brorsen, Maria del Carmen Caletrava Moreno, Julie Robson, and Phil Dickens. 2020. *"The Intellectual Property Implications of the Development of Industrial 3D Printing."* European Commission.

Monseau, Susanna. 2017. *Law, Technology, and Business The 21st Century Corporation and the Future of Work. Aspen Select Series*. Wolters Kluwer.

Palandri, Lucrezia. 2020. "Fashion as Art: Rights and Remedies in the Age of Social Media." *Laws* 9 (1). https://doi.org/10.3390/laws9010009.

Parker, Christine, Hope Johnson, and Janine Curll. 2019. "Consumer Power to Change the Food System? A Critical Reading of Food Labels As Governance Spaces: The Case of Açaí Berry Superfood." *Journal of Food Law & Policy* 15 (1): 1–48.

Paton, Elizabeth. 2016. "Fashion's Future, Printed to Order." The New York Times, December 5, 2016, sec. Business. https://www.nytimes.com/2016/12/05/business/fashions-future-printed-to-order.html.

Perez, Sarah. 2015. "Ex-Amazon Team Launches Mona, An App That Puts Personal Shopper In Your Pocket." Techcrunch. June 24, 2015. https://techcrunch.com/2015/06/24/ex-amazon-team-launches-mona-an-app-that-puts-a-personal-shopper-in-your-pocket/.

Prentice, Rebecca, and De Geet Neve. 2017. *Unmaking the Global Sweatshop, Health and Safety of the Worlds Garment Workers*. University of Pennsylvania Press.

Proposal for a Directive of the European Parliament and of the Council on Corporate Sustainability Due Diligence and Amending Directive 2019/1937. 2022.

Pucker, Kenneth. 2021. "Overselling Sustainability Reporting." *Harvard Business Review* 99 (3): 134–143.

"Remake—Let's Turn Fashion into a Force for Good." n.d. Remake. Accessed May 17, 2022. https://remake.world/.

"Renowned Chef Hajime Yoneda Joins Sony AI as an Advisor to Gastronomy Flagship Project: Owner-Chef of Michelin Three-Star Restaurant HAJIME to Advise Sony AI on Reimagining the Future of Restaurants with AI & Robotics." 2021. *PR Newswire*.

Robinson, Roxanne. 2021. "Sustainable in Sweden: Four Designers with an Eco-Positive Impact." *CFDA*. September 29, 2021.

Salerno-Garthwaite, Andrew. 2022. "The Dupe Killer: Tracking Copies with AI." Vogue Business, March 4, 2022. https://www.voguebusiness.com/technology/the-dupe-killer-tracking-copies-with-ai.

Scafidi, Susan. 2020. "Creation, Destruction, and the Future of Fashion." *Fordham Intellectual Property, Media and Entertainment Law Journal* 30 (2): 393–97.

Sibley, Jessica. 2015. "*The Eureka Myth: Creators, Innovators, and Everyday Intellectual Property.*" Suffolk University Law School Research Paper no. 15-7, February.

Siems, Mathias. 2019. "The Law and Ethics of "Cultural Appropriation"." *International Journal of Law in Context* 15 (4): 408–23.

Slotkin, Jason. 2017. "'Monkey Selfie' Lawsuit ends with Settlement Between PETA, Photographer." NPR, September 12, 2017. https://www.npr.org/sections/thetwo-way/2017/09/12/550417823/-animal-rights-advocates-photographer-compromise-over-ownership-of-monkey-selfie.

"Social Media Influencers and Counterfeit Goods Executive Summary." 2021. UK Intellectual Property Office. December 22, 2021. https://www.gov.uk/government/publications/social-media-influencers-and-counterfeit-goods/social-media-influencers-and-counterfeit-goods-executive-summary.

Sprigman, Christopher. 2017. "Copyright and Creative Incentives: What We Know (And Don't)." *Houston Law Review* 55 (2): 451–78.

Stroppa, Andrea, David Gatto, Lev Pasha, and Bernardo Parella. 2019. *Instagram and Counterfeiting in 2019: New Features, Old Problems*. Rome, New York 9 April 2019.

"Study on the Impact of Artificial Intelligence on the Infringement and Enforcement of Copyright and Design." 2022. Impact of Technology Deep Dive Report. European Intellectual Property Office. https://eur-lex.europa.eu/legal-content/EN/TXT/PDF/?uri=CELEX:52020SC0264&qid=1627664501586&from=EN.

Sulkowski, Adam. 2019. "Blockchain, Business Supply Chains, Sustainability, and Law: The Future of Governance, Legal Frameworks, and Lawyers?" *The Delaware Journal of Corporate Law* 43 (2): 303–345.

Sung, Morgan. 2022. "Creators Turn to Public Shaming to Seek Compensation from Brands They Say Don't Credit Them." NBC News. January 4, 2022. https://www.nbcnews.com/pop-culture/viral/creators-turn-public-shaming-seek-compensation-brands-say-dont-credit-rcna10062.

Sutor, Kristin. 2020. "Fast-Fashion, One Day You're In, and the Next Day You're Out: A Solution to the Fashion Industry's Intellectual Property Issues Outside of Intellectual Property Law." *The Michigan State Law Review* 2020 (3): 853–96.

Tashjian, Rachel. 2020. "In Fashion, Who Will Cancel the Cancelers?" GQ. July 1, 2020. https://www.gq.com/story/diet-prada-kanye.

TFL. 2018. "What Is Blockchain and What Can it do for the Fashion Industry." The Fashion Law. April 24, 2018. https://www.thefashionlaw.com/what-is-blockchain-and-what-can-it-do-for-the-fashion-industry/.

———. 2020a. "As Fast Fashion Gets Faster and Cheaper, the Giants Behind it are Facing Scrutiny." The Fashion Law. July 9, 2020. https://www.thefashionlaw.com/as-fast-fashion-gets-faster-and-cheaper-the-giants-behind-it-are-facing-scrutiny/.

———. 2020b. "As Young Designers Continue to Call "Copy!", What Can They Do to Protect Themselves?" The Fashion Law. August 19, 2020. https://www.thefashionlaw.com/as-young-designers-continue-to-call-copy-what-can-they-do-to-protect-themselves/.

———. 2021. "LVMH, Richemont and Prada Team Up for New Blockchain Venture Aimed at Tracing, Authenticating Luxury Goods." The Fashion Law. April 21,

2021.   https://www.thefashionlaw.com/lvmh-richemont-and-prada-team-up-for-new
-blockchain-venture-aimed-at-tracing-authenticating-luxury-goods/.

"The True Cost." 2015. The True Cost. Accessed May 17, 2022. https://truecostmovie
.com/.

Thomas, Dana. 2019. *Fashionopolis, The Price of Fast Fashion-and the Future of Clothes.*
Penguin Press; Illustrated Edition.

Turunen, Linda Lisa, and Mina Halme. 2021. "Communicating Actionable Sustainability
Information to Consumers: The Shades of Green Instrument for Fashion." *Journal of
Cleaner Production*, 297: 126605.

UN Office for Partnerships. n.d. "How Does UNOP Contribute to a More Sustainable
Fashion Industry?" UN Alliance For Sustainable Fashion. https://unfashionalliance.org
/members/unpartnerships/.

United Nations. 2018. *"Fashion Industry Charter for Climate Change."*

Vats, Anjali. 2020. *The Color of Creatorship.* Stanford University Press.

"Wardrobe Crisis." n.d. Wardrobe Crisis. Accessed May 17, 2022. https://thewardrobecrisis
.com.

Wicker, Alden. 2020. "Fashion Has a Misinformation Problem. That's Bad for the
Environment." Vox. January 27, 2020. https://www.vox.com/the-goods/2020/1/27
/21080107/fashion-environment-facts-statistics-impact.

Yang, Cindy, Kelly Bonner, Fiona Rodgers, and Michelle Ray-Jones. 2022. "Blockchain
and NFTs Are Smart, But Can They Revolutionize Fashion?" The Fashion Law.
January 13, 2022. https://www.thefashionlaw.com/blockchain-and-nfts-are-smart-but
-can-they-revolutionize-fashion/.

Index

Page numbers in *italic* denote figures.

For Product Safety Concerns and Information please contact our EU
representative GPSR@taylorandfrancis.com
Taylor & Francis Verlag GmbH, Kaufingerstraße 24, 80331 München, Germany